W9-BPK-858

SISTER IRENE'S
CULINARY JOURNAL

SISTER IRENE'S CULINARY JOURNAL

*A notebook filled with love, faith, and recipes
gathered over many blessed years of cooking, serving, and caring*

SISTER IRENE PSATHAS

PARACLETE PRESS

BREWSTER, MASSACHUSETTS

Library of Congress Cataloging-in-Publication Data

Psathas, Irene, 1931–
    Sister Irene's culinary journal: a notebook filled with love, faith, and recipes, from many blessed years
of cooking, serving, and caring / Irene Psathas.
            p.   cm.
    ISBN 1-55725-205-X
    1. Cookery, American. 2. Psathas, Irene, 1931–   —Diaries. 3. Nuns—Massachusetts—Orleans—Diaries.
4. Convents—Massachusetts—Orleans. I. Title.
    TX715.P9515   1998
    641.5973—dc21   98-7651
                                                                                     CIP

10 9 8 7 6 5 4 3 2 1

Illustrations and photos courtesy of the author and the Sisters of the Community of Jesus, Orleans, Massachusetts.

© 1998 by The Community of Jesus, Inc.
ISBN: 1-55725-205-X

All rights reserved. No part of this book may be reproduced in any form or by any means without the prior written
consent of the publisher, except brief quotations used in reviews.

Published by Paraclete Press
Brewster, Massachusetts
www.paraclete-press.com

Printed in the United States of America.

FOREWORD

At one point in my more than checkered career, I spent almost four years as Director of Trade Publishing for a fairly large cookbook publisher. What that rather ponderous title meant was that I oversaw the publication of everything else . . . the novels, the medical non-fiction, the biographies, the business how-to's—everything, in other words, that wasn't a cookbook.

Despite this compelling distinction, in those busy years I learned a great deal about cookbooks. Some of my understanding came by osmosis through simple proximity; but more of it came through the direct contact of lunchroom conversations and earnest requests from the other end of the hall for editorial second opinions. In the process of such frequent engagements, my colleagues taught me a number of things about good cookbooks, the principal one of which was that first and foremost a good cookbook is a good travel book. It helps, of course, if the food is also good; but even when a book's recipes and menus are both delicious and possible, they will not satisfy unless they also take the reader somewhere.

That somewhere may be simply another world of taste sensation that can be evoked by clear description and complementary juxtapositions. The somewhere may be another culture entered and grasped through the intimacy of its foods. It may be the soft world of remembrance laced with the gold of pleasant nostalgia. Or it may be the never-never land of an elegance and grandeur open to very few of us except in imagination. Whatever the somewhere, however, the good cookbook, the beloved one, the read and then re-read one, never forgets that its chief business is as much a thing of the armchair as a thing of the stove. The book you are about to read is a good cookbook.

I first came to the Community of Jesus in 1994—long enough ago, in other words, that I can no longer remember the exact experiences of that first stay in Bethany Guest House. Nor for that matter can I remember what my life was like without the ties of love, prayer, and shared Christianity that now bind me to that place and to the Brothers, Sisters and vowed laity who are the Community. It is enough that they are and I am and that we all know that together.

The religious have always fascinated the rest of us, I suspect. Certainly since the fifth century c.e., the religious who have chosen to live in community under the Benedictine rule have fascinated. The focus gained by the keeping of the Daily Offices, or appointed prayers, of the Church's liturgical day; the disciplined work of chant lifted in continuous praise to God the Father regardless of personal or communal circumstances; the elegance of hospitality and conduct in the midst of a studied simplicity; the difficult submission of the individual life to the Rule of the community's life before God: These set a mark most of us cannot attain while at the same time sustaining us with the possibilities of Heaven. And all these things are the life, the vocation, the sum of the Community of Jesus and of Sister Irene, a Senior Sister in Bethany Convent.

The recipes here are superb. They are lovely to the eye as well as the tongue, and they are kind to the cook. Indeed, I have eaten so many meals at Bethany's table by now that I recognize with glee some old favorites for which I have asked, but never received, the recipes. But the thing given us in the pages that follow is not food as such, but food in context. What we are given is food as it wells up from memory and ties us to what we have come from, food as it invites us to participate in the earth and its abundant cycles of giving and not giving, food that in its preparation becomes the objective, visible service of love. What we are given here is food as it constantly refines and expresses the spirit of the cook, food as it weaves community from shared satisfactions and the common table, food as it unites the individual with him- or herself by bringing together in one renewable and eucharistic congress all the pieces and parts—body, mind and spirit—of our humanness. What this cookbook gives, in other words, is transport into the world of Sister Irene Psathas and thereby into the world of the generous life.

Bon voyage.

Phyllis Tickle
Contributing Editor in Religion
Publishers Weekly

INTRODUCTION

I have a friend who is a strapping young fellow with a hearty appetite and an enthusiasm for food that makes me to *want* to cook for him. He is one of those people who not only enjoys eating most everything, but also appreciates it to the fullest. I have yet to offer him anything to which his immediate response after one taste hasn't been, "Awesome! Absolutely awesome!"

I have another friend, a woman considerably older, who is restricted to a very limited diet. She is a particularly sensitive, perceptive person with a rare sense of discrimination. To her, eating any meal, whether it be simply a piece of bread or a full-course dinner, is a sacramental experience in which she daily meets the Eucharist and all that it signifies to her. Her response is awesome in an entirely different sense.

Regardless of where one is on the continuum between these too extremes, there are few people whose hearts are not warmed or touched through food. Perhaps that is the reason why our Lord himself so often used food as a way to express care and concern for those he loved.

He prepared a cookout on the shore for his friends who were tired and hungry from fishing all night. He saw to it that lunch was provided for the multitude that followed him. His first concern for the young girl he raised from the dead was that she be given something to eat. One of the last things he did with his disciples before the crucifixion was to call them all together for a supper, and he made himself known to them in the breaking of the bread after his resurrection.

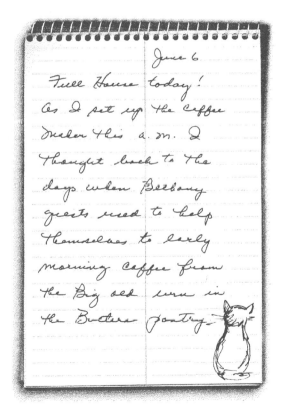

So after 30 years of life as a Sister of the Community of Jesus, I can understand why a friend recently referred to my work in the Community's kitchen as a holy vocation and of the kitchen at Bethany Retreat House especially as a sacristy.

I came to this place before there was a "Community" with or without a capital "C." No Convent, no Friary, no guest house, no abbey, just two Christian laywomen. It was in 1956, during a time of transition and questioning in my life, that I became aquainted with Cay Andersen and Judy Sorensen. These two devout friends lived and taught, informally, at Rock Harbor Manor, a guest house that Cay and her husband Bill owned in Orleans, Massachusetts. I had met the two women that same year at a conference in Swampscott, Massachusetts, on the north shore of Boston, where they had led a workshop I was attending. I liked what they had to say and felt that they could help me sort things out and discover what my priorities should be at that stage of my life.

One afternoon I decided to take a drive down to Cape Cod to see where they lived and to drop in for a chat. After a good visit, Cay and Judy invited me to stay for the night. Having other plans and not being prepared for an overnight, I thanked them and left to start home. But my car would not budge. Strange. This trusty little convertible had always taken me faithfully everywhere I wanted to go.

As I waited for help to arrive, Cay and Judy suggested I reconsider their invitation. No sooner had I said yes than every essential I needed appeared, including a bathing suit, sports clothes, and even a big beach towel. Maybe this wasn't a bad idea after all. At dinnertime I enjoyed my first tuna steak, caught fresh that day. Evening found me comfortably settled in a bedroom where from the back window I looked out on a lush locust grove and from the other, I saw the harbor, bustling with boats and fishermen. I loved it here and could not have felt more at home.

Little did I know on that first visit to Rock Harbor Manor, now our guest center and known as Bethany Retreat House, that a community was to form around this place, and that Cay and Judy would be the founders of that community and the spiritual mothers of a sisterhood of which I would become a member. Neither did I realize while staying in Bethany and eating in its lovely dining room, that I myself would someday spend many blessed years cooking, serving, and caring for others in this very place, and that this Community would be the mission field where I would spend the rest of my life seeing people helped and healed.

There are few things I find more rewarding than feeding people and giving them what I know they'll like, and I think it's impossible to determine who gets the most pleasure or blessing from it—the recipient or the giver.

In writing this book, I have looked back over past years in a way I never had before. Reliving one memory after another, I have been awestruck and amazed. My life has been so rich and so rewarding, blessed with the warmest relationships and most incredible experiences. I will always be grateful I made my way down to Rock Harbor. It was a journey that has paid off in rich dividends. So much so, that whenever guests say on their way out of Bethany, "We hate to leave this place," I understand exactly how they feel. That's why I'm still here.

Sister Irene Psathas

SISTER IRENE'S
CULINARY JOURNAL

JANUARY 1

Today starts a brand new year! It's unusually mild for January on the Cape. As I look out my window across the cleared, plowed-up space that used to be the welcoming lawn and circular driveway for Bethany House, I can see Bill Andersen sitting in his chair, his walker beside him, watching the construction. I know it has to be difficult for him to see buildings and grounds that he himself put in place many years ago, coming down before his very eyes to make room for a new church; but we have outgrown the Chapel of the Holy Paraclete that has served us so well for so long. The new church, massive and built of stone in the Italianate style of the early Church, will soon replace Holy Paraclete in our worship, but not in our memories. Watching Bill watch the building of the new church makes me think of the early days of this Community, of endings and beginnings.

For years the view out this window had been of a lovely rose garden encircling a bird bath where robins splashed and preened themselves. Just beyond the garden was the front door of Bethany Retreat House, framed with clematis vines, a beautiful maple tree on one side, forsythia and dogwood on the other.

Today the view is strikingly different. A dozen workmen in hardhats are orchestrating a building program, using as their tools a giant yellow Caterpillar, a huge crane, cement mixers, and jackhammers.

Outwardly the scene has drastically changed, yet in essence it remains unmistakably the same. While I miss the quiet, old familiar sight, I have a deep inner sense of expectancy about what is replacing it, and a strong conviction that what for so many years has beckoned people up the driveway to Bethany doorway, where they've been welcomed and invited to cross the threshold into another dimension of life, is even more alive and active now, still inviting those who choose to, to come and experience for themselves what might be waiting here for them.

at 37

I was thirty-seven when I came to be a novice, much older than the average young woman who is considering becoming a Sister. I was immediately assigned to work in the laundry, being responsible primarily for all the ironing, a job I never would have chosen. However, within a fairly short time I developed a system of praying for each person whose clothing I was ironing, and prayer turned the job into a rather satisfying experience.

The laundry room, being in the basement, and therefore out of the way of household traffic patterns, was generally nice and quiet. It was a pleasant enough place to be, and all things considered, I really preferred it to Mitzie's job of cleaning the guests' rooms in Bethany. She never seemed to be able to keep up, and was always charging into the laundry room to exchange soiled linens for clean ones.

One day, very unexpectedly, there were job changes. I was to do the shopping and cooking for the guest house, the Sisters, and the novices. I had always enjoyed cooking for myself or for a handful of invited friends, but cooking for twenty people on a regular basis presented a bit of a challenge, and quite frankly I was going to miss the laundry.

Hazel and I were talking recently about the early founding days of the Community when she temporarily lived with our novice class. She was a widow seriously considering making her home close to the Community, and while looking into the possibility of purchasing a house nearby, this was the only available place for her to stay.

Hazel has always remembered when I was assigned to do the cooking, for a group which at that time included overnight and longer-term guests, three original Sisters, and four novices, a total of about twenty people. Apparently the evening before a boiled-egg breakfast, I had asked each person how she wanted her eggs cooked. The previous cook had simply done them all hard or all soft, and Hazel confessed that at the time she had thought, "What a high-minded one this is. She thinks she's going to be able to boil eggs to suit each person?" She goes on to tell that that's precisely what happened. Each person's eggs were exactly to her liking, and she still marvels over this. As far as I was concerned, that's what Mama always did and would have done, so why wouldn't I?

It was known that the person responsible at that time for the menu planning kept a tight reign on the purse strings. Nothing was particularly wrong with that, except that at times we all felt a little uncomfortable being reminded that our numbers were increasing along with the cost of food. She took me on our first shopping trip and selected pork kidneys for the first meal I would be cooking, because they were quite low in price that week. In retrospect, it hardly seemed a fair way to introduce the new cook. Not that I myself had anything against kidneys of any kind. I just knew that they weren't too popular with the average person, pork ones in particular, because of their especially strong aroma. This assignment presented a bit of a challenge, but with a certain amount of determination and ingenuity, dinner turned out to be a delight to everyone—and there was not so much as a single slice of kidney left over for the cat.

Mama

JANUARY 7

The adage about reaching the heart through the stomach is by no means exclusive to men. Sister Marian reminded me of this today by telling me another story from the past that I had not remembered.

Marian was from a home that was very "big" on family, especially family birthdays. Her twenty-first birthday, as she had been quick to tell us, was, however, a disaster, coming as it did on the heels of a terminated engagement and a broken heart. Shortly after that sad birthday, she had come to live with the Sisters for a few months to sort things out and stayed longer than she had first intended. Suddenly her twenty-second birthday was approaching, and Marian was facing it with real trepidation.

It was 1974 and the Convent had not yet been built. We Sisters lived in different buildings on the grounds and ate all of our meals together in Bethany kitchen. Marian ate separately downstairs.

On her birthday her parents, who lived nearby, took her to lunch. She had a very nice time, but she now says, "What I have always treasured in my memory is my twenty-second birthday dinner. I was called up to Bethany dining room where the Sisters greeted me around a beautifully set table. I stood speechless (a rare state for me). I felt completely undeserving (also a rare state for me) of such love. The entire meal was indescribably delicious and served with such care.

"But it was the dessert that did me in—'Mama's Fluffy Maple Cake,' incredible both in taste and appearance. A single candle in a ring of fresh flowers flamed amidst swirls of fluffy maple frosting dusted with finely chopped walnuts. I was so moved! In that moment it hit me that the Sisters were my family and that this was where I belonged.

"Within a month, I became a novice—something I had resisted for almost five years. Now after so many years of being grateful for my life as a Sister, I look back on that birthday dinner as a turning point in my life. God knew the way to my heart! Fluffy Maple Cake!"

When my mother first came to America as a very young girl, her older sister found her a job doing household work for a wealthy family on Fifth Avenue in New York City. The lady of the house had a special liking for a certain cake from the bakeries of Abraham & Strauss: a tall, three-layered creation of light, moist, yellow cake, spread with creamy custard filling, frosted with generous swirls of maple-flavored divinity, and lavishly sprinkled with finely chopped walnuts.

My mother soon cultivated a taste for this culinary wonder also, and with her determination to make something from nothing and to please people's palates, she developed her own recipe for the cake by taste and instinct. Over the years it became a favorite in our family, and whenever my mother wanted to do something special for someone, she made them this cake. She named it "Fluffy Maple Cake" because of the lightness of texture of both the cake and the frosting. I have used it for years on retreats and for special birthdays, and have never yet come across anyone who hasn't been delighted with it.

My sister, Helen, was an excellent natural cook, and we both shared a love for coffee cakes and sweet rolls. I still use some of the recipes she passed on to me when she was a new bride so many years ago.

Helen

MAMA'S FLUFFY MAPLE CAKE

Cake:

2 cups sifted cake flour
3 teaspoons baking powder
Pinch of salt
½ cup (1 stick) butter,
    room temperature

1 cup sugar
1 teaspoon vanilla extract
Few drops lemon flavoring
3 eggs, separated
¾ cup milk

Filling:

2 cups milk
1 egg, separated
6 tablespoons sugar
2 tablespoons flour
2 tablespoons cornstarch

2 tablespoons butter
Pinch of salt
1 teaspoon vanilla extract
1 teaspoon banana flavoring

Fluffy Maple Frosting:

2 cups brown sugar
1 cup water
4 egg whites

Maple flavoring
Finely chopped walnuts

Yield: Makes one 8-inch cake

Cake: Prepare three 8-inch cake pans. Combine flour, baking powder, and salt. Cream together butter and sugar. Add vanilla extract and lemon flavoring. Beat in egg yolks. Add milk alternately with flour mixture. Mix well. Beat egg whites until stiff, and fold into cake batter. Bake at 350°F for about 30 minutes, or until cake tests done. Cool completely before filling and frosting.

Filling: Scald milk and let cool. Beat egg white to soft peaks. Beat egg yolk slightly and add to milk. Combine sugar, flour, and cornstarch. Add flour mixture to egg mixture, and add to scalded and cooled milk along with butter and salt. Bring to a boil, stirring constantly. Remove from heat and add vanilla extract and banana flavoring. Allow to cool before filling the cake.

Fluffy Maple Frosting: Melt brown sugar in the water. Boil 10 minutes or to about 240°F. Stiffly beat egg whites. While continu-

ing to beat, pour brown sugar mixture into egg whites. Add maple flavoring to taste; continue beating until cool.

Fill and frost the cake and cover with walnuts. Refrigerate until serving.

RASPBERRY CREAM CHEESE COFFEE CAKE

2¼ cups flour
¾ + ¼ cup sugar
¾ cup margarine
    or butter
½ teaspoon baking powder
½ teaspoon baking soda
¼ teaspoon salt

¾ cup dairy sour cream
1 + 1 egg
1 teaspoon almond extract
8 ounces cream cheese,
    softened
½ cup raspberry
    preserves
½ cup sliced almonds

Yield: Makes 16 servings

Preheat oven to 350°F. Grease and flour bottom and sides of 9- or 10-inch springform pan. In large bowl, combine flour and the ¾ cup sugar. Using pastry blender or fork, cut in margarine until mixture resembles coarse crumbs. Reserve 1 cup crumb mixture. To remaining crumb mixture, add baking powder, baking soda, salt, sour cream, 1 of the eggs, and almond extract; blend well. Spread batter over bottom and 2 inches up sides of prepared pan. (Batter should be about ¼ inch thick on sides.) In small bowl, combine cream cheese, the ¼ cup sugar, and the remaining egg; blend well. Pour over batter in pan. Carefully spoon preserves evenly over cheese filling. In small bowl, combine 1 cup reserved crumb mixture and sliced almonds. Sprinkle over top. Bake for 45 to 55 minutes or until cream cheese filling is set and crust is deep golden brown. Cool 15 minutes. Remove sides of pan. Serve warm or cool; cut into wedges. Refrigerate leftovers.

STREUSEL PUMPKIN SWEET ROLLS

Rolls:

4³/₄ to 5³/₄ cups flour, divided	1 pkg dry active yeast
½ cup sugar	1¼ cups milk
2 teaspoons grated lemon peel	1 cup canned pumpkin
1½ teaspoons salt	½ cup margarine or butter

Crumb Topping:

1½ cups flour	¼ teaspoon ground nutmeg
1 cup firmly packed	½ teaspoon ground allspice
brown sugar	¾ cup margarine or butter
1 teaspoon ground cinnamon	½ cup chopped nuts

Sweet Roll Glaze:

1 cup confectioners' sugar	1 to 2 tablespoons milk
½ teaspoon vanilla extract	

Yield: Makes 20 rolls

Note: Lightly spoon flour into measuring cup; level off.

Rolls: In large bowl, combine 1½ cups flour, sugar, lemon peel, salt, and yeast; mix well. In small saucepan, heat milk, pumpkin, and margarine until hot (120° to 130°F). Add hot mixture to flour mixture. Blend at low speed until moistened; beat 3 minutes at medium speed by hand; stir in 2½ to 3 cups flour until dough pulls away from sides of bowl.

On floured surface, knead in ¾ to 1¼ cups flour until dough is smooth and elastic, about 5 to 8 minutes. Place dough in greased bowl; cover loosely with plastic wrap and cloth towel. Let rise in warm place (80° to 85°F) until light and doubled in size, about 1 hour. Grease 15 x 10 x 1-inch pan.

Topping: In medium bowl, combine flour, brown sugar, cinnamon, nutmeg, and allspice. With fork or pastry blender, cut in margarine until mixture is crumbly.

Punch dough down several times to remove all air bubbles. On lightly floured surface, roll dough to 20 x 15-inch rectangle. Spoon 2½ cups of the crumb topping evenly over dough; sprinkle with nuts. Starting with 20-inch side, roll up tightly; press edges to seal. Cut into 20 slices; place cut side down in greased pan. Cover loosely with plastic wrap and cloth towel. Let rise in warm place until light and doubled in size, about 45 minutes.

Heat oven to 350°F. Uncover dough. Sprinkle with remaining crumb topping. Bake at 350°F for 35 to 50 minutes or until golden brown.

Sweet Roll Glaze: In small bowl, combine all glaze ingredients, adding enough milk for desired drizzling consistency; blend until smooth. Drizzle over warm rolls.

LEMON POPPY SEED MUFFINS

3 cups flour	1 cup sugar
1 tablespoon baking powder	1 tablespoon grated
½ teaspoon baking soda	lemon zest
½ teaspoon salt	2 large eggs
3 tablespoons poppy seeds	1½ cups plain low-fat
10 tablespoons butter,	yogurt
softened	

Syrup:

¼ cup sugar	¼ cup lemon juice

Yield: Makes 12 servings

Adjust oven rack to lower middle position and preheat oven to 375°F. Mix flour, baking powder, baking soda, salt, and poppy seeds in medium bowl; set aside.

Beat butter, sugar, and lemon zest with electric mixer on medium-high speed until light and fluffy, about 2 minutes. Add eggs, one at a time, beating well after each addition. Beat in one-half of the dry ingredients. Beat in one-third of the yogurt. Beat in remaining dry ingredients in two batches, alternating with yogurt, until incorporated.

Spray 12-cup muffin tin with vegetable cooking spray or coat lightly with butter. Use large ice cream scoop to divide batter evenly among cups. Bake until muffins are golden brown, 25 to 30 minutes. Set on wire rack to cool slightly, about 5 minutes.

While muffins are baking, prepare syrup. Heat sugar and lemon juice in small saucepan until sugar dissolves and mixture forms light syrup, 3 to 4 minutes.

Remove muffins from tin. Brush syrup over muffins and serve.

BLUEBERRY BUCKLE

Buckle:

½ cup vegetable shortening	2½ teaspoons baking powder
¾ cup sugar	¼ teaspoon salt
1 egg	½ cup milk
½ teaspoon lemon extract	½ teaspoon vanilla extract
2 cups flour	2 cups fresh blueberries

Topping:

½ cup sugar	¼ cup butter or margarine
⅔ cup flour	

Yield: Makes 12 servings

Preheat oven to 350°F.

Thoroughly cream shortening and sugar; add egg and lemon extract, and beat until light and fluffy. Sift together flour, baking powder, and salt; add to creamed mixture alternately with milk. Add vanilla extract. Spread in greased 11 x 17 x 1½-inch pan. Top with berries.

For the topping mix sugar and flour. Cut in butter until crumbly; sprinkle over berries. Bake for 50 to 55 minutes. Cool for ½ hour; cut in squares. Serve warm.

JANUARY 13

*The weather suddenly has turned raw and wintry, not the most
pleasant day for the arrival of Bishop Dalton,
who comes this afternoon for his annual visit and
retreat with the Community. I shall never forget his first time
with us almost twenty-five years ago.*

Beautiful," I said to myself, taking one more look at the table. I was so pleased with the way the centerpiece had turned out and the way in which it complemented the china. Mother Cay loved it and so did I. The morning sun beaming in through the big bay window gave an inviting warmth to the whole room—a perfect setting for breakfast with the bishop.

This was my first experience serving a bishop and I wasn't sure just what to expect. Everyone said he was very nice, but that didn't really soothe the part of me that often felt inadequate and intimidated by important people I did not yet know.

The menu included a light Dutch Apple Pancake that is baked at a high temperature, rises to a spectacular height, and remains there for a brief moment of glory, all golden and puffed up with its own breathtaking beauty, bringing exclamations from everyone at the table (providing, of course, it's brought there at just the crucial moment). This, I had perfectly planned and timed.

I left to start the coffee as another Sister came in to discuss with Mother Cay the temperature of the room and whether having a real fire lit in the fireplace might add even a bit more warmth and welcome to the atmosphere. The bishop arrived and after initial greetings all around, Mother Cay, knowing his love of tropical plants, asked if they could take a few minutes to show him her bird-of-paradise plant just come into bloom. "Fine," I replied, "Everything will be ready in about five minutes or less."

They went out to the porch, and I to the kitchen.

I peeked into the oven. My lovely culinary wonder could not have been cooperating more beautifully with all the rest of my best laid plans. Within minutes it would reach its peak of perfection. After filling the coffee and tea pots, I

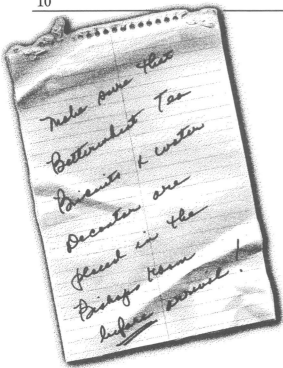

started back to the dining room, only to be suddenly seized with a tickle in my throat. This was no time to have a coughing spell and certainly not with a dangerously hot pot in each hand. As I turned the corner and was about to step over the threshold I was socked in the face by a blinding cloud of smoke pouring out of the fireplace in enormous billows. Through the entrance at the other end of the room came the bishop, gasping for breath, feeling his way through the haze, and shouting, "What is it? What's happening?"

Alarms started ringing, Brothers came running, and within minutes, sirens, trucks, and firemen followed. "The flue," shouted Mother Cay. "Is the flue open?" It was not, and thus unbelievably thick clouds of smoke wrapped themselves around us like heavy blankets. We threw open windows, turned on fans, and flung doors ajar in an attempt to save everyone from suffocation. By this time the room was filled as with a cast of thousands taking a curtain call after the finale of a grand opera performance.

The excitement died down a little, the air cleared a bit, and we all began to collect our wits. The bishop smiled and in his most gracious manner turned to the Mothers and then to all of us, addressing us in that distinctive way that only an English bishop can: "Well, I must say this has been quite an unforgettable reception you have given me. I have found it most moving, and I am impressed beyond words, but really you should not have gone to all this trouble."

For a certain retreat meal I had chosen Lemon Meringue Pie as a dinner dessert. The closer the meal came, the less time I had to make the pies. Unexpectedly, some day-old berry pies were given to us by a local grocery store. They could conceivably pass as a mediocre dessert for the retreat, and the convenience might compensate for the lack of freshness and flavor of the home-

made pies I had planned. I weighed this carefully in my mind through the afternoon, but try as I might, no matter how many times I felt inclined to settle on serving them, I could not bring myself to do so. It was not that I particularly like making lemon meringue nor that it is especially a favorite of mine. I simply did not feel at peace until I decided that, regardless of the pressure involved, I would launch into preparing the homemade pies as originally planned.

During those early days it was not at all uncommon for retreatants to experience healing during the course of a retreat and often through the most simple, unlikely, or even seemingly insignificant means. A flower in their room, a word casually spoken by someone in passing, the sound of a certain bird call—any one of such things could trigger an emotion or memory that was the key to unsolved problems they might have been wrestling with for years. This is still true today with guests and retreatants who come and spend time in such an environment of prayer.

There was one man on this particular retreat who had come for the first time. He had remained stony-faced from the time of his arrival, and from all outward appearances he was only enduring his time with us and benefiting very little, if at all, from anything taking place. Without dwelling on him, I prayed for him each time I noticed him. I've always been of the persuasion that no one's coming to Bethany is coincidental, but that there is a purpose behind every visit and that God has something to give to each person who comes. This being the case, it is our place to care for our guests and tend to their needs in a manner that will help this happen. So I prayed that this man would receive whatever God intended for him.

Late that evening, he appeared at the kitchen threshold. I had to look twice to make sure it was indeed the same person. Obviously having shed some tears, his eyes were red and swollen, but his face was soft with the faint hint of a smile at the corners of his mouth. With some effort to keep his voice from trembling he had come to thank me for the fresh Lemon Meringue Pie that was tart and runny, just the way his mother had always made it. He could not tell me all that it had meant to him, nor did he need to; some things are understood without ever having to be spelled out.

DUTCH APPLE PANCAKES

Cinnamon-sugar mixture	½ cup sugar
4 large apples, peeled and sliced	6 eggs
8 + 2 tablespoons melted butter	1 cup milk
1 cup flour	

Yield: Makes 8 to 9 servings

Sprinkle cinnamon-sugar mixture on apple slices and fry in the 8 tablespoons of butter until well cooked. Put apples in a 9 x 9-inch baking dish. Mix the 2 tablespoons of butter and the remaining ingredients in the blender. Pour over the apples and bake at 425°F for 15 to 20 minutes. Take out and sprinkle with more cinnamon-sugar mixture and dot with the remaining 2 tablespoons of butter. Bake 5 minutes more, or until fluffy.

JANUARY 20

Tonight at Church History Class I sat down next to Brother Jeremy. He was recalling his first retreat here. "I can still remember that chicken you cooked with peaches and black cherries in a tangy, mouth-watering sauce," he said, "and that was twenty-five years ago."

Here are some of the other favorite meals and desserts that I often repeated by special request in the old days for retreatants and guests:

POULET JUBILEE

2 broiler-fryers, cut up
1 teaspoon salt
¼ teaspoon pepper
¼ cup margarine, melted
2 cups Catalina® salad
   dressing

2 cups drained peach slices
2 cups drained dark
   sweet cherries
1 medium onion, sliced
½ cup chili sauce
   Hot cooked rice

Yield: Makes 6 to 8 servings

Preheat oven to 325°F. Place chicken, skin side up, in baking pan. Sprinkle with salt and pepper. Drizzle with margarine; broil until brown. Combine salad dressing, peaches, cherries, onion and chili sauce; spoon over chicken. Bake at 325°F for 1 hour or until chicken is tender. Serve over hot cooked rice.

WHOLE STUFFED BASS OR BLUEFISH

Stuffing:

3 cups dried bread cubes	1 cup minced celery
½ cup clam broth	¼ pound butter, melted
3 tablespoons chopped parsley	Salt and pepper
1 cup chopped onions	

Fish:

1 whole striped bass or bluefish	1 cup white wine
(about 4 pounds)	½ cup olive oil
Salt and pepper	1 tablespoon oregano
Melted butter	2 tablespoons chopped parsley
Juice of 1 lemon	

Savory sauce:

1 cup olive oil	½ cup tomatoes, fresh or
½ cup lemon juice	canned
3 bay leaves	1 tablespoon rosemary
1 crushed garlic clove	1 teaspoon sugar
	Salt and pepper

Yield: Makes 6 to 8 servings

Striped bass weighs 3 pounds or more; sea bass, 1 to 4 pounds. Have your butcher clean the fish and prepare for stuffing, leaving the tail intact.

Stuffing: Combine all ingredients and toss lightly.

Fish: Sprinkle inside of the fish with salt and pepper, and fill with stuffing, reserving leftover stuffing. Place carefully in a buttered baking pan, brush with melted butter, and sprinkle with salt, pepper, and lemon juice. Combine wine, olive oil, oregano, and parsley; beat with a fork, and pour over and around fish. Bake at 375 °F for 1 hour, basting frequently. Place the remaining stuffing in a casserole dish, dot with butter, cover with foil, and bake.

Sauce: Combine all ingredients and simmer for 20 minutes. Pour over baked fish before serving.

SHORT RIBS IN HORSERADISH SAUCE

1 cup dry white wine	1½ cups finely chopped celery
1 + 2 tablespoons minced garlic	1½ cups finely chopped onions
2 tablespoons Dijon mustard	5¼ cups chicken stock
1 teaspoon crushed red pepper	4 teaspoons fresh thyme, chopped
18 (3-inch to 4-inch) pieces meaty beef chuck short ribs	2 bay leaves
Salt and pepper	2 tablespoons horseradish
2¾ + 1 cup beef stock or broth	4 teaspoons cornstarch
2 tablespoons olive oil	¼ cup water
1½ cups finely chopped carrots	Fresh thyme sprigs

Yield: Makes 6 servings

Mix wine, 1 tablespoon garlic, mustard, and red pepper in large glass baking dish. Add short ribs; turn to coat. Cover and refrigerate 8 to 12 hours, turning occasionally.

Preheat oven to 500°F. Using tongs, transfer short ribs to a large roasting pan; reserve marinade. Sprinkle short ribs with salt and pepper. Roast until brown, turning once after about 30 minutes. Transfer short ribs to large bowl. Place the roasting pan over 2 burners. Heat juices over medium high heat. Add the 1 cup beef stock to the pan, and bring to a boil, scraping up any browned bits. Pour pan juices into the bowl with short ribs.

Reduce oven temperature to 350°F. Heat the olive oil in a heavy, large oven-proof pot over medium high heat. Add the carrots, celery, onions, and the 2 tablespoons garlic. Sauté until vegetables are tender, about 12 minutes. Add short ribs and pan juices, reserved marinade, the 2¾ cups beef stock, chicken stock, thyme, bay leaves, and horseradish. Bring to a boil. Cover pot and place in oven. Bake until short ribs are tender, about 2 hours.

Using tongs, transfer short ribs to a large bowl. Boil cooking liquid until reduced to a thin sauce consistency, about 25 minutes. Strain the liquid; discard solids and return liquid to the pot. Dissolve cornstarch in the water. Whisk into the cooking liquid. Boil until the sauce thickens and coats spoon, stirring constantly, about 2 minutes. Season with pepper. Return short ribs to pot. Simmer until heated through, about 3 minutes. Transfer to a platter. Garnish with thyme sprigs.

SPICED PORK TENDERLOIN WITH APPLE CHUTNEY

1/4 cup olive oil	1 1/2 teaspoons ground
3 tablespoons chopped garlic	cinnamon
4 1/2 teaspoons ground cumin	3 pounds pork tenderloin
1 1/2 teaspoons cayenne	Salt and pepper

Yield: Makes 6 servings

Combine oil, garlic, cumin, cayenne, and cinnamon in a bowl. Rub over the pork tenderloin. Cover the pork, and refrigerate at least 4 hours.

Preheat the oven to 400°F. Heat a large, nonstick skillet over high heat. Season pork with salt and pepper. Add pork to the skillet in batches and brown on all sides, about 5 minutes per batch. Transfer pork to a large baking pan. Roast pork until thermometer inserted into the thickest part registers 155°F, about 15 minutes. Transfer pork to a platter and let rest for 5 minutes.

Cut the pork into 1/2-inch-thick slices and arrange on plates; serve with chutney (recipe follows).

APPLE CHUTNEY

3 cups finely chopped and peeled (about 4 medium) Granny Smith apples	1 tablespoon peeled and chopped fresh ginger
1 cup chopped onion	1 1/2 teaspoons chopped garlic
1 cup packed brown sugar	1 teaspoon salt
1 cup water	1/4 teaspoon dried crushed red pepper
3/4 cup cider vinegar	1/4 teaspoon ground nutmeg
1/2 cup chopped red bell pepper	1/4 teaspoon ground allspice
1/2 cup dried currants	Pinch of cloves
	Extra salt and pepper

Yield: Makes about 3 cups

Combine all ingredients except extra salt and pepper in a heavy large saucepan. Bring to a boil over medium heat, stirring until sugar dissolves. Reduce heat and simmer until liquid is slightly syrupy, stirring occasionally, about 1 hour. Season chutney to taste with salt and pepper. Cool to room temperature. (The chutney can be prepared up to 1 week ahead. Cover and refrigerate. Bring to room temperature before serving.)

MUSTARD-GLAZED CORNED BEEF BRISKET

1 (4 to 5 pound) corned beef brisket	½ cup maple syrup
8 whole black peppercorns	⅓ cup sherry wine vinegar
2 bay leaves	⅓ cup firmly packed brown sugar
½ cup Dijon mustard	1 tablespoon oriental sesame oil
1 teaspoon dry mustard	

Yield: Makes 6 servings

Place brisket in large pot. Add water to cover, peppercorns, and bay leaves. Bring to a boil. Reduce heat; cover and simmer until tender, about 3½ hours. Drain brisket.

Transfer brisket to heavy shallow roasting pan, fat side up.

Preheat oven to 350°F. Whisk mustards in heavy small saucepan. Stir in remaining ingredients. Simmer 5 minutes, stirring constantly. Spread glaze evenly over top of brisket. Bake until heated through, about 45 minutes. Baste once or twice.

Note: Do not add peppercorns if they come with brisket.

BAKED SALMON WITH MUSTARD-CRUMB CRUST

2 tablespoons + 1 teaspoon distilled white vinegar	4 6- to 7-ounce salmon fillets
2 tablespoons sugar	Dried thyme
2 tablespoons Dijon mustard	Onion salt and pepper
1½ teaspoons dry mustard	1 cup fresh French bread crumbs
⅓ cup vegetable oil	

Yield: Makes 4 servings

Place vinegar, sugar, and both mustards in a blender. With blender running, slowly pour in oil and blend until medium-thick sauce forms. (Can be made 1 day ahead. Chill.)

Preheat oven to 375°F. Lightly grease a 13 x 9-inch baking dish. Arrange salmon in prepared dish, skin side down. Season with dried thyme, onion salt, and pepper. Spread 1 tablespoon mustard sauce over each fillet, covering completely. Press bread crumbs onto fish. Bake until salmon is cooked through and crumb topping is crisp and golden brown, about 18 minutes.

Using a large spatula, transfer salmon fillets to a platter. Serve, passing remaining mustard sauce separately.

VEAL MARSALA

1 pound thinly sliced veal	5 ounces beef bouillon
4 ounces freshly grated Parmesan cheese	⅔ cup water
½ pound fresh mushrooms	1 tablespoon Kitchen Bouquet ®
3 tablespoons butter	⅔ cup Marsala wine
	1 tablespoon chopped parsley Cooked linguini

Yield: Makes 4 servings

Cut veal into medallions and pound until thin; press Parmesan cheese into both sides of the meat. Sauté mushrooms in butter; remove mushrooms and sauté medallions until lightly browned. Return mushrooms to pan; add beef bouillon and Kitchen Bouquet ®. Cook 2 to 3 minutes over low heat. Add Marsala wine and cook 2 more minutes. Stir in the parsley. Pour over veal and serve with linguini.

GRILLED PORK CHOPS WITH HORSERADISH CREAM

1½ tablespoons olive oil (preferably extra-virgin)
3 teaspoons chopped fresh thyme or 1 teaspoon dried, divided
2 5- to 6-ounce boneless pork loin chops (each about 1 inch thick)
2 medium parsnips, peeled, cut diagonally into ¼-inch-thick slices
1 large tomato, cut in half crosswise
Salt and pepper
Onion salt
½ cup whipping cream
2 tablespoons prepared white horseradish

Yield: Makes 2 servings; can be doubled

Prepare barbecue (medium-high heat). Mix oil and half of the thyme in a small bowl. Sprinkle the pork, parsnips, and tomato with salt and pepper. Brush parsnips and tomato with thyme oil. Grill pork until no longer pink in center, turning occasionally, about 20 minutes total. After 10 minutes, place parsnips and tomato on barbecue. Grill tomato halves until softened but still holding shape, about 3 minutes per side. Grill parsnips until slightly charred and tender, about 5 minutes per side. Transfer pork and vegetables to a plate when done. Season with onion salt.

Meanwhile, simmer the cream in heavy, small saucepan over medium heat until reduced to ⅓ cup, about 5 minutes. Mix in horseradish and the remaining half of the thyme. Simmer sauce 1 minute longer, whisking constantly. Season with pepper.

Divide pork chops and vegetables between 2 plates. Spoon sauce over pork.

BEEF TENDERLOIN WITH ARTICHOKE PURÉE

Artichoke Purée:
1 (14-ounce) can artichoke hearts, drained well
3 tablespoons mayonnaise
3 tablespoons freshly grated Parmesan cheese
1 tablespoon fresh lemon juice
2 teaspoons chopped fresh tarragon or ¾ teaspoon dried
1 teaspoon grated lemon peel
1 garlic clove, minced
¼ teaspoon ground nutmeg
Generous pinch of cayenne
Onion salt and pepper

Steak:
2 8-ounce beef tenderloin steaks (each about 1 inch thick)

Yield: Makes 4 servings

Purée: Purée artichokes in a food processor until almost smooth. Add mayonnaise, grated Parmesan, lemon juice, tarragon, lemon peel, garlic, nutmeg, and cayenne. Process until well blended. Transfer to a small bowl. Season with onion salt and pepper.

Steak: Grill steak to desired doneness. Cut each steak across the grain into thin strips. Spoon purée over sliced steak and serve at once.

ROAST TURKEY WITH SWEET POTATO–APPLE HASH AND MARSALA SAUCE

Sweet Potato-Apple Hash:

1 + ½ teaspoons olive oil	1 cup chicken stock or canned
4 bacon slices, minced	chicken broth
½ cup chopped onion	2 tablespoons Frangelico®
2 cups diced, peeled	liqueur
sweet potatoes	¼ teaspoon chopped
1 cup diced, peeled Granny	fresh thyme
Smith apple	¼ teaspoon chopped
	fresh rosemary

Turkey:

1 2-pound boneless turkey	Onion salt and pepper
breast half, skin and visible	
fat removed	

Sauce:

1 cup + 2 tablespoons	¼ teaspoon chopped
dry Marsala wine	fresh thyme
2 teaspoons minced shallots	2 teaspoons arrowroot
½ teaspoon minced garlic	or cornstarch
4 cups canned	Salt and pepper
chicken broth	

Yield: Makes 4 servings

Sweet Potato-Apple Hash: Preheat oven to 450°F. Heat the 1 teaspoon oil in a large nonstick skillet over medium heat. Sauté bacon until it begins to brown, about 2 minutes. Add onion and sauté until tender, about 4 minutes. Add sweet potatoes and apple and sauté 2 minutes. Add stock and liqueur and bring to boil. Mix in thyme and rosemary.

Turkey: Place turkey breast in a large glass baking dish. Rub with the remaining ½ teaspoon of oil. Sprinkle with onion salt and pepper. Roast turkey 10 minutes. Spoon hash mixture around the turkey and continue roasting until a meat thermometer inserted into the thickest part of the turkey registers 165°F and the hash is tender, stirring occasionally, about 25 minutes longer.

Sauce: Combine the 1 cup Marsala wine, shallot, and garlic in a heavy, large saucepan and boil until reduced by half, about 8 minutes. Add broth and boil until reduced by half, about 20 minutes. Mix in thyme. Mix arrowroot with the remaining 2 tablespoons Marsala wine in a small bowl. Add arrowroot mixture to sauce and bring to a boil, stirring occasionally. Season to taste with salt and pepper.

Slice turkey and arrange on plates. Spoon hash alongside. Spoon Marsala Sauce over turkey and serve.

BEETS IN ORANGE SAUCE

4 large beets, trimmed	1 tablespoon grated
1 cup orange juice	orange peel (orange
2 tablespoons brown sugar	part only)
2 tablespoons (¼ stick) butter	2 teaspoons red wine vinegar
	Salt and pepper

Yield: Makes 4 servings

Preheat oven to 400°F. Wrap 2 beets together in foil. Repeat with remaining beets. Place on baking sheet. Bake until tender, about 1 hour and 15 minutes. Cool. Peel the beets. Cut each into 8 wedges.

Combine beets, orange juice, sugar, butter, orange peel, and vinegar in medium, nonaluminum saucepan. Simmer over medium heat until sauce is syrupy, stirring often, about 8 minutes. Season with salt and pepper. (Can be made 1 day ahead. Chill. Rewarm over low heat, stirring often.) Serve hot.

PARSNIP, CARROT, AND LEEK GRATIN

2 tablespoons (¼ stick) butter
2 pounds leeks (white and pale green parts only), halved lengthwise, rinsed, cut crosswise into 1-inch pieces (about 5 cups)
1½ pounds large carrots, peeled, cut diagonally into ¼-inch-thick slices
1½ pounds large parsnips, peeled, cut diagonally into ¼-inch-thick slices
2½ cups milk
2 tablespoons fresh sage, chopped, or 2 teaspoons dried rubbed
2 teaspoons Dijon mustard
¾ teaspoon onion salt
½ teaspoon pepper
½ cup coarsely grated Parmesan cheese

Yield: Makes 6 to 8 servings

Position rack in top third of oven and preheat to 400°F. Butter 13 x 9 x 2-inch glass baking dish. Melt butter in a heavy, large skillet over medium-low heat. Add leeks and sauté until soft and beginning to color, about 15 minutes. Transfer leeks to large bowl.

Cook carrots and parsnips in a large pot of boiling salted water until almost tender, about 3 minutes. Drain well; place in the bowl with the leeks. Whisk milk, sage, mustard, salt, and pepper to blend in a medium bowl. Pour milk mixture over vegetables and stir gently to combine. Transfer to prepared baking dish. Sprinkle with Parmesan. Cover the dish with foil. (Can be prepared 6 hours ahead; refrigerate. Let stand at room temperature for 30 minutes before continuing.)

Bake gratin for 30 minutes. Uncover and bake until vegetables are tender, top is golden brown, and cream is thickened, about 30 minutes longer. Let stand 10 minutes; serve hot.

SEAFOOD STRUDEL

Sauce:
2 tablespoons butter
2 tablespoons all-purpose flour
½ teaspoon Dijon mustard
Salt
Cayenne
¾ cup milk, room temperature
2 tablespoons whipping cream

Strudel:
¾ cup bread crumbs
¼ cup + 2 tablespoons freshly grated Parmesan cheese
¼ teaspoon dry mustard
½ pound phyllo pastry sheets or puff pastry
1 pound cleaned, shelled, cooked crab, shrimp, lobster, or tuna, or combination, in bite-size chunks
½ cup grated Swiss cheese
¾ cup sour cream
¼ cup chopped parsley
¼ cup minced shallots
2 tablespoons chopped chives
¾ cup (1½ sticks) butter, melted
2 tablespoons chopped parsley
Minced parsley

Yield: Makes 8 to 10 servings

Sauce: Melt 2 tablespoons butter in small saucepan over low heat. Stir in flour to make smooth paste and heat gently, stirring constantly, until mixture just begins to bubble. Remove from heat and add mustard, pinch of salt, and cayenne. Slowly stir in milk. Place over medium heat and cook, stirring constantly, until mixture bubbles and thickens. Add cream, taste for seasonings, and adjust if necessary. Cover and chill until very thick and firm, about 2 hours.

Strudel: Preheat oven to 375°F. Butter a baking sheet. Combine bread crumbs, the ¼ cup Parmesan, and dry mustard in small bowl. Sprinkle mixture on phyllo sheets. Layer seafood evenly on phyllo sheets and sprinkle with Swiss cheese. Dot with sour cream. Sprinkle with parsley, shallots, chives, and dot with chilled sauce.

Roll up phyllo into a log, placing seam side on prepared baking sheet, and brush with some of the melted butter. Bake 12 minutes. Remove from oven and brush with more melted butter. Slice loaf. Add parsley to remaining butter and brush again. Repeat brushing 3 more times during baking, reserving a little butter to brush on just before serving. Bake 35 to 40 minutes longer, until crisp and golden brown. Meanwhile, warm a large serving platter.

Remove strudel from oven and brush with remaining parsley-butter. Cool 10 minutes and transfer to warmed serving platter using long spatula. Dust with the remaining 2 tablespoons Parmesan cheese and minced parsley.

ALPINE CHICKEN

4 cups diced cooked chicken	1 teaspoon salt
2 cups sliced celery	Dash of pepper
2 cups toasted bread cubes	8 ounces shredded Swiss
1 cup mayonnaise-like	cheese
salad dressing	½ cup toasted slivered
½ cup milk	almonds
¼ cup chopped onion	

Yield: Makes 6 servings

Combine all ingredients except nuts. Pour into a 2-quart casserole; sprinkle with nuts. Bake at 350°F 30 to 40 minutes. (Can be made ahead. Cover unbaked casserole; refrigerate. When ready to cook, bake at 350°F for 50 minutes. Remove cover; continue to bake 10 minutes.)

KIELBASA AND CAULIFLOWER CASSEROLE

3 pounds cauliflower, untrimmed
1¾ pounds kielbasa

Sauce:

½ cup margarine, melted	1¾ cups milk (or more)
½ cup flour	Salt and pepper
¼ jar Dijon mustard	1½ cups cubed cheddar cheese
1¾ cups chicken bouillon	Freshly grated Parmesan
(or more)	cheese

Yield: Makes 8 to 10 servings

Cook cauliflower in a small amount of water until just tender. Do not overcook. Put sausage in a skillet. Cover with water and simmer for 10 minutes. Remove and cut into ½-inch slices. Heat the margarine in a saucepan and sauté kielbasa for 3 minutes. Stir in the flour and mustard; slowly add bouillon and milk and cook, stirring, until sauce is thickened and smooth. Don't make sauce too thick. Season to taste with salt and pepper. Put cauliflower on the bottom of a 9 x 13-inch, greased baking dish and tuck pieces of sausage and cheese in and around florets. Try to have just one layer. Pour sauce over all and sprinkle with Parmesan cheese. Bake at 350°F for 20 minutes until golden and bubbling.

EGGPLANT SOUFFLÉ

2 large eggplants	Milk
2 tablespoons or more butter	4 egg whites
3 egg yolks, slightly beaten	2 tablespoons blanched
½ cup thin cream or rich milk	almonds, toasted, finely
Onion salt and pepper	chopped
Ground nutmeg	2 tablespoons bread
½ cup soft bread crumbs	crumbs, toasted

Yield: Makes 6 to 8 servings

Cook eggplants in 2 quarts salted, slightly boiling water for 15 minutes or until tender. Remove skins and mash pulp; add 2 tablespoons butter, yolks, cream, and season to taste with onion salt, pepper, and nutmeg.

Soak bread crumbs in milk and squeeze crumbs in a dry cloth to remove the moisture. Add crumbs to eggplant. Fold in egg whites and turn into generously buttered soufflé dish. Sprinkle with almonds mixed with the same amount of toasted bread crumbs and a little melted butter. Bake for 30 minutes in a 400°F oven. Serve immediately in the baking dish.

ITALIAN EGGPLANT PARMESAN

2 small eggplants, about 2 pounds	1 cup chopped Italian parsley
2 cups ricotta cheese	Salt and freshly ground pepper
2 eggs	½ cup olive oil or more
¼ cup freshly grated Parmesan cheese	2 quarts Quick Tomato Sauce (below)

Yield: Makes 4 to 6 servings

Slice the eggplants. Preheat the oven to 400°F. Combine ricotta cheese, eggs, Parmesan, and chopped parsley. Season to taste with salt and pepper.

Heat 2 tablespoons of olive oil in a large skillet until oil begins to smoke. Add a single layer of eggplant slices, not overlapping. Turn slices quickly to coat both sides lightly with oil; reduce the heat slightly. Fry eggplant until lightly browned on both sides. (Do not add more oil after eggplant is in the skillet.) When slices are browned, remove to paper towels to drain. Pour 2 tablespoons more oil into the skillet and cook another layer of eggplant. Repeat until all eggplant pieces are cooked.

Spread ½ cup of the tomato sauce over bottom of an oval gratin dish measuring 9 x 12 inches. Arrange layer of eggplant slices over the sauce. Top each eggplant slice with a tablespoon of ricotta mix-ture. Repeat, arranging the next layer of eggplant slices to cover the gaps between slices in the first layer. Add more ricotta mixture. Add a final layer of eggplant, cover well with remaining tomato sauce, and spoon remaining ricotta mixture down center of the dish.

Set the dish on the middle rack of the oven and bake for 25 to 30 minutes, or until well browned and bubbling. Let stand for 10 minutes before serving.

QUICK TOMATO SAUCE

½ cup olive oil, best quality	⅛ teaspoon crushed red pepper
3 cups onions, finely chopped	¼ teaspoon oregano
2 medium size carrots, peeled and finely chopped	1 bay leaf
2 (28-ounce each) cans plum tomatoes, peeled, in tomato purée	1 cup finely chopped Italian parsley
1 tablespoon dried basil	4 garlic cloves, peeled and finely chopped
1 tablespoon dried thyme	1 tablespoon balsamic or other mild vinegar (optional)
1 teaspoon salt	

Yield: Makes 2 quarts

Heat the oil in a heavy pot. Add onions and carrots and cook, cov-ered, over low heat until vegetables are tender, about 25 minutes.

Add tomatoes, basil, thyme, salt, red pepper, oregano, and bay leaf. Cook over medium heat, stirring occasionally, for 30 min-utes. Remove the bay leaf and transfer tomato mixture to the bowl of a food processor fitted with a steel blade, (or use a food mill fit-ted with a medium disc) and purée.

Return sauce to the pot and set over medium heat. Add parsley and garlic and cook for another 5 minutes.

Taste and correct seasonings. Add balsamic vinegar if the sauce seems to lack intensity. Serve immediately or cool to room tem-perature, cover, and refrigerate, or freeze.

DATE-MACAROON PIE

3 egg whites
1 teaspoon almond extract
1 teaspoon water
½ teaspoon baking powder

1 cup sugar
½ cup walnuts
12 dates, chopped
12 saltine crackers, rolled (½ cup)
½ pint heavy cream, whipped

Yield: Makes 6 servings

Preheat oven to 325°F. Butter a 9-inch pie plate. Beat egg whites in a mixing bowl until stiff. Add almond extract and water. Mix baking powder and sugar together. Fold mixture of sugar, walnuts, dates, and saltines into egg whites. Bake for 30 minutes. Serve warm or cold with dollop of soft whipped cream.

SOUTHERN BLACK CHOCOLATE CAKE

Cake:

4 squares semi-sweet
  baking chocolate
½ cup boiling water
2 eggs
1½ cups sugar
½ cup cooking oil
½ cup sour cream

1 teaspoon baking soda
1½ cups flour
1 teaspoon almond extract
½ teaspoon vanilla extract
18 marshmallows, cut in
  thirds crosswise

Chocolate Frosting:

2 squares semi-sweet
  baking chocolate
¼ cup butter (½ stick)

¼ cup milk
1 cup sugar
1 teaspoon vanilla extract

Yield: Makes 12 servings

Cake: Preheat oven to 350°F. Grease a 9-inch square baking pan and place a sheet of greased, brown paper in the bottom. Combine chocolate and boiling water in a saucepan and heat until thick. Set the chocolate mixture aside to cool. Beat eggs in a mix-ing bowl. Add sugar and continue to beat until well mixed. Add oil and sour cream and mix well. Combine cooled chocolate mixture with egg mixture. Add baking soda to flour and combine with chocolate mixture. Add extracts. Pour mixture into pan and bake for 60 minutes.

Rinse marshmallow pieces in cold water. Remove cake from pan while it is still warm and cover the top with marshmallow pieces. When cake has cooled, cover with chocolate frosting.

Chocolate frosting: Melt chocolate and butter together in a medium sauce pan. Add milk and sugar and cook over medium heat until mixture comes to a rapid boil. Reduce heat and contin-ue cooking for 1 minute. Remove pan from heat, add vanilla extract, and beat mixture until thick enough to spread on the cake (but not quite so long as you would beat fudge) so that it will be creamy when cooled.

PLUM UPSIDE-DOWN CAKE

6 + 6 tablespoons (total 1½
  sticks) butter, room
  temperature
1 cup packed brown sugar
1 tablespoon honey
6 large plums, halved, pitted,
  each half cut into 6 wedges
1½ cups flour

2 teaspoons baking powder
½ teaspoon ground cinnamon
¼ teaspoon salt
1 cup sugar
2 large eggs
½ teaspoon vanilla extract
¼ teaspoon almond extract
½ cup milk

Lightly sweetened whipped cream

Yield: Makes 6 servings

Preheat oven to 350°F. Stir 6 tablespoons butter, brown sugar, and honey in heavy medium skillet over low heat until butter melts and sugar and honey blend, forming a thick, smooth sauce. Transfer to 9-inch-diameter cake pan with 2-inch-high sides. Arrange plums in overlapping concentric circles atop sauce.

Mix flour, baking powder, cinnamon, and salt in medium bowl. Using electric mixer, beat the remaining 6 tablespoons butter in large bowl until light. Add sugar and beat until creamy. Add eggs and beat until light and fluffy. Beat in extracts. Add flour mixture alternately with milk, mixing just until blended. Spoon batter evenly over plums. Bake cake until golden and tester inserted into center of cake comes out clean, about 1 hour and 5 minutes. Transfer to rack; cool in pan 30 minutes.

Using knife, cut around pan sides to loosen cake. Place platter atop cake pan. Invert cake; place platter on work surface. Let stand 5 minutes. Gently lift off pan. Serve cake warm with whipped cream.

FRESH RHUBARB BETTY

1¾ cups sugar
1 tablespoon flour
¼ teaspoon salt
1 teaspoon grated orange peel, divided
5 cups cubed rhubarb (1½ pounds)

1 orange, peeled, cut into cubes
3 + 1 cups bread cubes
¼ + ¼ cup butter
½ cup coconut

Yield: Makes 12 servings

Preheat oven to 375°F. Combine sugar, flour, salt, and ½ teaspoon orange peel. Stir in fruits. Add the 3 cups bread cubes and ¼ cup butter. Mix together and put into a 9 x 13-inch baking dish. Mix the remaining ½ teaspoon orange peel, the 1 cup bread cubes, the remaining ¼ cup butter, and the coconut, and sprinkle on top. Bake for 35 to 40 minutes or until tender. This recipe may be frozen for use later.

BLUEBERRY-SOUR CREAM PIE

Crust:
1¼ cups flour
½ cup (1 stick) chilled butter, cut into pieces
2 tablespoons sugar

Pinch of salt
4 tablespoons (approximately) ice water

Filling:
1 cup sour cream
¾ cup sugar
2½ tablespoons flour
1 egg, beaten

¾ teaspoon almond extract
¼ teaspoon salt
2½ cups fresh blueberries

Topping:
6 tablespoons flour
¼ cup (½ stick) chilled butter, cut into pieces

¼ cup finely chopped pecans
¼ cup sugar

Yield: Makes 8 servings

Crust: Blend flour, butter, sugar, and salt in a food processor until of consistency of coarse meal. With the processor running, add water by tablespoonfuls until clumps form. Turn dough out onto a floured surface. Gather dough into a ball. Flatten to a disk. Wrap in plastic; chill until firm, at least 30 minutes.

Preheat oven to 400°F. Roll out dough on a floured surface to a 13-inch round. Transfer to a 9-inch glass pie plate. Trim the edge to ½-inch overhang. Fold edge under and crimp. Freeze for 10 minutes. Line the crust with foil; fill with beans or pie weights. Bake until sides are set, about 12 minutes. Remove foil and beans.

Filling: Mix sour cream, sugar, flour, egg, almond extract, and salt in a medium bowl to blend. Mix in blueberries. Spoon filling into the crust. Bake until filling is just set, about 25 minutes.

Topping: With fork, mix the flour and butter in a medium bowl until small clumps form. Mix in pecans and sugar. Spoon topping over the pie. Bake until topping browns lightly, about 12 minutes. Cool pie to room temperature.

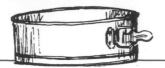

COFFEE–TOFFEE CRUNCH TORTE

Crust:

1 cup almonds, toasted

1½ cups ground sugar cookies

½ cup English toffee, chocolate-covered, coarsely chopped

5 to 6 tablespoons butter, melted, hot

Ganache:

½ cup whipping cream

1 teaspoon vanilla extract

2 tablespoons dark corn syrup

6 ounces chocolate, bitter-sweet (not unsweetened) or semi-sweet, chopped

Mousse:

1 cup sugar

6 large egg yolks

⅓ cup water

4 tablespoons instant espresso powder

½ teaspoon ground nutmeg

2½ cups chilled whipping cream

2 tablespoons coffee liqueur

1 teaspoon vanilla extract

1½ cups (about 9 ounces) English toffee, chocolate-covered, coarsely chopped

20 (approx.) whole almonds, toasted

Yield: Makes 12 servings

Crust: Grind nuts with cookies and toffee in a processor. Add 5 tablespoons butter; blend until nuts are finely chopped. To moisten the crumbs, if necessary, blend in 1 tablespoon butter. Using plastic wrap as an aid, press mixture onto bottom and up the sides of a 9-inch-diameter springform pan with 2¾-inch-high sides. Freeze 15 minutes.

Preheat oven to 350°F. Bake crust until golden, about 12 minutes. Freeze crust.

Ganache: Bring cream, vanilla extract, and syrup to a simmer in a heavy medium saucepan. Remove from heat. Add chocolate; whisk until melted and smooth. Cool to room temperature.

Mousse: Whisk sugar, yolks, water, and espresso powder in a large metal bowl. Set the bowl over a saucepan of simmering water (do not allow bowl to touch water); whisk until a candy thermometer registers 160°F, about 3 minutes. Remove the bowl from over the water. Add nutmeg. Using an electric mixer, beat the egg mixture until it is cool and thick, about 5 minutes.

Beat cream, liqueur, and vanilla extract until stiff peaks form. Fold the cream mixture and toffee into the egg mixture. Spoon half the mousse into the crust. Drizzle ¼ cup of ganache over mousse. Using the tip of a knife, swirl the two mixtures together. Carefully spoon in the remaining mousse; smooth the top. Cover and freeze the torte overnight. Cover remaining ganache; chill.

Rewarm remaining ganache over low heat, whisking just until slightly softened but not melted. If necessary, let stand until firm enough to pipe. Spoon ganache into a pastry bag fitted with a star tip. Run a sharp knife around the torte pan sides. Release the pan sides. Pipe ganache in a lattice design atop the torte. Pipe the ganache in star shapes around the border. Garnish with almonds. (Can be prepared up to 1 week ahead. Freeze until lattice sets, then cover and keep frozen.)

CAPPUCCINO CREAMS

Nonstick vegetable oil spray
1 2½-inch piece vanilla bean, split lengthwise
½ + 1¼ cups whipping cream
2 ounces white chocolate, good-quality (such as Lindt® or Bakers®), finely chopped
8 tablespoons sugar
4 large egg yolks
1 large egg
¼ cup sour cream
4 teaspoons clear (white) rum
Pinch of salt
6 teaspoons instant espresso powder

Yield: Makes 6 servings

Preheat oven to 350°F. Coat 6 (¾-cup) ramekins or custard cups with nonstick spray. Place ramekins in a 13 x 9 x 2-inch baking pan. Scrape seeds from vanilla bean into a small saucepan; add bean. Mix in the ½ cup cream and the chocolate. Stir over low heat just until smooth.

Whisk the remaining 1¼ cups cream, sugar, yolks, egg, sour cream, rum, and salt in medium bowl until smooth. Strain the white chocolate mixture into the egg mixture, and whisk to blend. Pour ¼ cup custard mixture into each ramekin; reserve remaining custard. Set ramekins in a baking pan; pour enough hot water into baking pan to come halfway up sides of ramekins. Bake until custards set, about 30 minutes. Let stand 5 minutes.

Add espresso to remaining custard mixture; stir until dissolved. Spoon espresso custard over white chocolate custards, dividing equally.

Bake until custards set, about 30 minutes. Remove from baking pan. Chill uncovered until cold, about 3 hours. (Can be made 24 hours ahead. Cover; keep chilled.)

Cut around ramekin sides to loosen custards. Turn onto plates.

PEARS POACHED IN PORT AND CRANBERRY JUICE

1 750 ml bottle ruby port
½ cup cranberry juice cocktail
Dash of fresh lemon juice
6 tablespoons sugar
1 (5 x 1-inch) strip orange peel (orange part only)
1 teaspoon anise extract
3 large pears, firm but ripe, Bosc or Bartlett (about 8 ounces each), peeled, halved, cored
1 cup plain low-fat yogurt
2 tablespoons confectioners' sugar
Mint sprigs (optional)

Yield: Makes 6 servings

Combine port, juices, sugar, orange peel, and anise in a heavy medium saucepan. Bring to a boil, stirring twice. Reduce heat to medium; simmer for 5 minutes. Add pear halves to the liquid. Simmer pears uncovered until tender, turning occasionally, about 20 minutes.

Using a slotted spoon, transfer the pears to a large bowl. Boil the cooking liquid until it is reduced to a thin syrup (about 1¼ cups), about 15 minutes. Pour the syrup over the pears in the bowl. Cool to room temperature. Cover and chill until cold, about 4 hours. (Can be made 24 hours ahead. Keep chilled.)

Mix yogurt and sugar in a small bowl. Spoon the cold syrup onto plates. Place 1 pear half, flat side down, on each plate. Spoon yogurt mixture over pears. Garnish with mint, if desired, and serve.

Afternoon coffee hours were one of the first regularly scheduled activities in the Community. At first they were held in one of the Community houses. These were times for the whole Community family to stop work and get together for an hour of fellowship, refreshment, and relaxation. For a period of time, novice Mitzie had some responsibility for preparing the drinks and setting things up for this occasion. Punctuality was not one of her strengths, and I can still see her at 2:50 PM clutching the coffee urn to her chest and her short legs doing double time as she tried to get to her appointed place in time to do her job. But there was no way the coffee was going to be perked by 3:00, and once again I knew that everyone would be starting with cookies and having their drinks later on.

In the beginning the Sisters did all the baking for these times. Then as we grew in numbers, Community houses took turns providing them. Eventually the location was moved to the Fellowship Room or to Bethany front lawn whenever weather permitted.

A favorite at coffee hour in those days were warm carmelitas. The recipe for these was taken from the back of an empty oatmeal bag that I just happened to salvage from the trash one day. It combined oatmeal, chocolate chips, chopped nuts, and caramel sauce into a delightfully chewy bar that few people, young or old, could resist, especially when the bars were freshly baked. They remained high on the popularity list with all of us for many years.

Interesting and significant things often took place at these coffee hours. One afternoon as I was just about to take a seat on the front lawn, I glanced down toward the harbor and saw a tiny woman, timid in appearance, looking our way. She took several steps toward us, hesitated, and then turned the other way without going too far. Was she wondering whether she could join us? When I went down to find out, I came face to face with a lady whose eyes registered fear, hurt, and desperation.

An accumulation of painful experiences had resulted in her coming close to taking her own life. She was reaching out for help, hoping she might find it here. She stayed for some time that day, then returned to coffee hour day after day and attended any events and services open to the public, while all the time maintaining her membership and attendance at the local Catholic church. With the encouragement and approval of her priest, she began to spend time on a regular basis with the Sisters, working in the art department each morning for several hours after coming from Mass.

We all grew to love Millie and looked forward to her quiet presence with us in the Convent. She became a dear, devoted friend who maintained a close bond with us until the day she died.

Among the coffee hour favorites were these snacks:

CARMELITAS

Crust:

1 cup flour	¼ teaspoon salt
1 cup rolled oats	¾ cup butter, melted
¾ cup brown sugar	1 teaspoon vanilla extract
½ teaspoon baking soda	1 teaspoon maple flavoring

Filling:

1 cup (6 ounces) chocolate chips	¾ cup caramel ice cream topping
½ cup chopped pecans	3 tablespoons flour

Yield: Makes 24 bars

Preheat oven to 350°F. In a large mixing bowl, combine all ingredients for the crust. Blend well to form crumbs. Press half of the crumb mixture into the bottom of a 9 x 12-inch pan. Bake for 10 minutes. Remove pan from oven and sprinkle with chocolate chips and pecans. Blend together caramel topping and flour, and spread over chocolate chips and pecan mixture. Sprinkle the remainder of crumb mixture over the top. Bake for 15 to 20 minutes or until golden brown. Cool until warm and loosen from the edges of the pan before completely cooled.

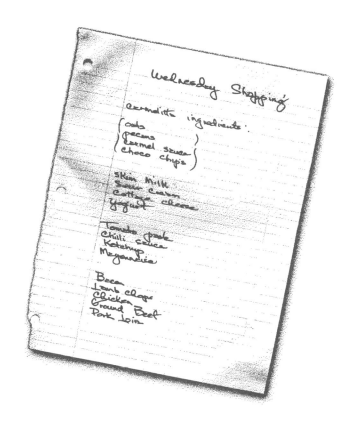

RASPBERRY BARS

3 cups flour
1 teaspoon baking powder
2 eggs, beaten
1 cup sugar

1 cup shortening
2 teaspoons almond extract
Raspberry jam
Nuts (optional)

Yield: Makes 14 to 16 bars

Preheat the oven to 350°F. Combine flour, baking powder, eggs, sugar, shortening, and almond extract. Mix lightly by hand. Spread more than half the dough on ungreased cookie sheet. Spread a layer of jam over top. Sprinkle with nuts, if desired. Sprinkle the remaining dough over top. Bake for 20 to 30 minutes.

BUCKEYES

1 pound creamy peanut butter
½ pound butter
1½ pounds confectioners' sugar

1 pkg. (12 ounces) chocolate chips
¼ bar paraffin

Yield: Makes 12 servings.

Mix peanut butter and butter together with confectioners' sugar until smooth. Form small balls and refrigerate. Slowly melt chocolate chips and paraffin together in double boiler. Use toothpick to dip cold candies in chocolate, covering the peanut butter ball halfway with chocolate. Let dry on waxed paper. Best stored in freezer.

COCONUT OAT CRUNCHIES

1 cup butter
1 cup sugar
1 cup brown sugar
1 egg
1 cup vegetable oil
1 teaspoon vanilla extract
1 cup rolled oats

1 cup crushed cornflakes
½ cup shredded coconut
½ cup chopped walnuts or
  pecans
Rind of 1 orange, grated
3½ cups flour
1 teaspoon baking soda
1 teaspoon salt

Yield: Makes 8 dozen

Preheat oven to 325°F. Cream butter and sugars until light and fluffy. Add egg, oil, and vanilla extract. Mix well. Add oats, cornflakes, coconut, nuts, and orange rind. Stir well. Add flour, soda, and salt. Stir until well blended. Drop by teaspoonfuls on ungreased cookie sheets. Flatten with fork dipped in water. Bake 15 minutes.

JANUARY 24

*Today's lunch was so satisfying, enjoyed by everyone—a delicious
potato-carrot soup with freshly baked bread. People's satisfaction
with it confirms my feeling that sometimes simpler is better.*

The Mothers' vision for Bethany Retreat House cooking was that it be a tangible means of ministry to guests and retreatants. Great emphasis was always placed on any special dietary needs of our visitors. They felt it was of prime importance that people felt cared for through the food served to them. This did not necessarily mean the food had to be expensive or elaborate. The very first retreat meal I ate in Bethany was a plain roast chicken leg, mashed potatoes and gravy, and some vegetable that now escapes my memory. Neither chicken legs nor mashed potatoes have ever been among my favorite foods, but that meal tasted heavenly to me. I've never forgotten it because it blessed me so much.

POTATO-CARROT SOUP

2 carrots, chopped	1 turnip, peeled and diced
1 rib celery, chopped	3 to 4 cups chicken broth
1 onion, chopped	1½ cups milk
3 tablespoons butter	1½ cups sour cream
2 medium potatoes, peeled and diced	

Yield: Makes 6 servings

Cook carrots, celery, and onion in the butter in a covered saucepan on low heat, until tender. Add potatoes and turnip and cover with chicken broth and simmer until all the vegetables are tender, about 30 minutes. When vegetables are cooked, mash or purée.

Mix together milk and sour cream; add to puréed vegetables. Add enough additional milk or broth until of consistency desired. Do not boil. Serve.

Note: This soup may also be served cold.

JANUARY 31

Tea with Sally was most rewarding, as it always is when she comes to visit. As we said goodbye I saw one Sister after another heading down the road toward the barn. I knew they were all going to see Duchess and her newborn calf that had arrived last night at midnight, and I wanted to see her too.

Everyone loves Duchess, our little brown Jersey cow and a fairly new Community member. From the very beginning of the Community, we have had goats. They have been very entertaining and have brought us a lot of joy, along with the chickens, but there is something so different about this little brown cow. With one look of her limpid eyes, she succeeds in melting the hardest of hearts and endearing herself to everyone.

Because she so much loves being with people, Brother Jacob often used to bring her to graze in the upper garden across from the Convent, where people passed regularly on their way to and from the parking lot. Her loud lowings were music to our ears and tempted many a distractable Sister to slip away from her work for a visit with Duchess.

After Duchess was bred, there was a great deal of anticipation as she approached motherhood. It was going to be a first-time experience for many of us, this birth of a little calf. Our cheese-making Sister even started calculating the amount of milk Duchess would be giving and laid plans for experimenting with different types of homemade cheeses.

I thought back to the early days of the Community when the first child was born, another first-time experience in our Community family. It happened in the middle of the night. A call went out to all the houses for everyone to come to the chapel where the announcement of the new arrival was made, and we all joined in a prayer of thanksgiving for the safe delivery. This was a rather novel experience the first several times, but when the number of births increased, more than one Sister praying for an expectant mother would secretly beseech God to bless her with a daytime delivery.

At that time, the Brothers and Sisters each had an hour-long nighttime

prayer vigil, which meant that the already too short night of sleep was interrupted by an hour of intercessory prayer in the chapel. Add to that another trip back to the chapel to give thanks for a new baby, and one's good nature could really be tested. I shall never forget one disgruntled Sister, to whom sleep was most precious, muttering aloud as she pulled her coat tightly around her and stepped out into the cold night air, "I think this celebration of new birth should be reserved only for those who experience the joys of motherhood, and that Sisters should be exempt from having to participate in it!" I doubt the decision actually was influenced by her bold complaint, but very soon after, this little tradition ceased, to the relief of many—married and celibate alike.

Brother Jacob and I share a mutual love for the gardens. We agree on many things: for example, that zucchini and peas should be picked young and tender, tomatoes should be left on the vine till fully ripened, and lettuce planting should be staggered to provide a steady supply all season long. We also agreed about the kale, or so I thought until recently.

Late last month, I returned from visiting my brother in Florida. While there, I had been shocked to discover that kale was selling for four dollars a pound, and it was not at all of the quality we grew back home. I couldn't wait to surprise my brother with a bag of kale freshly picked from our own garden—a perfect little expression of thanks for all that he and his wife had done for me during my stay with them. It would cost only two dollars to mail a generous package of it.

I took my knife and a basket and headed to the kale patch, only to be stopped short in my tracks. There was no kale patch. Not a speck of green was to be seen where just before my trip there had been a profusion of crisp, curly leaves. What had happened? Had Brother Jacob plowed it under after we had agreed to leave it growing through the mild winter, with the frost nipping it and giving it a much sweeter flavor than the summer crop? I could not figure this out. No, it had not been plowed under, but closer examination revealed that it had been chewed down to the very roots; not even a nubbin was left above ground. And then I spied hoof marks and it all made sense. Duchess had been here.

When Brother Jacob gave me a cheery welcome home, I met him with anything but a pleasant response. "Why would you put the little cow in that garden when you know how we count on that kale for a fresh green vegetable through the winter months?" I demanded. Speechless, he shook his head. "I'm sorry," he stammered. "I just never thought she'd do that, and to have put her in the other garden would have jeopardized the Brothers' newly planted grapevines that they're cultivating for making communion wine." So we had saved the Brothers' grapes and lost the Sisters' kale—a not too happy predicament, in my opinion.

In an effort to appease me, Brother Jacob promised me the first rhubarb of the season and choice strawberries from the Friary garden, and he assured me that he blessed the kale patch and prayed over it every time he walked by it in hopes that it would miraculously spring back, which eventually it did make a feeble attempt to do.

After my wrath had subsided, and I was calm enough to consider the matter sanely, I felt very bad for Brother Jacob, especially when I remembered that I had offered some kale to Duchess in the summer, and she had shown no interest in it. Why should he expect her to devour the patch? Suddenly I understood what had happened—like any normal pregnant mother, Duchess had been seized with a craving, and hers happened to be for sweet frost-bitten kale.

All this passed through my mind as I approached the barnyard gate and peeked in. The sight before my eyes was priceless: dear, dear Duchess with a tiny replica of herself. I stood staring, speechless for some time. Then leaning toward her, I stroked her head and whispered in her ear, "Your little one is so beautiful, Duchess. I can't think of any way I would rather have had that kale put to use."

STRAWBERRY–RHUBARB PIE

Crust:

See recipe for Basic Pie Crust

Filling:

4 cups (generous) chopped rhubarb	⅔ cup flour
1 cup (generous) chunked strawberries	½ teaspoon salt
1½ cups sugar	1 tablespoon butter
	1 egg
	2 tablespoons water

Yield: Makes 8 to 10 servings

Lightly toss together the filling ingredients and turn into pastry-lined pan. Dot with butter. Cover with crust, making slits in the top. Combine egg and water and brush on top crust. Sprinkle the top generously with sugar. Bake at 450°F for 10 minutes and then at 325°F for 45 minutes. Cover with foil if pie starts to get too brown.

BASIC PIE CRUST

2 cups flour	¾ cup shortening
1 teaspoon salt	5 to 6 tablespoons cold water

Yield: Makes pastry for one 2-crust pie

In a medium bowl with a fork, lightly stir together the flour and salt. With a pastry blender or 2 knives used scissor-fashion, cut in shortening until the mixture resembles coarse crumbs. Sprinkle in the cold water, a tablespoon at a time, mixing lightly with a fork after each addition, until pastry just holds together. With your hands, shape pastry into a ball. (If it is a hot day, wrap in waxed paper and refrigerate 30 minutes.) Divide pastry into 2 pieces, one slightly larger, and gently shape each piece into a ball.

On a lightly floured surface with a lightly floured rolling pin, roll larger ball into a ⅛-inch-thick circle, 2 inches larger all around than the pie plate. Roll half the circle onto the rolling pin; transfer the pastry to the pie plate and unroll, easing it into the bottom and side of pie plate.

Fill as recipe directs. For the top crust, roll the smaller ball as for bottom crust. With a sharp knife, cut a few slashes or a design in the center of the crust; center over the filling. With scissors or a sharp knife, trim pastry edges, leaving a 1-inch overhang all around the pie plate rim. Fold overhang under; pinch a high edge; make a decorative edge. Bake pie as recipe directs.

Papa

Mike's

FEBRUARY 11

Today got off to a wonderful start, even if it was a little overcast. As I was checking my mailbox, one of our favorite cats, Elijah, appeared, rubbing up against my leg. He wasn't demanding to be fed or to be let out; he was just being friendly. I picked him up and we sat on the couch for almost five minutes, he purring and kneading my knee, me scratching his ears. Such a nice way to start the day. I thought back to my youth, to my childhood cat, and to my father.

Papa began work in a restaurant in New York City as soon as he arrived from Greece. After a few years of experience, he went into business for himself in Olean, New York—the city in which I was born. His restaurant was considered one of the finest in town, not only because of the food, but also because it was the only establishment in town with a ballroom and live music. Saturday was a big night out for everyone in the area, and people came from all the surrounding small towns to "Mike's" for dinner and then dancing.

It was a big night for me, too, because that was the night our whole family went to Papa's restaurant, and he would cook dinner for us. Sometimes we ordered from his very extensive menu. When we did, I would always order scallops. Other times he would do the deciding and serve us sizzling steaks or luscious lamb chops. Many times he would serve wild game, such as venison, rabbit, or woodchuck that Skinny Joe had caught. Skinny Joe was the tallest, thinnest man I'd ever known. He was a widower who loved to hunt and fish, but he had no one to cook what he caught, so he would take it to Papa, and Papa would prepare it for him as well as us, a very nice arrangement for us all.

One of the first things Papa did when he moved into our house in Olean was to plant a row of grapevines across the backyard. In time they formed a natural canopy as they grew up over a trellis that connected to the back roof of the house. My cat, Greyboy, used Papa's grapevine to make his way up to my bedroom window, where he would wait for his breakfast every morning.

Greyboy also trained Papa to stop by our house on his way back from the market with Greyboy's favorite treat——a generous serving of fresh chopped meat, a specially ground blend of veal, beef, and pork, the only meat Papa used in his Salisbury steak, a very popular luncheon entree at Mike's. The sight of Papa's blue DeSoto turning into the drive brought Greyboy like a streak of lightning across the empty lot, and he would always manage to be sitting at the head of the drive waiting for the chef to serve him his very own Salisbury steak just the way he liked it: tartare.

Papa butchered most of his own meat. Customers who knew him well enough to frequent his kitchen would gather around his old worn butcher's block, spellbound, watching him as he sharpened his knife against the steel and then, with a deftness that awed me, effortlessly and skillfully carve up a side of beef into steaks, chops, roasts, and stew meat, while all the time carrying on a conversation about the latest local concerns. I would secretly be bursting with pride at the expertise with which he carried this out, and I could think of nothing more fascinating than to be as dexterous a butcher when I grew up.

Because nothing was ever wasted, we often had many of the parts of the calf or steer not always found in the grocery stores. Tripe was a favorite dish in our home, as were kidneys, brains, and sweetbreads. When I see people sometimes cringe at the mention of these, I always think, "If only you could have tasted them the way Papa cooked them."

Meat juices were considered precious, and every bit was saved and scraped from the roasting or cooking pan. Meat bones and poultry carcasses were always cooked down for their natural juices or to make soup or sauce bases. When someone says, "Oh, that's the secret to your flavorful sauce," I have to smile because to me it's no secret, just the obvious thing to do. Vegetables were always cooked in the smallest possible amount of water, and the juice was never discarded, but always saved as a drink or added to soup.

One time the local newspaper published an article on Papa's restaurant. One of the things that particularly captured the attention of the journalist was that Papa used an old-fashioned stockpot, something most restaurants by that time no longer utilized. Throughout the day vegetable peelings, trimmings from roasts, and prime rib bones would be tossed into the simmering pot where they cooked down into a rich, flavorful broth that was drained off at the end of

Papa 1955

the day and used for soup du jour the following day. Papa had a reputation for serving the best soup in town, and much of the reason was the use of his faithful old stockpot.

MANHATTAN CLAM CHOWDER

1 pint clams, shucked or 2 (6½-ounce) cans clams, minced	2 cups finely chopped, peeled potatoes
3 slices bacon	½ teaspoon dried basil or crushed marjoram
1 cup chopped celery	
1 cup chopped onion	¼ teaspoon pepper
1 (28-ounce) can tomatoes, cut into bits, undrained	1 teaspoon onion salt

Yield: Makes 4 servings

Chop shucked clams, reserving juice. Strain clam juice to remove bits of shell. (Or, drain canned clams, reserving juice.) If necessary, add water to juice to equal 1½ cups. In a large saucepan cook the bacon until crisp. Remove the bacon, reserving drippings. Drain the bacon on paper towels; crumble.

Cook celery and onion in reserved bacon drippings over medium heat about 5 minutes or until tender. Drain. Stir in reserved clam juice, tomatoes, potatoes, basil or marjoram, and pepper. Bring to boiling; reduce heat. Cover and simmer for 20 to 25 minutes or until vegetables are tender.

With the back of a fork, slightly mash vegetables against side of the pan. Stir in clams. Return to boiling; reduce heat. Cook 1 to 2 minutes more. Sprinkle each serving with bacon.

AVGOLEMONO (GREEK EGG-LEMON SOUP)

8 cups chicken broth	4 eggs, separated
Salt	Juice of 2 lemons
1 cup rice	Lemon slices for garnish

Yield: Makes 6 servings

Bring chicken broth to a boil; salt to taste. Add rice and simmer, covered, for 20 minutes; remove from heat. In a bowl, beat egg whites until stiff; add yolks and beat well. Slowly add lemon juice to the eggs, beating constantly; add 2 cups of the hot chicken broth and do not stop beating. (Constant beating is the secret to prevent curdling of this delicate soup.) When the eggs and broth are well mixed, pour this mixture back into the remaining broth and rice. Stir well over heat, but *do not allow to boil*. Serve at once in bowls; garnish soup with thinly sliced lemons.

OXTAIL SOUP

1 oxtail (2 to 2½ pounds), cut into 2-inch pieces	1 dried red chili
2 cups pearl barley	4 cups beef broth
1 medium onion, quartered	Salt and freshly ground pepper
4 cloves garlic, peeled and crushed	½ cup coarsely chopped fresh parsley
3 fresh parsley sprigs, chopped	
1 teaspoon ground cumin	

Yield: Makes 8 servings

Place the oxtail, barley, onion, garlic, parsley sprigs, cumin, and chili in a heavy soup pot. Add the broth and enough water to cover the ingredients by 1½ inches.

Bring just to a boil, reduce the heat, and simmer, covered, for 1¼ hours, skimming any foam that rises to the surface. Season with salt and pepper, and cook, uncovered, for another 15 minutes. The oxtail should be very tender; remove pot from heat.

Remove oxtail and shred meat from the bones, discarding bones and any fat. Cover meat and refrigerate.

Strain the broth twice through a very fine strainer. Reserve barley mixture. Cool broth for at least 1 hour so that fat rises to top. Skim off all fat and discard.

Return broth to the soup pot. Bring to a boil. Return shredded meat to broth and cook another 5 minutes. Stir in parsley and cook 1 minute longer.

Reheat barley mixture. Divide barley mixture among 8 soup bowls and ladle the hot soup atop. Serve immediately.

VENISON STEAKS

Marinade:

1 cup white wine	½ cup vinegar
½ cup olive oil	Pinch of ground cloves
1 bay leaf, crushed	Pinch of thyme
2 garlic cloves, minced	Pinch of oregano
6 venison steaks	

Sauce:

1 onion, minced	1 cup white wine
1 garlic clove, minced	Salt and pepper
¼ pound (1 stick) butter	Melted butter
¼ cup chopped parsley	
4 fresh tomatoes, peeled and chopped, or 1 (16-ounce) can whole tomatoes	

Yield: Makes 6 servings

Combine ingredients for the marinade, pour over steaks, and marinate for at least 2 hours. Remove steaks from marinade, reserving marinade, and place steaks on paper to dry. Sauté onion and garlic in the butter; add parsley and tomatoes, and cook until the onions are tender. Pour this sauce into the reserved marinade; add white wine, salt, and pepper to taste; stir well and simmer for 25 minutes. Meanwhile brush the steaks with melted butter, and

broil on both sides, being careful not to overcook. (The timing depends upon thickness of the steaks.) When cooked, place the steaks on a platter, and pour hot sauce over top.

BRAISED RABBIT

1½ cups dry red wine
1 cup chicken broth
1 cup beef broth
2 onions, sliced
4 garlic cloves, halved
2 bay leaves
½ teaspoon oregano
1 (3½-pound) rabbit, cut into 6 pieces
Salt and pepper
3 tablespoons olive oil

Yield: Makes 4 servings

Whisk wine, both broths, onion, garlic, bay leaves, and oregano in a large bowl. Add the rabbit. Cover and refrigerate 8 to 12 hours, turning occasionally.

Remove rabbit from marinade, reserving the marinade. Pat rabbit dry. Season with salt and pepper. Heat the oil in a heavy large skillet over high heat. Add rabbit to the skillet and cook until brown, about 4 minutes per side. Add reserved marinade. Bring to a boil. Reduce heat to medium-low. Cover and simmer until the rabbit is cooked through, about 25 minutes.

Using tongs, transfer rabbit to a platter. Tent with foil to keep warm. Boil cooking liquid until reduced to 1½ cups, about 20 minutes. Discard garlic and bay leaves. Season the sauce to taste with salt and pepper. Return rabbit to skillet, and simmer until heated through, about 5 minutes. Arrange the rabbit on the platter and pour the sauce over top.

SALISBURY STEAK

Steak:
1 pound ground meat (I prefer a mixture of ground beef and ground turkey)
⅓ cup dry bread crumbs
2 eggs
¼ cup finely chopped onions
1 teaspoon onion salt
½ teaspoon pepper
¼ cup finely chopped fresh parsley

Sauce:
1½ cups sliced mushrooms
¼ cup Marsala wine
Meat juices and pan drippings
Juice of ½ fresh lemon

Yield: Makes 6 servings

Steak: Mix all the steak ingredients together thoroughly. Shape meat mixture into patties and cook in a skillet over medium-high heat until brown on each side. Remove from the pan and keep warm. Reserve juices and pan drippings.

Sauce: Add mushrooms and Marsala wine to remaining meat juices and simmer for a few minutes. Add lemon juice. Pour over the steaks and serve at once.

CREOLE TRIPE

2 pounds tripe
1 onion, quartered

2 bay leaves
1 clove garlic, halved

Sauce:

1 onion, thinly sliced
3 tablespoons butter
1 garlic clove, minced
4 fresh tomatoes, peeled
   and diced, or 1 (16-ounce)
   can whole tomatoes

2 bay leaves
Dash of oregano
½ cup white wine
Salt and pepper
Chopped fresh parsley

Yield: Makes 4 to 6 servings

Wash the tripe in cold water. Drain well. Place tripe in a pot with onion, bay leaves, and garlic; cover all with water. Bring to a boil; simmer, covered, for 2 hours. Drain tripe and cut into strips. In a skillet, sauté sliced onion in 3 tablespoons butter until onions are soft; add garlic, tomatoes, bay leaves, oregano, wine, salt, and pepper. Stir and simmer for 5 minutes. Add tripe and a little water to the sauce, if necessary, to cover tripe. Simmer, covered, over low heat for 45 minutes. Garnish with chopped parsley. This is delicious served over rice pilaf.

SPANAKOPITA (SPINACH PIE)

3 pounds fresh spinach
2 bunches green scallions,
   finely chopped
½ + ½ cup olive oil
½ cup minced parsley
½ teaspoon dill (optional)

8 eggs, beaten
1 pound feta cheese,
   crumbled
Onion salt and pepper
½ pound phyllo pastry sheets
1 cup butter, melted

Yield: Makes 10 to 15 servings

Preheat oven to 350°F.

Wash spinach, cut off stems, dry completely with towels, and chop. Brown scallions in ½ cup olive oil until tender. Combine spinach, parsley, dill (if desired), eggs, and cheese; add cooked scallions, season with onion salt and pepper to taste, and mix well.

Grease a 9 x 13-inch baking pan and line with 5 of the phyllo sheets. Combine the melted butter and the remaining ½ cup olive oil; brush each phyllo sheet with butter and oil mixture. Spread the spinach mixture over phyllo, and top with remaining sheets, brushing each with butter and oil mixture. Bake for 45 minutes. Cool and cut into squares (for best results cut through the phyllo with a razor blade).

This may be served hot or cold, as an appetizer in small squares, or as a vegetable side dish in larger squares.

ATHENIAN RICE PUDDING

⅓ cup rice
½ cup water
   Pinch of salt
1 quart milk
4 egg yolks
¾ cup sugar

   Rind of 1 orange or 1
   lemon, grated
1 teaspoon vanilla extract
   Ground cinnamon
   Ground nutmeg

Yield: Makes 6 servings

Parboil rice in water with salt for 5 minutes; drain. Scald milk; add the drained rice, and cook over low heat, stirring occasionally for 45 minutes. Beat egg yolks with sugar. Remove rice mixture from heat, and slowly stir in egg yolks, mixing well. Add orange or lemon rind (or a combination of both), return to low heat, and stir constantly until creamy and thick. Add vanilla extract, mix well, and pour into sherbet glasses or dessert bowls. Sprinkle with cinnamon and nutmeg to taste, and let cool. This may be served with thick cream.

BAKLAVA (GREEK PASTRY)

Syrup:
2 cups honey
2 cups water
2 cups sugar

2 cinnamon sticks
1 teaspoon grated orange peel
1 teaspoon vanilla extract

Baklava:
1 pound butter, melted
1 pound phyllo pastry sheets
1 pound shelled walnuts, coarsely ground or chopped

2 teaspoons ground cinnamon
1 teaspoon ground allspice
⅔ cup sugar

Yield: Makes 3 dozen servings

Syrup: Combine all ingredients for the syrup in a saucepan, bring to a boil, and simmer for 10 minutes. Strain, and allow to cool.

Baklava: Mix walnuts thoroughly with cinnamon, allspice, and sugar. Brush a 9 x 13 x 2-inch pan with butter. Lay a sheet of phyllo in the bottom, brush with butter, cover with another sheet of phyllo, brush with butter, and repeat this process until you have used a dozen sheets. Spread one thin layer of nut mixture on top of the phyllo; cover with another sheet, brush with butter, cover with another layer of nuts, and repeat the process until all nuts are used. Cover with the remaining phyllo sheets, brushing each sheet with butter.

With a very sharp knife, cut the top phyllo sheets (down to the first layer of nut mixture, approx. ⅝ inch) into triangles, cutting diagonally across the pan. Bake at 350°F for 1½ hours.

When Baklava is evenly browned, remove from the oven, and pour the cooled syrup evenly over top of it, so syrup penetrates layers and covers the Baklava. Allow to cool several hours before serving.

FEBRUARY 20

*Sister Patience is setting up work projects down in the Retreat
Kitchen for the young Community girls. These high schoolers always
look forward to working with the Sisters in the Retreat Kitchen during their school breaks. I remember how eager I used to be to work
in the kitchen with my father when I was their age.*

When I was twelve years old, Papa let me start working for him on
Saturday nights. Besides all the people who came for dinner, many
others came just for sandwiches and drinks. I had two main jobs.
One was to line up all the sandwich orders, lay out the bread, and keep the supply of ingredients replenished. At the same time, I had to keep my eye on the
dishes returning from the dining room, stack them in racks, and wash them in
a hand-operated dishwasher.

Whenever there was a lull between sandwich orders and dishes, I would slip
out to watch the dancing in the ballroom. Before the evening's work began, I
would visit with Pat Ringrose, a smiling, blue-eyed Irishman with snow-white
hair. He was Papa's bartender and we were friends. He let me sample the different liqueurs in fancy bottles displayed behind the bar. Apricot brandy and
crème de menthe became my favorites.

At the time I started high school, my brother, Bud, who was eight years older than I, was Papa's day chef. This meant he went to work around 6:00 AM to do the day's cooking.

The school was just up a steep hill from Papa's restaurant, and I would ride my bike to the restaurant, leave it there for the day, and then walk up the hill. But first, I would always stop in to see my brother. He would just be taking the freshly roasted meats out of the oven. He would let me sample each. After I had decided which I liked best, he would make me two generous sandwiches to take with me for lunch. Then he would tease me about my appetite and punch me in the arm, saying, "That's okay, Toots, you're still a cute kid, and you're solid as a rock." I liked stopping by to see my brother. It gave the day a nice start.

Years later, when he had his own successful eating place, renowned for its fabulous buffet, I still liked stopping in to see him. He let me sample the jumbo shrimp and many of his original dishes, like tangy Marinated Eggplant, a special Seafood Salad, and a surprising Strawberry Ham creation, alive and sharp with flavor. Then he would tease me about my appetite.

Now when I visit him, retired now, but never having given up cooking, he prepares my favorite foods for me, and then . . . he teases me about my appetite.

It has been said that Greeks are addicted to greens, and it is well known that beans and greens are an old standby in every Mediterranean household.

Take any fresh greens (I prefer dandelions when available, but endive, Swiss chard, kale, spinach, or turnip greens are also good this way). Stir-fry them in a little olive oil with crushed fresh garlic, and add cooked beans such as fava, navy, or chickpeas. Cover and cook till greens are soft and well done. Let sit until flavored all the way through. Wonderful!

MARINATED EGGPLANT

1 medium eggplant (about 1½ pounds)	½ teaspoon dried oregano leaves
1 small onion, chopped	½ teaspoon salt
2 tablespoons white wine vinegar	¼ teaspoon pepper
1 clove garlic, chopped	¼ cup olive oil

Yield: Makes 4 to 6 servings

Cut the eggplant into ¾-inch cubes (about 5 cups). Heat a small amount of salted water (½ teaspoon salt to 1 cup water) to boiling. Add the eggplant. Heat to boiling, reduce heat. Cover and cook until tender, about 10 minutes; drain.

Place the eggplant and onion in a glass or plastic bowl. Mix the vinegar, garlic, oregano, salt, and pepper, and pour over the eggplant and onion. Toss. Cover and refrigerate at least 6 hours. Just before serving, stir in oil.

SEAFOOD SALAD

1 cup chopped lobster	½ cup minced celery
1 cup chopped crab	1 tablespoon minced shallots
1 cup chopped shrimp	Dash of cayenne
½ cup Homemade Mayonnaise (see recipe p. 141)	

Yield: Makes 4 to 6 servings

Combine all ingredients, mixing lightly, and serve on lettuce.

STRAWBERRY HAM

8 ounces mustard	1 jar (12 ounces) pineapple jelly
1 jar (5 ounces) horseradish	1 sugar-cured ham, cut into bite-sized pieces
1 jar (12 ounces) strawberry preserves	

Yield: Makes 3 (1-cup) servings of sauce

Blend all ingredients except ham together and refrigerate. Heat and serve over ham.

GRILLED BUTTERFLIED LEG OF LAMB

6 medium garlic cloves
½ teaspoon ground pepper
2 tablespoons minced fresh rosemary
4 tablespoons + ½ cup extra-virgin olive oil
½ cup + 3 tablespoons red wine
¼ cup prepared mustard

1 (6-pound) leg of lamb, trimmed, boned and butterflied
Fresh rosemary sprigs
Bay leaves
Fresh thyme sprigs
Salt and freshly ground pepper

Yield: Makes 6 to 8 servings

Have the butcher bone and butterfly the lamb for you. Marinate 8 to 12 hours for best flavor. Rosemary, thyme, and bay leaves strewn over the cooking coals will lightly scent the meat.

Grind garlic, pepper, and rosemary to paste in mortar and pestle. Mix in the 4 tablespoons olive oil and the ½ cup wine. Arrange lamb, cut surface down, in glass baking dish. Cut slits over surface using small knife. Spoon and press garlic mixture into slits. Rub mustard over entire surface of lamb. Combine the ½ cup oil and the 3 tablespoons wine and pour over meat, turning to coat. Refrigerate lamb 8 to 12 hours. Let stand at room temperature for 1 hour before grilling.

Prepare barbecue grill with medium-hot coals. Drain lamb, reserving marinade. Arrange lamb, boned side down, on grill. Grill 15 minutes, basting frequently with rosemary sprigs dipped in marinade. Turn over and grill 5 minutes, basting frequently. Scatter rosemary, thyme and bay leaves over coals. Continue grilling lamb until thermometer inserted in thickest part registers 130°F for medium-rare. Transfer lamb to platter; let stand 10 minutes. Thinly slice across grain. Sprinkle with salt and pepper; garnish with rosemary.

STUFFED MUSHROOMS

1 pound mushrooms (caps should be 2 to 3 inches in diameter)
5 tablespoons butter, divided
3 tablespoons finely chopped onion
¼ cup Madeira
¼ cup fine, dry bread crumbs

¼ cup grated Swiss cheese
¼ cup grated Parmesan cheese
4 tablespoons minced parsley
½ teaspoon tarragon
¼ teaspoon pepper
2 tablespoons heavy cream

Yield: Makes 6 to 8 servings

Preheat oven to 375°F.

Remove stems from mushrooms. Melt 2 tablespoons butter and brush caps. Place caps, hollow side up, in a roasting pan. Mince the mushroom stems and squeeze in a towel to remove moisture.

Sauté onions in 1 tablespoon butter to soften. Add mushroom stems and cook over high heat, stirring frequently, about 5 minutes, or until most moisture has disappeared. Add Madeira; boil until mostly evaporated. Remove from heat.

Mix in bread crumbs, cheeses, parsley, tarragon, and pepper. Bind together with cream. Fill mushroom caps with stuffing. (Mushrooms can be prepared ahead to this point. Refrigerate until ready to use.)

Just before baking, top with drops of remaining 2 tablespoons butter, melted. Bake 15 minutes or until caps are tender and stuffing is slightly browned.

FEBRUARY 22

A strong wind is whipping up from the harbor tonight as I sip my hot tea and look over the guest list. I see we have a variety of people coming to Bethany soon, and I am reminded of some of the guests who have come and gone over the years.

There is always this to consider when feeding visitors from abroad. Should we give them American-style food or try to cater to the tastes of their homeland? It is nice to do both, depending on the number of meals they will be eating with us.

We usually try to plan a meal of fresh cod for visitors coming to the Cape for the first time. Most everyone seems to enjoy it simply broiled or else baked with a lightly buttered golden crumb topping. Unless we know that whoever is coming prefers a rich sauce or is partial to having it deep fried, we serve it one or the other of the first two ways.

When Metropolitan Emilianos first visited us, I knew he had been traveling and had not been in his native land for a good while before arriving on the Cape. I suspected that with his monastic background he would favor fish over meat and that he would be inclined toward simplicity in his eating. I also had the feeling that, being Greek, he might appreciate having cod prepared the way Papa always cooked it, the whole fish (head included) slowly baked in a bed of onions, celery, green peppers, fresh tomatoes, and olive oil, and then allowed to sit in these juices, absorbing the flavors for some time before serving, so I opted for that way of preparing it. Since he is a genuinely humble man, I now know that I could have served him most anything and he would have been satisfied and grateful.

But I shall never forget the light in his eye and the simple statement he made when he came to the table and sighted the Greek-baked cod. "This," he said, shaking his head in amazement and holding out his hands as though he had been presented with the greatest of gifts, "this makes me feel that I am now at home."

One afternoon I walked into Bethany Kitchen and was surprised to see Sister Maxine hovering over quite a collection of teapots spread out on the table at the end of the room. "What's all this?" I inquired.

"I'm preparing for the British. They're coming next week, you know," she answered. "Simple tea trays have the potential for producing more problems than the serving of an entire retreat meal. I'm getting ready ahead of time."

I thought she was taking the matter a little too seriously, but we did want this group from England to have a positive experience visiting for the first time. It also does pay to plan ahead, so I withheld my judgment while she went on explaining.

"Canon Albright will be in room number 3. He's been here many times and always likes this large, round-bellied, silver pot. Mrs. Phillips will be in number 5. She drinks Lapsang Souchong tea. I thought the Oriental china would be perfect for her. There's a couple in number 1. I picked this tea service for them. Then there are six individual pots for the six single rooms. We have two people in the Little House, six ladies in the Lower Dorm, and six men in Alpha and Omega Dorm. They will all want tea first thing in the morning. That's twenty-four people all needing tea at the same time, and it's so important to them how it's prepared. You know, bringing the cold water to a boil, heating each pot, and steeping the tea for just the right length of time."

Everything she said made sense, although it did seem to be turning into a major production. Happy that she was taking her responsibility so seriously, I decided to make no comment.

The British arrived on schedule. All went smoothly getting them settled in and serving them dinner the first night. Maxine, clipboard in hand, had by now recruited six Sisters to assist in making and serving morning tea trays. Snow had started to fall late in the evening, adding to her anxiety about executing her plan, since some of the trays needed to be taken out of doors to separate buildings. So, to be safe, she added two more Sisters to her morning tea crew just to ensure nothing would go amiss.

By this time, even she was chuckling about the absurd proportions this operation had taken on. I left and gave it no more thought until the next morning when I came up from the Retreat Kitchen where breakfast was in prepara-

tion to find Maxine frantically filling the large coffee urn. Tea trays were haphazardly scattered throughout the kitchen, and Sisters were scurrying around gathering cups and spoons. "Now what's happening?" I questioned. Simultaneously bordering on tears and laughter, she replied, "My British friends have all requested coffee for 'wake up' like the Americans, and they'd like their tea with breakfast instead."

Since this episode, we have adopted a lovely custom we picked up during our many visits to England. We put an electric teapot, with cups and saucers, tea, and coffee makings as a nice welcome in each room. It is a happy solution to an otherwise all too unpredictable problem.

GREEK–BAKED FISH

1 tablespoon + ½ cup olive oil
½ + ½ cup finely chopped parsley
3 to 4 pounds striped bass, sea bass, halibut fillets, or whole fish
Salt and pepper
Juice of 1 lemon
3 onions, thinly sliced
2 green peppers, cut in strips
4 stalks of celery, cut in diagonal slices
1 (16-ounce) can whole tomatoes
1 cup white wine
1 cup clam broth
3 to 4 fresh tomatoes, sliced
Oregano

Yield: Makes 6 servings

Grease a baking pan with the 1 tablespoon olive oil, and spread ½ cup of chopped parsley on bottom of the pan. Lay the whole fish or fish fillets on the parsley, season with salt and pepper, and pour lemon juice over the fish. Combine onions, peppers, celery, the remaining ½ cup parsley, canned tomatoes, wine, and clam broth with the remaining ½ cup olive oil; mix and pour over the fish. Place fresh tomato slices on top of fish; sprinkle with oregano; bake at 350°F for 1 hour, basting occasionally.

48

FEBRUARY 23

Looking out Bethany kitchen window this morning at the harbor beginning to freeze over, I remembered one more guest of note that I neglected to write about last night.

Sometimes, in our quest to anticipate the needs and desires of guests, we succeed. And sometimes we fall short!

A precocious ten-year-old accompanying his parents quickly conveyed to us that he was a seasoned world traveler and accustomed to going first class. His immediate demand on arriving was for the elevator to his room, something we did not have. This met with obvious displeasure on his part, even though we saw to it that all his bags and belongings were quickly whisked up to his room while he was checking out the dining facilities to see if they were to his satisfaction.

Sister Carol, who takes great pleasure in offering guests hot or cold drinks as soon as they are settled in, was just about to do so, when the young man spoke up and ordered an ice bucket and Perrier water for each of their rooms. I could see Sister Carol wince inwardly as she politely smiled and hurried off to fill his request. Barely had she gotten the tray together to take up the stairs when there was a loud rapping on the banister rail and in a very condescending tone of voice our young guest called out, "Bellboy, ding ding. Are the drinks on the way yet? And can you tell me where to find the pool?"

The color in Carol's face deepened noticeably. I could barely keep a straight face while she tried with little success to sell him on the idea of a nice refreshing swim at the beach just off the harbor. I knew we had to come up with some way to disarm this fellow and compensate for the three strikes he had already chalked up against us. There had to be a little boy somewhere inside this sophisticate—if only one could find the right key.

At that moment I suddenly remembered what I had just taken out of the oven before this family had driven in: warm cowboy cookies! These are a glorified chocolate chip cookie with nuts and oats added for crunchiness. Quickly running a plate of them up the stairs, I slipped them onto Carol's tray and disappeared. A while later she came into the kitchen with a look of triumph on her

face. It had worked! She had won him over and succeeded in satisfying him, at least in some way.

The rest of the stay was much less stressful, and you might even say the young man and Sister Carol became friends, of a sort. He ordered cowboy cookies from her quite often, but he never did address her by her own name. He much preferred the nickname he had coined for her, "Sister Bellboy"!

COWBOY COOKIES

1 cup flour, sifted
½ teaspoon baking soda
½ teaspoon baking powder
1 teaspoon salt
½ cup vegetable shortening
½ cup sugar

½ cup brown sugar
1 egg
1 cup rolled oats
2 cups chocolate chips
1 teaspoon vanilla extract

Yield: Makes 2 dozen cookies

Preheat the oven to 350°F. Sift together the flour, baking soda, baking powder, and salt in a bowl and set aside. Cream together the shortening, sugar, brown sugar, and eggs. Add the flour mixture and beat. Add the oats, chocolate chips, and vanilla extract. Drop by teaspoonfuls onto an ungreased cookie sheet and bake for 8 to 10 minutes, or until golden and slightly set. Remove from oven and put on racks until cool.

I was never too surprised at the different people who showed up unannounced at the Bethany front door, no matter how out of the ordinary they might be. But I must admit that the arrival of Aunt Alice, whom I unexpectedly found sitting on the antique chair in the front hall, was a bit unnerving.

If the doorbell had been rung at all, it had not been firmly rung or I had failed to hear it in the kitchen, unlikely as that might be. Whatever the case, when I did hear something in the hall, I looked out the kitchen window and was somewhat surprised to see a limousine pulled up at the door.

It was summer and the front screen door was closed but unlocked, allowing anyone to enter. I went to see who was there, and was totally unprepared for what met my eyes. There stood a very tanned young man (nothing so unusual about that on the Cape in the summer), very blonde (nothing so unusual about that either, except that this blonde head was without question artificially colored), and there were definite signs of makeup on his face and around his eyes. He was dressed in a tight-fitting, powder blue outfit, open from the neck to the waist, exposing a bare chest on which glittered a bright gold chain and medallion.

For a moment, I could not decide whether I had been mysteriously transported to a West Coast nightclub or its entertainment had been transported here. Standing beside him with the air of a bodyguard was a uniformed chauffeur looking rather like a member of the Mafia. I was speechless, as my unidentified guests likewise seemed to be. It was as though we were all participating in a strange drama of some sort and had each lost our lines. Finally I summoned the wit to mutter, "May I help you?"

The chauffeur remained silent and staring with penetrating eyes. The person in powder blue seemed to have great difficulty finding words to express himself, which seemed to me very incongruous with his flashy attire. Anxiously wringing his hands, while taking little mincing steps forward and then backward, he finally managed to mumble something very garbled about the conference center in a neighboring town having referred him to us. Then with a nervous, almost terrified gesture, he pointed to a wooden box on the antique chair by the grandfather clock. My first fleeting thought was that it contained a time bomb set to go off any second.

"Aunt Alice," he finally stuttered. "It's Aunt Alice, she's in there."

I gasped, but tried to maintain some degree of composure. This was not the usual manner in which to be introduced to someone's aunt, but then there was nothing usual about this whole bizarre encounter.

Gradually, bit by bit, the picture came into focus, and it was all quite simple. Aunt Alice had lived on the Cape all her life. She had been particularly fond of Rock Harbor and wanted to have her ashes sprinkled on the waters of Cape Cod Bay. Here was her sole survivor asking for a little help in carrying out Aunt Alice's last request. Happy to be able to assist, I made a call to the clergy and turned my visitors over to them without trying to gather any further information about the young man himself.

As I returned to my cooking in the kitchen, I couldn't help thinking to myself, "I know there are some people who have the idea that the life of a Sister in a quiet retreat house must be very dull and uneventful." I have never yet found it to be so.

FEBRUARY 24

This morning I came upon my first clump of crocuses poking their way up through the soil, just ready to burst into bloom, a happy harbinger of spring and Easter. Tomorrow is Ash Wednesday already, so tonight we're having our traditional pancake dinner. This year we're doing Blinis—light little pancakes two of our sisters discovered while being with the nuns in the Pühtitsa Russian Orthodox convent in Estonia three years ago.

Lent has always been observed in the Community as a special time of preparation for Easter. One of the customs of the early days, which continued for many years, was our Saturday night Lenten meals. As a help to understanding and appreciating the significance of these days preceding Christ's death and resurrection, we met as a family for a simple meal that was planned to remind us of the last meal Jesus ate with his disciples.

We used rough, textured napkins and heavy, brown, pottery bowls, dishes, and mugs, with no silverware. We decorated the bare wooden tables with fresh fruit, figs, dates, grapes, and nuts, which were eaten as the dessert, and jugs or pitchers of grape juice, which was the beverage. The rest of the meal consisted of loaves of homebaked whole wheat bread, butter, honey, cheese, sardines, and boiled eggs. Each person received a selected word or Scripture at his place. Sisters sang old Lenten songs recalling Christ's passion. This was a sober meal and purposely so.

Over the years, at different periods of time such as Lent and Advent, we would observe special days of fasting. Abstinence from foods normally eaten on a regular basis can be a very fruitful and enlightening experience and can result in many benefits, not the least of which is an appreciation for what we often take for granted. I think this was one of the reasons Mother Cay encouraged light eating; at one point she suggested that the sisterhood have an evening meal once a week of only homemade bread and applesauce.

Although I still love my applesauce with ham, roast pork, or many other foods, never was it more enjoyable to me than when eaten with only a plain piece of bread during those several months that we had those suppers. Similarly, when we had fast days of only bread and water, we came into a new reverence, if you will, for this staff of life, as we might never have had otherwise. It also pushed some of the cooking Sisters into baking different types of breads, which up until then they had had no interest in doing. Among those that became favorites were Portuguese Sweet Bread, Dill Bread or Rolls, and English Muffin Bread.

But the one variety that has remained the most desired, long after each of the others have run their course of popularity, is our plain, old-fashioned whole wheat bread made from wheat berries that we ourselves grind. A solid, good, textured loaf with a bit of honey giving it just a suggestion of sweetness, it still remains a great classic, like a fine piece of music in the standard repertoire.

BETHANY WHOLE WHEAT BREAD

6 cups warm water (105° to 115°F)	1 tablespoon salt
1¾ ounces yeast	2½ cups flour
¾ cup oil	7½ cups whole wheat flour (freshly ground is preferable)
¾ cup honey	

Yield: Makes 4 loaves

Pour water in a mixing bowl; add yeast. Once the yeast is active, add the remaining ingredients, mixing on low speed in an electric mixing bowl with a bread paddle or by hand until smooth, about 5 to 10 minutes. Continue to add whole wheat flour until the dough pulls away from the sides of the bowl and forms a ball. Dough will be barely sticky when it is ready. (Too much flour will make the bread very heavy.)

Divide the dough into four pieces measuring approximately 2 to 2⅛ pounds. Knead the dough and place in well-greased bread pans. Let rise for 15 minutes or until the dough is about 1½ to 2 inches above the pan. Bake in a 375°F oven for 40 minutes. Transfer to a wire rack to cool.

PORTUGUESE SWEET BREAD

2 pkgs. yeast
1 teaspoon + 1 cup sugar
½ cup warm water
½ cup water
4 tablespoons powdered
   milk

1 stick butter, softened
3 eggs, lightly beaten,
   + 1 egg, well beaten
2 teaspoons salt
4 to 4½ cups flour

Yield: Makes 2 loaves

Combine yeast, the 1 teaspoon sugar, and ½ cup warm water in a large bowl, and allow to proof. Combine the ½ cup water and powdered milk, and heat until warm in a pan. Put the butter in the warm milk, add the 1 cup sugar, and blend well. Add to the yeast mixture and stir to combine the ingredients. Add 3 eggs and salt and mix well. Add 4 cups of flour, 1 cup at a time, kneading with your hands in the bowl, to make a soft dough. Turn out on a floured board and knead until dough is smooth and elastic. Use only enough flour to prevent from sticking. Put dough in a buttered bowl and let rise until doubled in bulk. Punch down and divide into two equal pieces. Place in two buttered skillets 9 inches in diameter at the top, or you can use two loaf pans. Cover loosely and let rise again until doubled in bulk. Brush the loaves with the well-beaten egg, and bake in a 350°F oven for about 30 minutes. Cool on racks before slicing.

DILL BREAD OR ROLLS

2 pkgs. yeast
½ cup warm water
1½ cups lukewarm milk
½ cup sugar
2 teaspoons onion salt

2 eggs
½ cup shortening or
   margarine
6 + 1 to 1½ cups flour

Yield: Makes 3 dozen rolls or 2 loaves

Preheat oven to 375°F. Dissolve yeast in warm water; add milk, sugar, onion salt, eggs, shortening or margarine, and 6 cups of flour. Mix well. Add enough of the remaining flour to make a soft dough. Knead until smooth and elastic. Place in a greased bowl, cover, and let rise until doubled in bulk (about 1 hour). Punch down and form into rolls. Place on a greased pan and let rise until doubled in bulk. Bake at 400°F for 12 to 15 minutes.

ENGLISH MUFFIN BREAD

3 + 2½ to 3 cups flour
2 pkgs. yeast
1 tablespoon sugar
2 teaspoons salt
2 cups milk

½ cup water
½ cup cooked
   Cream of Wheat ®
Cornmeal

Yield: Makes 2 loaves

Combine 3 cups of the flour, yeast, sugar, and salt. Heat milk and water until very warm (120° to 130°F). Add liquid mixture to dry mixture; beat well. Add Cream of Wheat ®. Stir in more flour to make a stiff batter. Spoon the batter into two 8½ x 4½-inch pans greased and sprinkled with the cornmeal. Sprinkle tops of the loaves with cornmeal. Cover and let rise in a warm place for about 45 minutes. Bake at 400°F for 25 minutes. Remove from pan immediately and let cool.

MARCH 2

*I just came over from the Convent kitchen where Evelyn is shredding
up a mountain of cabbage for tonight's dinner. She's making
Bahmi, an Indonesian pork dish her great-grandparents brought
back from that country after serving as missionaries there for years.
It's a favorite in the sisterhood.*

More than a few of our Sisters are from outside the United States. Their influence on our cooking has been unique and refreshing. I sometimes marvel at the variety of interests and skills we have here, culinary and otherwise. Such a diversity of backgrounds, interests, and creative gifts provides a richness to our life together. It also affects our menu planning and meal preparations and contributes to the wide variety of recipes in our General Recipe Box.

Basically we keep our meals simple, providing a wholesome, well-balanced diet, low in fats and meats and high in grains, fresh fruits, and vegetables. But with so many creative cooks, we seldom have very plain cooking for any length of time. Someone is always eager to try something new and different.

One young Sister has spent a number of missionary terms teaching in Korea. She has brought back to the sisterhood her knowledge and love of Korean cooking, which every so often manifests itself on a special occasion. Suddenly the chopsticks come out, the kimchee and pulgogi appear—sometimes even kimonos on the serving Sisters!

Two of our sisters were born and raised in Bermuda. They introduced us to Cassava Pie—a dish I've never tired of, and a recipe I was very glad to have during a period of time when we raised our own chickens for cooking and I needed a way to use poultry that was not tender enough for roasting.

We have another young Sister who loves life in the wild. She initiates clambakes on the beach and camping trips for Sisters during September. By then the busy summer schedule eases a bit, and groups of Sisters take a weekend or several overnights to camp out. She is always the first to remind me that our shellfish licenses need renewing, and she is ever eager to recruit Sisters for clam-

ming, oystering, and mussel-gathering expeditions. Her enthusiasm about getting the shellfish always pleases me. Her enthusiasm about steaming them in wine and garlic does not. To me (and I'm inclined to believe to the shellfish as well), it is unforgivable to adulterate their pristine flavor in such a way, so we have endless arguments about this. Neither of us ever wins or gives up our opinion about it. We just prepare our shellfish both ways.

I cannot ever remember being told to eat everything on my plate. It never occurred to me not to. Nor can I remember disliking any food. Mama had been born in Ukraine of poor peasant stock. She had grown up on a diet of mainly cabbage, onions, and potatoes, seasoned with a trace of meat on special holidays. The family was so poor that forks were a luxury, and the children took turns using the few they had.

Papa had come from Greece, bringing with him a love of lamb and rice. We had Italian, Syrian, and Irish neighbors, so we ate foods native to each of their countries, and I cultivated a taste for all of them. I was equally as happy with Mama's Ukrainian pierogies, a kind of Ukrainian version of Italian ravioli, as I was with Mrs. McGranagan's Irish lamb stew.

Long before yogurt was sold commercially Mama was making it, and she always had a culture of it going in the refrigerator. This was Papa's favorite dessert, along with a few spoonfuls of homemade grape jelly or Rose Petal Sweets and a demitasse.

From our Syrian neighbors we acquired a taste for Syrian bread, and we made our own pita pockets and pizzas—before the general public ever knew what either of them was.

Laura grew up helping her mother in the kitchen. With a natural love for homemaking, and an instinctive sense about cooking, she came into the sisterhood with a wealth of good old "home cooking" type recipes from her mother as well as some of her own she had accumulated as a young career woman.

One of the choicest recipes in the General Recipe Box is her mother's torte. A surprising combination of textures and flavors, this marvelous creation combines a rich cake with a crunchy, slivered-almond meringue baked onto the layers. The layers are put together with a creamy custard filling and topped with whipped cream and sliced peaches—incredibly delicious! This summer I prepared it with fresh strawberries for some old friends, and they were so taken with it they named it Strawberry Splendor. Another old treasure is her mother's sausage stuffing—and her Annie Q's Biscuits still remain my first choice as a rich dessert biscuit.

One of our first three Sisters is a native Cape Codder. Although she now lives and serves in Canada, she has never lost her love for all that is indigenous to the Cape, such as cranberries, rose hips, and beach plums. We have her to thank for a number of good old reliable recipes in our General Recipe Box, such as Cape Cod Cranberry Torte and Orange-Cranberry Bread—both of which are very popular with guests and retreatants.

She always kept a keen eye on the beach plums and rose hips to ensure our having a good supply of jelly from each. To a true Cape Codder this is essential to survival through the winter months.

It was Karen who first discovered Mr. McGuire, a fellow Cape Codder. Karen could spot a beach plum bush from any distance, especially when she was on a beach plum hunt, and this man's yard was a haven for them. He was an elderly widower, living alone in what appeared to be an abandoned house. She approached him one day as he was walking along Rock Harbor Road and inquired about the house and the bushes. "Oh, that's where I live and those are my bushes. They're loaded with plums this year. Help yourself," was his generous response to her inquiry.

Karen couldn't have been more elated if she had inherited an unexpected fortune. From that day on, Sisters picked from Mr. McGuire's bushes and kept him supplied with jelly and visits through the long winter months. When we learned that one of his favorite meals was clam pie, I would always make one for him whenever we had a successful clamming trip. He was a delightful old gentleman, who for years blessed us all by sharing so freely, not only the fruit of his bushes, but his warm friendship as well.

In actuality, we have only two Italian Sisters in the sisterhood, but one

58

would think we had at least fifty by the preference shown for the Italian food. For most of the Sisters it seems we can never have it often enough.

Some typical Sisters' meals include lots of soups and salads. We often have a Baked Potato Bar, with assorted vegetables such as chopped broccoli, onions, peppers, mushrooms, tomatoes, bacon bits, and cheese sauce, and frequent Salad Bars, which include a grain salad made from lentils, chickpeas, barley, or black-eyed peas. These are examples of some favorite dishes:

MINESTRONE SOUP

1 cup water	1 teaspoon salt
½ cup dried great Northern, navy, or kidney beans	½ teaspoon dried basil leaves
4 cups chicken broth	⅛ teaspoon pepper
2 small tomatoes, chopped	1 bay leaf
2 medium carrots, sliced	4 ounces green beans, cut
2 cups shredded carrots	into 1-inch pieces (about
1 stalk celery, chopped	¾ cup)
1 medium onion, chopped	2 small zucchini, cut into
¼ head shredded cabbage	1-inch slices
½ cup macaroni, uncooked	Freshly grated Parmesan
1 tablespoon snipped parsley	cheese

Yield: Makes 5 servings

Heat water and dried beans to boiling in a Dutch oven; boil for 2 minutes. Remove from heat. Cover and let stand for 1 hour; pour off soaking water. Add enough fresh water to cover beans. Heat to boiling; reduce heat. Cover and simmer until tender, 1 to 1½ hours (do not boil or beans will burst).

Add chicken broth, tomatoes, carrots, celery, onion, cabbage, macaroni, parsley, salt, basil, pepper, and bay leaf to beans. Heat to boiling; reduce heat. Cover and simmer for 15 minutes. Add green beans and zucchini. Heat to boiling; reduce heat. Cover and simmer until macaroni and vegetables are tender, 10 to 15 minutes. Remove bay leaf. Serve with Parmesan cheese.

GREEN BEAN, ZUCCHINI, AND POTATO STEW

¼ cup olive oil
1 cup onion, chopped
1 pound fresh green beans, trimmed, halved crosswise
¼ teaspoon cayenne
8 ounces zucchini, cut into 1-inch-thick slices
8 ounces russet potatoes, peeled, cut into 1-inch-thick cubes

¾ cup fresh chopped Italian (flat-leaf) parsley
Pinch of oregano
1 (28-ounce) can Italian style tomatoes, drained and chopped, juices reserved
Salt and pepper

Yield: Makes 6 to 8 servings

Heat oil in a heavy large nonstick skillet over medium-high heat. Add onion and sauté 5 minutes. Add green beans and cayenne, and sauté until onion is translucent, about 3 minutes. Add zucchini, potatoes, parsley, tomatoes, and tomato juices. Bring to a boil; reduce heat. Cover and simmer until potatoes are tender, stirring frequently, about 45 minutes. Season to taste with salt and pepper. Remove from heat. (Can be prepared 24 hours ahead. Cover and refrigerate.) Serve warm or at room temperature.

BROCCOLI BAKE

2 egg whites
¼ cup mayonnaise
3 tablespoons grated Parmesan cheese
2 tablespoons chopped parsley
Peel of ½ lemon, grated

2 pounds broccoli, fresh, or 2 (10-ounce) pkgs. frozen broccoli spears, cooked, drained
2 tablespoons butter, melted
Paprika

Yield: Makes 4 to 6 servings

Preheat oven to 450°F.
Beat egg whites until soft peaks form. Fold in mayonnaise. Stir in cheese, parsley, and lemon peel. Arrange cooked broccoli in oven-proof serving dish. Pour melted butter over broccoli. Top with egg white mixture. Sprinkle with paprika. Bake 5 minutes or until puffy and lightly browned.

CRISPY CHICKEN

1 (2½- to 3-pound) broiler-fryer chicken, cut up
¼ cup butter, melted

3 cups saltine cracker crumbs
2 teaspoons onion salt

Yield: Makes 6 servings

Rinse the chicken; pat dry. Sprinkle with onion salt and pepper. Brush chicken with melted butter. Roll chicken pieces in crumbs. In a 15 x 10 x 1-inch or 13 x 9 x 2-inch baking pan arrange chicken pieces, skin side up, so pieces do not touch. Drizzle any remaining butter atop.
Bake in a 375°F oven for 45 to 55 minutes or until tender and no longer pink. Do not turn.

PASTA PRIMAVERA

2 cups broccoli, peeled
  and cut into small florets
2 cups diced yellow squash
  or zucchini
1 cup diced carrots
1 cup diced tomatoes
1 + 2 tablespoons butter
1½ cups heavy cream

½ to ¾ cup freshly grated
  Parmesan cheese
1 pound pasta, such as
  fettucini, linguini, or
  spaghetti
Salt and freshly ground
  pepper

Yield: Makes 4 to 8 servings

Separately blanch broccoli, squash, and carrots until barely tender. Drain. Sauté tomatoes for 1 to 2 minutes in 1 tablespoon butter. Heat cream, cheese, and the remaining 2 tablespoons butter together; keep warm. Cook pasta in boiling salted water until just tender. Drain and place in a large sauté pan. Add cream mixture and three-fourths of the blanched vegetables. Cook for 1 to 2 minutes, tossing gently, until hot. Season with salt and pepper, turn out on a platter, and top with the remaining blanched vegetables and tomatoes. Serve with additional grated cheese.

ZUCCHINI LASAGNA

2 tablespoons olive oil
2 medium garlic cloves,
  minced
1 (28-ounce) can tomatoes,
  crushed
2 tablespoons fresh basil
  or parsley leaves, chopped
Salt and pepper
15 dried 7 x 3½-inch,
  no-boil lasagna noodles

3 cups roasted zucchini
  (see preparation instructions
  below), divided
1 pound mozzarella cheese,
  shredded (about 4 cups),
  divided
5 ounces Parmesan cheese,
  grated (about ⅔ cup),
  divided
Cooking spray for foil

Yield: Makes 6 to 8 servings

Heat oil and garlic in a 10-inch skillet over medium heat until fragrant but not brown, about 2 minutes. Stir in tomatoes; simmer until thickened slightly, about 10 minutes. Stir in basil or parsley and add salt and pepper to taste. Pour into a large measuring cup. Add enough water to make 3½ cups.

Spread ½ cup sauce evenly over bottom of a greased 9 x 13-inch lasagna pan. Lay 3 noodles crosswise over sauce, making sure they do not touch each other or sides of pan. Spread ¾ cup prepared zucchini evenly over noodles, ½ cup sauce evenly over zucchini, and ¾ cup mozzarella and 2 generous tablespoons Parmesan evenly over sauce. Repeat layering of noodles, zucchini, sauce, and cheeses 3 more times. For fifth and final layer, lay final three noodles crosswise over previous layer and top with remaining 1 cup tomato sauce, 1 cup mozzarella, and 2 tablespoons Parmesan. (Can be wrapped with plastic and refrigerated 8 to 12 hours or wrapped in plastic and aluminum foil and frozen for up to 1 month. If frozen, defrost in refrigerator.)

Adjust oven rack to the middle position and preheat oven to 375°F. Cover pan with large sheet of foil greased with cooking spray. Bake 25 minutes (30 minutes if chilled); remove foil and continue baking until top turns golden brown in spots, about 15 minutes. Remove pan from oven and let lasagna rest 5 minutes. Cut and serve immediately.

Roasted zucchini: Adjust oven racks to upper and lower-middle positions and preheat oven to 400°F. Slice zucchini lengthwise in ⅜-inch-thick slices. Toss with 3 tablespoons olive oil, 4 minced garlic cloves, and salt and pepper to taste. Spread out zucchini on two baking sheets; roast, turning occasionally, until golden brown, about 35 minutes.

Note: This can be made with raw lasagna noodles instead of the no-bake ones, but lasagna must sit 12 hours or be frozen before baking.

SAUSAGE AND CHEESE STRATA WITH TOMATOES

12 ounces hot Italian sausages, casings removed
3½ cups milk
8 eggs
2 teaspoons minced fresh thyme or ¾ teaspoon dried
1½ teaspoons onion salt
¼ teaspoon pepper
3 fresh tomatoes
11 slices white sandwich bread (about 1 pound), crusts trimmed, bread cut into 1-inch pieces
½ cup chopped onion
½ cup freshly grated Parmesan cheese (about 1½ ounces)
1 cup (packed) grated mozzarella cheese (about 4 ounces)
¼ cup feta cheese, crumbled
Chopped fresh parsley

Yield: Makes 8 servings

Sauté sausages in a heavy medium skillet over medium heat until cooked through, breaking up with the back of a spoon, about 5 minutes. Using a slotted spoon, transfer the sausage to paper towel and drain well.

Butter a 13 x 9 x 2-inch glass baking dish. Whisk milk, eggs, thyme, onion salt, and pepper in a large bowl to blend. Add tomatoes, sausage, bread, onion, and Parmesan cheese and stir to blend. Transfer to prepared baking dish. Cover and refrigerate at least 4 hours.

Preheat oven to 375°F. Bake the strata, uncovered, until puffed and golden brown, about 45 minutes. Sprinkle with mozzarella and feta cheese and bake until the mozzarella melts, about 5 minutes. Transfer pan to rack and cool 5 minutes. Sprinkle with parsley.

TUSCAN GRILLED BREAD SALAD

4 ¾-inch-thick slices of Italian bread (each about 3 x 5 inches)
1 green bell pepper, seeded, quartered
1 large tomato, cut into ½-inch-thick slices
4 1½-inch-thick onion slices (preferably sweet onion, such as Vidalia)
3 + 3 tablespoons bottled olive oil vinaigrette
1 (15 ounce) can cannellini beans (white Italian kidney beans), rinsed, drained
¼ cup fresh basil, thinly sliced
Salt and pepper
Fresh basil sprigs (optional)

Yield: Makes 2 servings

Prepare the barbecue grill (medium-high heat). Arrange bread and vegetables on a baking sheet. Brush bread and vegetables lightly with 3 tablespoons of the vinaigrette.

Grill pepper and onion for 6 minutes, turning occasionally. Place bread and tomato slices on the grill. Continue to grill until pepper and onion are slightly charred, bread is toasted, and tomatoes are heated through, turning occasionally, about 3 minutes longer. Transfer vegetables and bread to work surface; cut into bite-size pieces.

Place cannellini beans, sliced basil, and the remaining 3 tablespoons vinaigrette in a large bowl and toss to coat. Mix in grilled vegetables and bread. Season salad to taste with salt and pepper; garnish with basil sprigs, if desired.

PUFFY EGGPLANT CASSEROLE

1 large eggplant	¼ + ½ cup saltine cracker crumbs
½ cup mushroom soup	3 + 3 tablespoons butter, melted
⅓ cup mayonnaise	1 cup grated sharp cheese
1 egg	Salt

Yield: Makes 5 servings

Peel eggplant, chop, and cook (boil or steam). Drain. Mix soup, mayonnaise, egg, ¼ cup crumbs, 3 tablespoons butter, and cheese; add salt to taste. Add to eggplant. Put in a greased pie plate. Mix the remaining ½ cup crumbs and 3 tablespoons butter and sprinkle on top. Bake at 350°F until brown and puffy. This is good as a lunch casserole served with hard rolls and salad.

WILTED CABBAGE WITH CARROTS AND BACON

4 bacon slices, cut into ½-inch pieces	2 carrots, coarsely grated
1 medium onion, thinly sliced	¼ cup washed, dried, and chopped fresh parsley
3½ cups cabbage, thinly sliced (about ¾ pound)	Salt and pepper

Yield: Makes 2 servings

In a large nonstick skillet, cook the bacon over moderate heat until crisp and transfer with a slotted spoon to paper towels to drain. In the fat remaining in the skillet, cook onion over moderately low heat, stirring, until softened. Add cabbage and carrots, and cook, stirring, over moderate heat until crisp-tender, about 5 minutes. Stir in bacon and parsley, and season with salt and pepper.

ORANGE–ROSEMARY CHICKEN

1 12-ounce container frozen orange juice concentrate, thawed	4 teaspoons soy sauce
	2 teaspoons hot pepper sauce (such as Tabasco®)
⅓ cup dry white wine	1 large garlic clove, chopped
⅓ cup honey–Dijon mustard	Onion salt and pepper
2 tablespoons finely chopped fresh rosemary or 2 teaspoons dried	2 7-pound chickens, each cut into 8 pieces (breasts halved if large)

Yield: Makes 6 servings

Blend orange juice, wine, mustard, rosemary, soy, hot sauce, and garlic in processor to make orange glaze.

Prepare barbecue grill (medium heat). Sprinkle chicken with onion salt and pepper. Grill until golden, turning occasionally, about 5 minutes per side. Continue grilling chicken until cooked through, brushing glaze over chicken and turning occasionally, about 25 minutes longer. Transfer to platter to serve.

CHICKEN HEROES

¾ cup mayonnaise and
extra for spreading
5 green onions, including tops,
thinly sliced
1 (8-ounce) can water chestnuts,
drained and coarsely chopped
4 teaspoons Dijon mustard
1 teaspoon Worcestershire sauce
1 teaspoon salt
5 to 6 drops Tabasco® sauce

4 cups cooked, diced chicken
1 + 1 cups shredded
Monterey Jack cheese
1 baguette loaf French
bread
Minced fresh parsley
Sliced green onions
Sliced black olives
¼ cup sliced almonds,
toasted

Yield: Makes 6 to 8 servings

In a large bowl, combine the ¾ cup mayonnaise, green onions, water chestnuts, mustard, Worcestershire, salt, and Tabasco®. Stir in the chicken and 1 cup of the cheese. Up to this point, the chicken mixture can be prepared ahead, covered, and refrigerated for up to 24 hours.

Split the baguette in half lengthwise. Trim any uneven crust from the bottom so the loaf rests evenly. Place bread halves, cut side up, on a baking sheet. Spread mayonnaise on the bread. Spread chicken mixture evenly over each bread half and sprinkle with the remaining 1 cup of cheese. Bake until cheese is bubbly and lightly browned, about 10 minutes. Transfer to a long cutting board. Garnish with parsley, sliced green onions, olives, and almonds. Slice to serve.

The yellow blossoms that form on the end of zucchini and summer squash have a distinctive flavor, but since they usually last only a day before shriveling up, it is important to pick them first thing in the morning.

They are equally as tasty prepared in the Italian manner as Rosie, our neighbor, always made them, dipped in batter and fried, or the Greek way stuffed with a lamb and rice filling and steamed. I knew Papa liked them the latter way, so when I was living at home I would always fix them whenever he was going to be eating at home. They became my specialty. I don't remember his ever commenting on them, but I was always pleased when he reached for seconds, and even more pleased when the platter was emptied.

BATTER-FRIED SQUASH BLOSSOMS

½ cup corn oil   1½ cups milk
1 cup flour, sifted   18 squash blossoms
1 teaspoon salt   Unseasoned flour for coating
1 egg   Frying oil

Yield: Makes 6 servings

Blend oil, flour, and salt. Add egg and milk. Beat with an electric mixer until smooth; the batter will be thin. Coat blossoms generously with unseasoned flour. Dip in batter, letting excess drip off. Fry in oil (375°F) 3 to 4 inches deep until golden brown.

STUFFED SQUASH BLOSSOMS

16 squash blossoms   ½ cup chicken broth
2 cups rice filling

Yield: Makes 8 servings

Fill each squash blossom with generous tablespoon of rice filling as used in Dolmades (see recipe p. 93). Place in a covered baking dish with broth. Bake until broth is absorbed, about 30 minutes.

CAPE COD CRANBERRY TORTE

3 eggs, separated
½ + ½ cup sugar
1 teaspoon vanilla extract
1 teaspoon almond
   extract
1 cup fine graham
   cracker crumbs
½ cup nuts, chopped
1 can (1 pound) whole
   cranberry sauce
½ cup brown sugar
1 small pkg. of
   strawberry gelatin (.44 oz.)
½ cup heavy cream

Yield: Makes 6 to 8 servings

Preheat oven to 350°F. Beat egg yolks until thick. Gradually beat in ½ cup of the sugar and keep beating until very light. Beat in extracts and mix in crumbs.

Beat whites of eggs until foamy throughout; add the remaining ½ cup sugar a tablespoon at a time, and beat until shiny and stiff enough to stand in peaks. Fold this mixture into the beaten egg mixture and blend in nuts.

Spread beaten egg mixture into two 8-inch (or one 10-inch) buttered pie plates. Bake for 20 to 25 minutes or until set. Take from the oven and place on racks to cool.

In a saucepan, mix together the cranberry sauce and brown sugar. Place over moderate heat and stir constantly until mixture comes to a boil. Take from heat and add gelatin. Stir to dissolve and let cool until partially set. Whip the cream.

Spread a thin layer of the cooled cranberry mixture on the torte shells. Then add a layer of whipped cream. Continue this pattern, ending with whipped cream, until all is in the shell. Let stand until cranberry portion is completely set.

ORANGE-CRANBERRY BREAD

2 cups flour
1 cup sugar
1½ teaspoons baking powder
½ teaspoon soda
1 teaspoon salt
¼ cup shortening
¾ cup orange juice
1 tablespoon grated
   orange rind
1 egg, well beaten
1 or 2 cups cranberries,
   fresh or frozen, coarsely
   chopped

Yield: Makes one loaf

Sift together flour, sugar, baking powder, soda, and salt. Cut in shortening until mixture resembles coarse cornmeal. Combine orange juice and grated orange rind with the egg. Pour all at once into dry ingredients, mixing just enough to dampen. Carefully fold in the cranberries. Spoon into a greased 9 x 5 x 3-inch loaf pan. Spread corners and sides slightly higher than the center. Bake in a moderate oven, 350°F, about one hour, or until the crust is golden brown and a toothpick inserted in the center comes out clean. Remove from pan. Cool. Store overnight for easy slicing.

MRS. HILL'S TORTE

Cake:

½ + 1 cups sugar
  ½ cup softened butter
  2 egg yolks
  1 teaspoon baking powder
  1 cup flour, sifted
  4 tablespoons milk,
    room temperature

1 + 1 teaspoons vanilla extract
4 egg whites
  Sliced Almonds
  Sweetened whipped cream
  Fresh fruit or canned
  peaches

Custard filling:

¼ cup sugar
  1 tablespoon cornstarch
  1 egg yolk, beaten

1 cup milk
  Vanilla extract
  Butter

Yield: Makes 6 to 8 servings

Cake: Cream ½ cup of the sugar with softened butter. Add egg yolks and blend well. Add baking powder to flour, and add alternately to the sugar mixture with milk and 1 teaspoon vanilla extract. Spread in 2 well-greased and floured cake tins.

Beat the 4 egg whites until stiff, slowly adding the remaining 1 cup sugar and 1 teaspoon vanilla extract. Spread over cake batter, and sprinkle with sliced almonds. Bake at 350°F for about 30 minutes. (Poke down through meringue with a knife to make sure the cake is done.)

Custard filling: Combine sugar, cornstarch, egg yolk, and milk in a medium saucepan. Bring to a boil, stirring constantly. Cool. Add vanilla and a little butter.

When set and cooled, spread custard between the two cake layers. Just before serving, spread top layer with sweetened whipped cream, and decorate with sliced fresh fruit or sliced canned peaches.

ANNIE Q'S BISCUITS

2 cups flour
2 teaspoons sugar
½ teaspoon cream
  of tartar
½ teaspoon salt

4 teaspoons baking powder
1 stick margarine or
  ½ cup vegetable
  shortening
⅔ cup milk (at room
  temperature)

Yield: Makes 6 to 8 servings

Mix dry ingredients. Add margarine (or shortening) and work with a pastry cutter until mixture resembles cornmeal. Add milk and mix lightly. Put on a floured board. Pat to ¾-inch thickness and cut into rounds or squares. Bake at 450°F for 8 to 10 minutes or until lightly brown.

BRAISED LAMB SHANKS WITH ROSEMARY

6 lamb shanks (about 5 pounds total)
  Onion salt and pepper
2 tablespoons olive oil

2 medium onions, chopped
3 large carrots, peeled, cut
  into ¼-inch-thick rounds
2 garlic cloves, minced
1 (750-ml) bottle dry red wine
1 (28-ounce) can diced
  tomatoes with juices
1 (14½-ounce) can
  chicken broth

1 (14½-ounce) can beef
  broth
5 teaspoons chopped
  fresh rosemary
2 teaspoons chopped
  fresh thyme
1 teaspoon grated lemon
  peel

Yield: Makes 6 servings

Sprinkle shanks with onion salt and pepper. Heat oil in a heavy large pot over medium-high heat. Working in batches, add shanks to pot and cook until brown on all sides, about 8 minutes. Transfer shanks to a bowl.

Add onions, carrots, and garlic to pot and sauté until onions are golden, about 10 minutes. Pour in all remaining ingredients. Return shanks to the pot, pressing down to submerge. Bring the liquids to a boil. Reduce the heat to medium-low. Cover; simmer until the meat is tender, about 2 hours.

Uncover pot; simmer until the meat is very tender, about 30 minutes longer. (Can be made 1 day ahead. Chill until cold; cover and keep chilled. Rewarm over medium heat before continuing.) Transfer shanks to a platter; tent with foil. Boil juices in the pot until thickened, about 15 minutes. Season with onion salt and pepper. Spoon over shanks.

SYRIAN (PITA) BREAD

2 pkgs. yeast	1 tablespoon salt
1/3 teaspoon sugar	6 cups flour (you can use
1/2 + 1 1/2 cups warm water	white, wheat, or a mixture)
1/4 cup olive oil	

Yield: Makes 8 or 9 pitas

Dissolve yeast and sugar in 1/2 cup of the warm water in a large mixing bowl and allow to proof. Add the remaining 1 1/2 cups water along with the oil, salt, and 5 cups of the flour, mixing in the flour 1 cup at a time. The dough will be quite sticky. Turn out on a floured board and work in the remaining cup of flour, or more if the dough is too sticky. Knead for 10 minutes or more until the dough is smooth and elastic. Shape dough into a ball and place in a buttered bowl. Cover and let rise for 1 1/2 to 2 hours, or until doubled in bulk.

Punch down the dough and divide into 8 or 9 equal pieces, shaping each piece into a ball. Let rest for about 10 minutes. Preheat the oven to 500°F. Flatten each ball with a well-floured rolling pin and roll to 1/8-inch thickness. Dust two baking sheets with cornmeal and place two circles on a sheet. Cover and let rest for about 1/2 hour.

Put one sheet at a time in the middle of the oven. Bake for 10 to 13 minutes or until puffed up and lightly browned. Repeat with the remaining pans, unless you can fit two side by side. Remove pitas from the pan when done baking to prevent a crispy crust from forming. These can be frozen and reheated for 10 to 15 minutes.

HOMEMADE YOGURT

1 1/2 quarts milk	2 tablespoons yogurt

Yield: Makes about 1 1/2 quarts

Bring milk to a boil slowly over low heat, stirring constantly to prevent sticking. Simmer for 10 minutes, remove from heat, and cool. Dilute yogurt in a little of the milk, and add to the remaining milk. Blend well, and pour into small jars. Cover and leave in a warm place overnight. When yogurt is set, store in refrigerator.

ROSE PETAL SWEETS

4 cups fresh rose petals	1 tablespoon fresh lemon juice
2 cups water	3 tablespoons fruit liqueur
2 + 1 cups sugar	Pinch of salt

Yield: Makes 4 1/2 pints

Note: It is essential that only fragrant red rose petals be used; approximately 1 dozen roses equals 4 cups of petals.

Remove the base end of the rose petals, wash gently, and drain. Bring the water, 1 cup sugar, and lemon juice to a boil in a saucepan; add rose petals gently, in layers. Boil for a few minutes, slowly stir in the remaining 1 cup of sugar, and stir until sugar is dissolved. Bring to a full boil, lower heat, and simmer about 10 minutes, or until the syrup forms a ball when dropped from the tip of a spoon on a saucer. Skim the syrup, add 3 tablespoons of fruit liqueur, pour into sterilized jars, seal with paraffin, and store.

BAHMI GORENG
(INDONESIAN PORK)

Marinade:
- ½ cup soy sauce
- 1 tablespoon sugar
- ½ teaspoon red pepper flakes
- 1 clove garlic, minced

Main dish:
- 3 pounds pork, sliced thinly in strips
- 4 leeks, thinly sliced
- 3 cloves garlic, minced
- ½ cabbage, shredded
- 1 pound egg noodles
- Soy sauce to taste (approx. ⅛ cup)
- ½ cup small shrimp, cooked (optional)

Sweet and Sour Sauce:
- ½ cup molasses
- 1 tablespoon soy sauce
- 1 tablespoon water

Yield: Makes 8 servings

Marinate the pork in soy sauce, sugar, red pepper flakes, and garlic for at least an hour (more is fine). In a wok or deep fry-pan cook leeks, garlic, and cabbage in oil until soft. Remove from heat.

Drain pork from marinade and fry in oil until thoroughly cooked.

Cook egg noodles in salted water and drain. Add noodles, cabbage mixture, and shrimp to the pork and cook together quickly, adding soy sauce to taste.

Sauce: Mix molasses, soy sauce, and water.

Serve Bahmi Goreng hot with the Sweet and Sour Sauce. Make plenty because your guests will want seconds.

CASSAVA PIE

- 12 pounds frozen ground cassava
- 2 pounds sugar
- 1 can condensed milk
- 27 eggs, unbeaten
- 2 pounds butter, melted
- 2 teaspoons ground nutmeg
- 3 tablespoons salt
- Brandy to taste
- 5 pounds chicken
- 2½ pounds cubed pork
- Salt and pepper

Yield: Makes 16 servings

Put cassava in a large bowl. Cover with sugar. Add condensed milk, eggs, butter, nutmeg, and salt. Blend thoroughly. Place half this mixture in a large greased baking pan or use several small ones, making sure there are at least 1½ inches of batter in each one.

Put chicken and pork in a large pot, cover with water, and add salt and pepper. Bring to a boil and simmer until meat is just tender. Remove chicken meat from the bones; ladle meats over the cassava batter, adding a little stock. Cover the meat filling with remaining cassava, leaving a small hole in the center for basting.

Bake at 350°F for one hour. Reduce heat to 250°F and bake another 3 hours. Baste hourly by pouring stock through the hole in the crust. Cool in pan.

MARCH 5

*Sister Linda is asking for help in the greenhouse
transplanting seedlings. What memories of
growing up with my mother this brings back!*

Each year, early in the spring, I would come home from school one day to find a wooden table in front of the window in my bedroom. It would be covered with tuna cans containing seedlings that Mama had started from seeds she had dried and saved from the choicest tomatoes, cucumbers, squash, and other vegetables the year before.

As far back as I can remember, I was surrounded by growing things, and to this day, the sight of a garden never fails to delight me. Coming across an open market has always been one of the highlights of my travels.

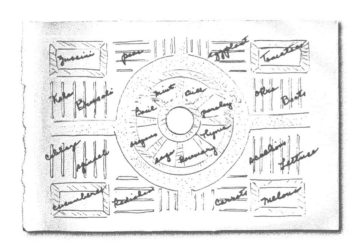

APRIL 2

Now that the cold weather is past and we won't be using the black stove for heat, I need to remind Sister Marjorie to do something about the chimney.

Elijah is a snow-white feline with a neck as thick as a wrestler's, a scar on his nose, and one permanently turned-down, chewed-up ear. How he acquired these battle scars, no one really knows. We can only surmise. He was a stray that the vet wanted to find a home for, and the Sisters are softies when it comes to situations like these. We took him to live with us, and he has won the heart of every Sister, even those who aren't cat lovers.

Once in a while a bird makes its way into the stovepipe leading from the chimney into our black stove. When this happens, as it did today, Elijah goes wild, pacing all around and across the stove, pawing and scratching at the stovepipe from every angle trying to get to the captive. He always comes away from these experiences very frustrated. Sister Marjorie is going to figure out how to put a little screen across the chimney to prevent this from recurring. I hope she doesn't get around to it too soon. I like seeing Elijah all smudged from the stove black, looking like a Mary Poppins chimney sweep. It makes him even more endearing.

APRIL 6

Casually thumbing through Mother Cay's old recipe box late this afternoon, my eyes fell on a recipe that suddenly catapulted me back over more than thirty years to South America.

Before I became a Sister, I had worked in the inner city with a young Catholic priest who ran a coffee house in the South End of Boston. With a passion for the poor and needy, he organized a trip that took ten of us from different walks of life to Colombia. Two priests, a *New York Times* editor and his wife, a recovered alcoholic, a Reformed minister, a Boston physician and his wife, a widow, and I all spent two weeks together experiencing firsthand the poverty and need of that country.

Everything about our time there appealed to me. I can still picture that young mother surrounded with her children, weaving the vividly colored serape I brought back with me. Forever etched in my heart will be the memory of one of her little dark-eyed boys sweeping me up into a lively dance in the village street. So many of the Latin American children had flashing smiles, rhythmic feet, and outgoing personalities.

But the memory evoked by the recipe in Mother Cay's box was of the convent where I stayed along with Alice, the widow in our group. It was a very dark, Spanish-looking building surrounded by a high, black, wrought-iron fence with a heavy locked gate. Approaching it after dark our first night, I thoroughly expected to be let in by a Spanish-speaking nun in traditional long black habit. I was not prepared for the figure in sweatshirt and jeans who unlocked the gate, introduced herself in English (with a marked Jersey accent) as Sister Mary Rose, and invited us in. Nor was I at first prepared for what we met within—five more American sisters, all attired like the one who had greeted us, more or less lounging around a television as several played guitars. This was my very first time inside a convent, and the romantic image I had had of the monastic life temporarily suffered a mild blow. Thirty-five years later, after many visits to various convents at home and abroad, I have come to understand that each has its own distinctive spirit or ethos, and this particular one had a strong American influence and happened to be very contemporary, liberal, and casual.

We were shown to our rooms and told to help ourselves to whatever we might find or like in the refrigerator, then come "hang around" with the Sisters in the living room if we wanted to. Alice quickly took them up on their offer, going immediately to explore the refrigerator.

She quickly spread out a little buffet for us, and I have no recollection of what it consisted of except for one dish over which I, for some reason, completely lost my senses. It was a spongy, almost colorless, molded dessert with the tang of fresh lemon that captivated my taste buds and left me feeling like a Greek god feasting on ambrosia. None of the nuns seemed to know much about it, who had made it, or where it had come from. I was tempted to believe that an angel had prepared it exclusively for me. Then on the day of our departure, Sister Mary Rose handed me a scribbled piece of paper with the directions, more or less, for making this magical dessert. She wasn't sure they were accurate, and she didn't really know the name of it, but she thought it was called something like Snow Pudding.

I looked at the faded old recipe card written in Mother Cay's hand. Returning it to the box, I wondered how Mother Cay had been introduced to Snow Pudding, and why she had kept it among her favorites. I would have loved to hear her story about it.

SNOW PUDDING

1 envelope unflavored gelatin	½ cup fresh lemon juice
2 tablespoons cold water	1 teaspoon lemon rind, grated
1 cup boiling water	1 cup whipping cream
1 cup sugar	Fresh orange slices for garnish

Yield: Makes 8 servings

Soften gelatin in cold water. Stir in the boiling water. Add sugar and stir until dissolved. Add lemon juice and lemon rind; stir. Refrigerate until slightly thickened, but not set.

Whip cream until thick and fold into gelatin mixture. Chill. If desired, fresh fruit may be folded in when gelatin is partially set. Garnish with orange slices before serving.

APRIL 10

Two freshly picked daffodils just greeted me as I opened the door. On the ledge in the hallway stands a lovely alabaster figure of the Madonna and Child that I brought back from Italy long ago. Every now and then a little bunch of daisies, a few pansies or herbs, or perhaps a branch of quince silently appears at her feet, placed there by an anonymous Sister—a tribute to Mother and Child and a joy to me. Never do I cease to be thrilled by a little floral gesture that comes my way, and this one took me back to my roots—literally!

I pulled the lid down on the mailbox and, still holding the letter in my hand, closed my eyes and prayed, "Lord, please let this letter result in whatever you want it to." I dropped it in, closed the lid, and crossed the street to Oppenheim's, Olean's leading florist located uptown in the Olean House Block, the finest section of the city.

The letter I had just mailed was an application for work in this establishment. I was in my last year of high school, and it was time to start earning my own living. I could think of no other place I would rather do so than in this shop, which, to me, was the closest thing on earth to the garden of Eden.

I stood transfixed, staring into the windows, inhaling the fragrance through the open door. To be able to earn my living in such an environment would be nothing short of an unrealistic dream come true.

I rehearsed again, from memory, the carefully calculated letter just posted, especially the ending: "I have majored in both business and art with above-average grades in each, but have no training in working with flowers. However, I would be willing to accept any position available in order to obtain work in your shop."

If I slept at all that night, it could not have been more than a wink, and when the next day Joe Oppenheim called me, I went weak in the knees. "Who wrote that letter you sent me?" he asked. "I found it quite impressive for a teenager." His bookkeeper was leaving him soon, and she would start training me the next day. On the side we'd see how adept I might or might not be with flowers.

How could this be true? God really loved me that much to give me the very thing I most desired? I was deeply moved.

Everything about my new job was even more than I had fantasized it would be. I loved the shop itself, the bookkeeping, the flowers of course, and the people I worked with.

Lillian, a tall, thin, fast-moving, energetic expectant mother devoted more time to telling me about life with her alcoholic husband and introducing me to her Polish way of cooking than to teaching me bookkeeping. I have never since then been able to eat a potato golompki without recalling our days together when she taught me the ropes on my first real job.

Joe Oppenheim was a fun-loving daredevil who loved to tease, challenge, and play tricks on people. He saw to it that I had a quick initiation into my job. Within a week he taught me to drive the delivery truck, sent me out alone to the cemetery at night to collect baskets, took me to a mortuary and placed my hands on a corpse so that I would be comfortable and at ease pinning a corsage on a deceased person and arranging flowers in and around caskets, and took me for a flight in an open plane, which included stunts and flying upside down.

Mrs. Oppenheim, who doted on her only son, Joseph, regularly brought him homemade chicken soup, cheese blintzes, or her own corned beef and tongue, always including some for me. She made sugar cookies that were out of this world, substituting chicken fat for butter, which gave them a texture and flavor that was incomparable.

Joe's way of finding out whether I was adept at working with flowers was to hand me an order and tell me to fill it—no instructions, no sample to copy or follow, no guidelines.

After I was finished, he would tell me how it could be improved or changed. But he always challenged me to just get in there and do it, and the results were often surprising—even to me.

The flower business was not his first love. His heart was in the sky. He was a private pilot for an executive, who often called him without a moment's notice to fly him somewhere. This, of course, left us in a lurch in the shop, especially if we were in the middle of several weddings or funerals, which was often the case. But he was very considerate about making up to us for the inconvenience he caused and would bring me a deluxe banana cream pie from the Olean House.

One time when I went to cut into the pie given me the day before, I found my Bible, which I kept at the shop, opened and propped up beside it. A large portion of the pie was missing, and there was a big red arrow, drawn unmistakably by Joe's hand, pointing to the verse, "The Lord giveth and the Lord taketh away."

If I should ever be forced to choose only one dessert that I could make or eat, it would be my version of this pie, which I have developed over the years. Experience has taught me that the most important thing to remember in making it is to immediately store it in a cool place under lock and key!

The Olean House featured many fine foods, some of which have stuck with me as "old faithfuls" over the years. The pecan rolls from their coffee shop were nonpareil! Served with several chilled curls of butter, they were generous in size, individually baked with whole pecan halves, and with an almost mahogany glaze over each. They had a perfect firm texture, with sugar and cinnamon running through them. But it was the subtle, almost unidentifiable hint of nutmeg that distinguished them from so many other coffee rolls.

One could almost tell time by the stream of merchants, salespeople, and shopkeepers making their way at mid-morning each day to the Olean House for this coffee break par excellence.

They also served a marvelously rich, moist, chocolate layer cake for lunch that was equally as popular. But they were best known for their roast duckling à l'orange.

Work hours at the flower shop were often irregular, especially around holidays such as Easter, when we would have to make hundreds of corsages the day before. On some occasions we worked straight through the night. At times like these, we staggered our breaks and meal times.

One evening around Easter time, I went into the Olean House for dinner and decided to pull out all the stops and splurge. I had been working very hard, so I decided to reward myself with nothing less than roast duckling à l'orange, even though the price was an exorbitant $7.95. I didn't do this very often.

Hardly had I placed my order when Mrs. Oppenheim walked in. Her eyes lit up when she saw me, and she came straight to my table. "I'm treating you tonight," she announced. I squirmed in my seat, protesting. "Don't argue with me," she insisted. "I don't know what we'd do without you." I could feel my face turning scarlet, and not from the compliment. I was suddenly feeling less hungry than when I'd come in, but when she ordered the crabcake special at $2.50 for herself, I lost my appetite completely.

For years after, whenever she and I wanted a good laugh, we would pull out the roast duckling incident. Mrs. Oppenheim said she learned from that experience never to offer to pick up the tab for anyone without first finding out what they had ordered.

When it came to be that I was working full time with flowers and another bookkeeper had been hired, Joe's trips became more frequent, and it was obvious that flying was to be his full-time career. Ella Morey bought the shop and gave me a raise in salary, along with more responsibility.

She had two passions besides flowers. One was high-style fashions, and the other was bridge. It seemed to me that her interest in the latter was increasing, and that she was always having the girls for bridge on the day the displays in the windows needed redoing.

That in itself did not bother me. I had grown to love doing window displays. What bothered me was that so often when it was my turn to redo them, there was no new merchandise to display, as there always seemed to be when it was her turn. Whenever I complained about this, she would simply light up a cigarette, smile, and say, "But Irene, you're so good at making something from nothing." Then draping her beaver-lined cape around her, off she'd go to Bridge Club. Exasperating!

She had one favorite menu for Bridge Club which she took great pride in preparing: chicken crêpes with green grapes and a wonderfully rich English trifle saturated with sherry. To placate me, she would always save me a serving for lunch the day after walking out on me.

CHICKEN-MUSHROOM CRÊPES

Crêpes:

1 cup flour	1¼ cups milk
Pinch of salt	1 tablespoon butter, melted
2 eggs	Vegetable oil

Filling:

4 tablespoons butter	6 tablespoons sour cream
2 onions, chopped	2 tablespoons sherry
½ pound fresh	Salt
mushrooms, sliced	½ cup parboiled
½ cup parboiled	asparagus tips
2 cups coarsely chopped,	
cooked chicken	

Sauce:

6 tablespoons butter	¾ cup freshly grated
6 tablespoons flour	Parmesan cheese
½ cup sherry	½ cup grated Swiss or
2 cups chicken stock	Gruyere cheese
1 cup milk	Salt

Yield: Makes 8 servings

Crêpes: Sift flour and salt into a bowl. Make a well in the center and add eggs and a little of the milk. Beat well with a wooden spoon, working in all the flour. Gradually beat in remaining milk until bubbles form on top of batter. Stir in butter.

Add a small amount of oil to a 7-inch crêpe pan—enough to barely cover the base—and place over high heat. Pour in 2 to 3 tablespoons of the batter and quickly tilt the pan so that batter covers the base thinly and evenly. Cook for about 1 minute over high heat until lightly browned. Turn crêpe with a metal spatula and cook the other side for about 30 seconds. Keep crêpe warm. Continue until the batter is used.

Filling: Melt butter in a large skillet. Add onions and sauté until soft. Add mushrooms and sauté for a few minutes. Remove from heat. Add chicken, sour cream, sherry, and salt to taste. Stir until well blended. This mixture may be made ahead and refrigerated. Before heating, fold in asparagus tips and reheat.

Sauce: Melt butter and remove from heat. Add flour and stir until smooth. Stir in sherry, stock, and milk. Return pan to heat and cook, stirring constantly, until mixture is thick and comes to a full boil. Reduce heat and simmer. Add cheeses and salt to taste. Stir over low heat until cheeses melt. Remove pan from the heat and cover with waxed paper so that a skin does not form. The sauce may be frozen.

To assemble: Fill crêpes with warmed filling, roll up, and place side by side in a baking dish. Spoon some of the sauce over the crêpes and bake at 350°F for 15 minutes. Reheat the rest of the sauce gently and serve separately.

ENGLISH TRIFLE

Custard:

3 beaten eggs	¼ cup sugar
2 cups milk or light cream	1 teaspoon vanilla extract
Sponge Cake (see directions)	2 tablespoons toasted
6 tablespoons cream sherry	sliced almonds
¼ cup strawberry preserves	½ cup whipping cream
2 cups cut-up strawberries	1 tablespoon sugar
	½ teaspoon vanilla extract

Yield: Makes 8 servings

Custard: Combine eggs, milk, and sugar in a heavy medium saucepan. Cook and stir this mixture over medium heat. Continue cooking until egg mixture coats a metal spoon. Remove from heat. Stir in vanilla extract. Quickly cool the custard by placing saucepan in a sink or bowl of ice water for 1 to 2 minutes, stirring constantly. Pour custard mixture into a bowl. Cover surface with clear plastic wrap. Chill until serving time.

Cake: Prepare sponge cake as found in recipe for Whipped

Cream Rolls on p. 166. Cut cake into 1-inch cubes (you should have about 5 cups). Reserve remaining cake for another use.

To assemble: In a 2-quart serving bowl, layer half the cake cubes. Sprinkle with half the sherry. Dot with half the preserves. Top with half the fruit and half the almonds. Pour half the custard over all. Repeat layers. Cover and chill for 3 to 24 hours. To serve, beat whipping cream, sugar, and vanilla extract until soft peaks form. Spread over trifle.

PECAN ROLLS

2 + 2 to 2½ cups flour
1 pkg. active dry yeast
1 cup milk
1 + 1 cups sugar
⅓ + ¼ cup + 3 tablespoons butter
½ teaspoon salt
2 eggs

⅔ cup brown sugar
2 tablespoons light corn syrup
Pecan halves
1 teaspoon ground nutmeg
2 teaspoons ground cinnamon

Yield: Makes 24 servings

Combine 2 cups flour and the yeast. Heat and stir milk, 1 cup sugar, ⅓ cup butter, and salt until liquid is warm (120° to 130°F) and the butter almost melts. Add to the flour mixture along with the eggs. Beat with an electric mixer on low speed for 30 seconds, scraping the bowl. Beat on high speed for 3 minutes. Using a spoon, stir in as much of the remaining 2 to 2½ cups of flour as you can.

Turn out onto a lightly floured surface. Knead in enough of the remaining flour to make a moderately stiff dough that is smooth and elastic (6 to 8 minutes total). Shape into a ball. Place in a lightly greased bowl; turn once. Cover; let rise in a warm place until doubled (about 1 hour).

While dough is rising, combine brown sugar, ¼ cup butter, and light corn syrup. Cook over medium heat and stir until combined. Pour into greased muffin tins and sprinkle pecan halves in each.

Punch dough down. Divide in half. Cover; let rest 10 minutes. Roll one half of the dough into a 12 x 8-inch rectangle. Melt the 3 tablespoons butter; brush half over the dough. Combine the remaining 1 cup sugar and cinnamon; sprinkle half of the mixture over the dough. Roll up from one of the long sides. Seal seams. Slice dough into 12 pieces. Repeat with the remaining dough, butter, and sugar and cinnamon mixture. Place the rolls in greased muffin tins. Cover; let rise until nearly doubled (about 30 minutes). Bake in a 375°F oven for 20 to 25 minutes. Invert onto a serving plate.

CRÈME DE CASSIS CHOCOLATE CAKE

Crème anglaise:
2 cups half-and-half
1 vanilla bean, split in half

½ cup sugar
4 large egg yolks

Cake:
10 ounces bittersweet (not unsweetened) or semi-sweet chocolate, chopped
¾ cup (1½ sticks) butter
½ cup unsweetened cocoa powder

½ cup crème de cassis liqueur
5 large eggs
1 cup sugar

Chocolate–Cassis Icing:
¼ cup whipping cream
8 ounces bittersweet (not unsweetened) or semi-sweet chocolate, chopped

6 tablespoons + ¾ cup crème de cassis liqueur
Fresh mint sprigs

Yield: Makes 12 servings

Crème anglaise: Bring half-and-half to simmer in heavy medium saucepan. Scrape in seeds from vanilla bean; add bean. Whisk sugar and yolks in bowl. Gradually whisk in half-and-half mixture. Return mixture to saucepan; stir over medium-low heat until custard thickens and leaves path on back of spoon when finger is drawn across, about 5 minutes (do not boil). Strain sauce. Cover; chill until cold, at least 4 hours.

Cake: Preheat oven to 350°F. Butter 9-inch-diameter spring-form cake pan with 2¾-inch-high sides. Line bottom with parchment; butter parchment. Dust pan with flour; tap out excess. Melt chocolate and butter in heavy medium saucepan over low heat, stirring until smooth. Cool slightly. Whisk in cocoa and liqueur. Using electric mixer, beat eggs and sugar in large bowl until mixture whitens and triples in volume, about 6 minutes. Add chocolate-butter mixture and fold together.

Pour batter into prepared pan. Bake until top forms crust and tester inserted into center comes out with very moist crumbs attached, about 40 minutes. Cool cake in pan on rack 5 minutes. Press down on crusty portion of cake to even. Release pan sides from cake. Turn cake onto rack; peel off parchment and cool completely.

Chocolate–Cassis Icing: Bring cream to simmer in heavy medium saucepan. Add chocolate and 6 tablespoons liqueur; whisk until smooth. Let icing stand until cool but still spreadable, about 15 minutes.

Place cake on plate. Spread icing over top and sides. Chill 1 hour. (Can be made 1 day ahead. Cover; chill. Let stand 2 hours at room temperature before serving.)

Simmer ¾ cup liqueur in heavy small saucepan until reduced to a generous ½ cup, about 5 minutes. Cool.

Spoon crème anglaise onto the plates, forming a pool. Spoon reduced liqueur decoratively atop sauce and swirl with knife. Slice cake and place 1 slice in center of each plate. Garnish with mint.

ROAST DUCK À L' ORANGE

Duck	Salt and pepper
½ lemon	

Orange sauce:

1 cup port or dry red wine	Dash of freshly ground
½ cup orange juice	black pepper
2 teaspoons lemon juice	⅛ teaspoon Tabasco ®
1 tablespoon cognac	Pinch of ground allspice
1 teaspoon Kitchen	2 tablespoons cooked and
Bouquet ®	puréed duck liver
1 tablespoon cornstarch	Orange slices
½ teaspoon salt	Watercress

Yield: Makes 6 servings

Duck: Preheat oven to 350°F. Rub the skin of the duck with lemon. Sprinkle inside of the duck with salt and pepper. Place duck on a rack in a roasting pan and roast, without basting, about 12 minutes per pound, or longer. Fifteen minutes before duck is done, sprinkle the outside with salt and pepper. (Before roasting, fill cavity of the duck with stuffing, if desired. Roast a stuffed duck approximately fifteen minutes per pound.)

Sauce: In a saucepan, blend together ingredients for the sauce. Cook, stirring constantly, until sauce thickens. Garnish with orange slices and watercress.

BANANA CREAM PIE

Crust:

1¼ cups flour
½ cup (1 stick) chilled
   butter, cut into pieces
2 tablespoons sugar

Pinch of salt
4 tablespoons
   (approximately) ice water

Filling:

¾ cup sugar
¼ cup cornstarch or
   ½ cup flour
3 cups milk
4 eggs, separated
1 tablespoon margarine
   or butter

1 teaspoon banana
   flavoring
½ cup whipped cream
2 ripe bananas
2 cups heavy cream
2 tablespoons
   confectioners' sugar

Yield: Makes 8 servings

Crust: Blend flour, butter, sugar, and salt in a food processor until coarse meal forms. With processor running, add water by tablespoonfuls until clumps form. Gather dough into a ball. Flatten to a disk.

Preheat oven to 400°F. Roll out dough on a floured surface to a 13-inch round. Transfer to a 9-inch glass pie plate. Trim the edge to ½-inch overhang. Fold edge under and crimp. Freeze for 10 minutes. Line the crust with foil; fill with beans or pie weights. Bake until sides are set, about 12 minutes. Remove the foil and beans.

Filling: In a medium saucepan combine sugar and cornstarch or flour. Gradually stir in milk. Cook and stir over medium-high heat until mixture is thickened and bubbly. Reduce heat; cook and stir for 2 minutes more. Remove from heat.

Beat the egg yolks lightly with a fork. Gradually stir about 1 cup hot filling into the yolks. Return all to saucepan; bring to a gentle boil. Cook and stir for 2 minutes more; remove from heat. Stir in the margarine and banana flavoring. Pour half the hot filling into the crust. Chill in refrigerator. Cool the other half of filling. When thoroughly cooled, fold the whipped cream into cooled filling. Slice 2 ripe bananas onto first layer of chilled pie; add remaining half of filling. Top entire pie with thickly whipped heavy cream sweetened with confectioners' sugar.

GOLOMPKI
(POTATO DUMPLINGS)

4 pounds potatoes, peeled
Salt
Water

2 teaspoons onion salt
1 egg

Yield: Makes 70 to 75 servings

In a medium saucepan, place one-third of the potatoes with enough salted water to cover. Bring to a boil over high heat. Reduce heat to medium. Partially cover; cook for 20 minutes or until tender. Drain; let cool. Grind cooked potatoes into a large bowl.

Grate remaining raw potatoes onto a piece of doubled cheesecloth about 20 inches x 12 inches. Gather ends of cheesecloth so grated potatoes are enveloped in a ball. Squeeze excess potato juice into a medium bowl by twisting cheesecloth ends. Reserve potato juice.

Stir squeezed raw potatoes into cooked potatoes. Add 1 teaspoon salt and egg. Work mixture together for 3 to 4 minutes. From reserved potato juices, spoon off and discard all but the bottom 2 tablespoons of potato juice, which contains potato starch. Stir starchy juice into potatoes.

Boil the salted water in a large pot. Using your hands, roll 1 heaping teaspoon potato mixture into a ball. Drop potato dumplings into boiling water. Boil until potatoes are cooked and dumplings float, about 7 minutes.

CHEESE BLINTZES

Crêpes:

½ cup flour	1 large egg
2 tablespoons sugar	½ cup milk
½ teaspoon baking soda	1 + 2 tablespoons butter
Pinch of salt	

Filling:

1½ cups ricotta cheese	½ teaspoon grated
2 tablespoons sugar	orange zest
½ teaspoon grated lemon zest	½ teaspoon vanilla extract

Confectioners' sugar (optional)

Yield: Makes 4 servings (about 10 blintzes)

Crêpes: Stir together the flour, sugar, baking powder, and salt in a mixing bowl. In a separate bowl, stir the egg and milk. With a fork, quickly stir the egg mixture into the flour mixture. Melt 1 tablespoon butter in a 5-inch crêpe pan, pour it into the batter, and stir to mix. Leave melted butter coating in pan.

Heat the pan over moderate heat. Ladle in only enough of the batter to cover the bottom of the pan, swirling the pan to coat it evenly. Cook the crêpe just until its edges turn golden, then remove it with a spatula and flip it, cooked side up, onto a kitchen towel, folding the ends of the towel up over it. Repeat the process with the remaining batter, stacking the crêpes inside the towel.

Filling: In a mixing bowl, stir together the ingredients for the filling.

To Assemble: Take a crêpe and place it, cooked side up, on a work surface. Spoon about 1 tablespoon of the filling across the center of the crêpe. Fold opposite sides over the ends of the filling; fold the other 2 sides over to enclose the filling. Repeat with the remaining crêpes and filling.

Melt the remaining 2 tablespoons butter over moderate heat in a skillet large enough to hold all the blintzes without crowding. When butter sizzles, add the blintzes, seams down, and fry them until golden brown, 3 to 4 minutes per side. Sprinkle with confectioners' sugar before serving, if desired.

CRISPY SUGAR COOKIES

2 cups flour	1 cup sugar
1 teaspoon baking powder	1 egg
½ teaspoon salt	¼ cup milk
½ cup clarified chicken fat,	½ teaspoon lemon extract
or butter	½ teaspoon lemon zest

Yield: Makes 5 dozen

Sift together flour, baking powder, and salt. Cream together the chicken fat and sugar, and mix in egg. Add dry ingredients alternately with milk, lemon extract, and zest; blend. Chill dough overnight.

Preheat oven to 400°F.

Roll the dough to ⅝-inch thickness on a floured board. Press out the desired shapes. Transfer to greased cookie sheets and bake 7 to 10 minutes.

Dear Lord —
On this night of Passover,
Help me to recall all that
you suffered & endured to
obtain my salvation.
As you have given
yourself for me, may I
freely give myself entirely
to you —

APRIL 22

Tonight we commemorate the Passover with a special meal,
which for many Community members has become their
favorite meal of the year.

Although it is not as somber as the Lenten meals of previous weeks, there is a sense of seriousness about the Passover meal. Each household first gathers to read together from the Book of Exodus the scriptural account of the first Passover. Here the Israelites were instructed to prepare and eat, in haste, a meal of lamb and bitter herbs before leaving the land of Egypt, marking the lintel of their door with the blood of a lamb as a sign of protection from the death angel who would pass over the marked homes.

After reading the story we go quickly to an assigned home where, standing, we eat our symbolic meal of lamb, endive, and pita bread.

From there we go to the chapel where we have our last Eucharist service preceding Easter, followed by the stripping of the altar and sanctuary in preparation for Good Friday.

For years we had an Easter dinner for the entire Community family. Lilies, daffodils, forsythia, and other spring flowers were lavishly placed everywhere from the chapel down to the Fellowship Room. Brightly colored place cards added to the festivity of the decorations.

Most often the meal was planned around some kind of chicken, such as Spring Stuffed Chicken Breast or Cumberland Chicken, with its wonderful sauce of currant jelly, ginger, and sherry. With this, we always served a fresh spring vegetable such as asparagus or tender green beans and some type of light pasta or new potatoes.

Dessert would be something like Daffodil Cake, a lemon-custard-filled angel food frosted with flavored whipped cream, or Fresh Strawberry Crumb Pie or Apricot Pear Lattice Tart.

In more recent years, we have begun to celebrate this day with an early breakfast before the church service in two locations—the Friary and the Convent—and each person is free to go to either place or to both. An identical buffet is served at each place with brunch-type foods, always including a fresh fruit cup or platter, some kind of egg dish, bacon and sausage, coffee cake, muffins, or French toast.

Regardless of what is served, our Easter meal is always a joyous occasion.

SPRING STUFFED CHICKEN BREASTS

6 whole boneless chicken breasts
4 leeks (white part and 1 inch green), halved lengthwise and well rinsed
4 tablespoons + 9 teaspoons unsalted butter
12 ounces fresh mushrooms, sliced lengthwise
¾ cup coarsely chopped fresh parsley

2 tablespoons chopped fresh rosemary leaves, or 2 teaspoons crumbled dried
Grated zest of 2 lemons
12 thin slices prosciutto
12 thin slices (2½ x 1 inches) Monterey Jack cheese
Freshly ground black pepper
1 cup Madeira or dry sherry

Yield: Makes 6 servings

Rinse chicken pieces well and trim away any excess fat. Pat dry. Place the breasts on a cutting surface skin side down. Remove the fillets (the finger-size muscle on the back of each breast half) and reserve for another use. Place a piece of waxed paper or plastic wrap over each breast, and pound with the flat side of a meat pounder until thin.

Bring a saucepan of water to a boil. Add leeks, and simmer for 1 minute. Drain, separate the leaves, and pat dry.

Melt the 4 tablespoons of butter in a skillet, and sauté the mushrooms over medium heat until just tender, 5 minutes. Drain well.

Preheat the oven to 350°F. Combine the parsley, rosemary, and lemon zest in a bowl and mix well.

To assemble the rolls, lay the chicken breasts flat, skin side down. Place one slice of prosciutto lengthwise on each side of the breasts. Divide the leeks evenly among the breasts, laying the leaves lengthwise. Arrange the mushrooms down the center of each breast. Sprinkle the parsley mixture over all, and top with 2 slices of cheese, lengthwise. Sprinkle with pepper.

Starting on one long side, roll the breasts carefully, making about 3 turns to form a tight roll. Tie the roll together with kitchen string.

Line a shallow roasting pan with aluminum foil, and place the chicken rolls, seam side down, in the pan. Sprinkle the chicken with pepper, and place 1½ teaspoons of the remaining butter on top of each roll. Pour Madeira into the pan.

Bake, basting frequently, until golden, 35 minutes. To serve, slice the rolls into ½-inch-thick rounds. Arrange them decoratively on dinner plates, and spoon some of the pan juices over them.

CUMBERLAND CHICKEN

Onion salt and pepper	1 large bag Pepperidge
8 boned chicken breasts	Farm® corn stuffing,
1 cup melted butter	ground fine in blender

Cumberland Sauce:

1 jar (10 ounces) red currant jelly	1 (6-ounce) can frozen orange juice concentrate,
4 tablespoons sherry	thawed
⅛ teaspoon ginger	1 teaspoon dry mustard
	¼ teaspoon Tabasco®

Yield: Makes 8 servings

Sprinkle onion salt and pepper over the chicken breasts, dip in melted butter, roll in stuffing crumbs, and place in shallow pan. Bake approximately 45 minutes to 1 hour at 350°F and serve with Cumberland Sauce.

Combine sauce ingredients until smooth, warming, if necessary, to melt the jelly. Serve with wild rice.

FRESH STRAWBERRY CRUMB PIE

Crumb crust and topping:

1 cup hazelnuts or almonds (about 4 ounces)	½ cup sugar
2 cups flour	¾ cup (1½ sticks) butter, chilled, cut into small pieces

Filling:

½ cup sugar	2 pints whole strawberries
1½ tablespoons cornstarch	

Yield: Makes 6 servings

Crust and topping: Preheat oven to 350°F. Spread nuts in a medium baking pan. Roast the nuts, stirring occasionally, until toasted, about 10 minutes. Remove nuts from oven and turn out onto a cloth towel. Rub off and discard the papery skins; increase oven temperature to 450°F. In a food processor fitted with a metal blade, process the nuts until finely ground, about 10 seconds.

In a large bowl, mix together the nuts, flour, and sugar. Using a pastry blender or 2 knives, cut butter into flour mixture until coarse crumbs form. Using fingers, evenly press half the mixture into the bottom and up sides of an 8- or 9-inch tart pan.

Filling: Mix together the sugar and cornstarch in a medium bowl. Gently fold in berries. Spoon berry mixture into crust, spreading evenly. Sprinkle berry mixture evenly with the remaining crumb crust and topping. Bake until topping is golden and filling is bubbly, 30 minutes. Transfer pan to a wire rack to cool for 10 minutes. Serve warm.

Baking tip: Watch nuts very carefully when you are grinding them in the food processor. If you grind too long, the result will be nut butter.

APRICOT-PEAR LATTICE TART

Crust:

2½ cups flour
1 teaspoon salt
2 teaspoons sugar
8 tablespoons (1 stick)
  cold butter, cut into pieces
6 tablespoons vegetable
  shortening
5 to 6 tablespoons ice water

Filling:

1 (16-ounce) can apricot
  halves in light syrup,
  drained
1 (29-ounce) can pear
  slices in light syrup,
  drained
⅓ cup firmly packed
  brown sugar
3 tablespoons sliced
  almonds, toasted
½ teaspoon ground
  cinnamon
¼ to ½ teaspoon grated
  lemon peel
1 egg yolk, beaten
1 teaspoon water

Glaze:

⅓ cup apricot preserves

Yield: Makes 8 to 10 servings

Crust: Combine flour, salt, and sugar in a mixing bowl. Add the butter and shortening; working quickly, using a pastry blender, cut in the ingredients until the mixture resembles coarse crumbs. Sprinkle ice water over the mixture 1 or 2 tablespoons at a time, and toss after each addition. When you can gather the dough into a ball, you've added enough water (usually 5 to 6 tablespoons).

Transfer the dough onto a cool, lightly floured surface; using the heel of your hand, smear the dough away from you, about ¼ cup at a time. Repeat until all the dough has been smeared. (This will blend in the butter and shortening and make the pastry flakier.) Gather the dough into a ball, using a dough scraper; divide the ball in half. Flatten each half slightly, wrap in wax paper, and refrigerate for 30 minutes to 1 hour. (You can freeze the dough at this point. Wrap well in plastic wrap.)

Prepare pie crust, using 9-inch tart pan with removable bottom or 9-inch pie pan. Place one half of the prepared crust in pan; press in bottom and up sides of pan. Trim edges if necessary. Heat oven to 400°F.

Filling: Arrange apricots and pears in crust-lined pan. In small bowl, combine brown sugar, almonds, cinnamon, and lemon peel. Sprinkle evenly over fruit.

Top: Cut the remaining crust into ½-inch wide strips, and arrange to form a lattice top. Trim and seal edges. In small bowl, combine egg yolk and water; gently brush over lattice.

Bake at 400°F for 45 to 55 minutes or until crust is golden and fruit is soft when skewer is inserted. Heat preserves in small saucepan over low heat; brush over tart.

SWISS OMELET ROLL WITH MUSTARD SAUCE

Omelet:

½ cup mayonnaise
2 tablespoons flour
1 cup milk
12 eggs, separated
½ teaspoon salt
⅛ teaspoon pepper
1½ cups finely chopped ham
1 cup (4 ounces) Swiss cheese
¼ cup chopped green onion
  Watercress (or parsley) and
  tomato slices for garnish

Mustard Sauce:

1 cup mayonnaise
2 tablespoons prepared mustard
2 tablespoons chopped
  green onion

Yield: Makes 6 to 8 servings

Omelet: Combine mayonnaise and flour. Gradually add milk and beaten egg yolks; cook, stirring constantly over low heat until thickened. Remove from heat; cool 15 minutes. Fold mayonnaise mixture and seasonings into stiffly beaten egg whites. Pour into 15½ x 10½-inch jelly roll pan lined with wax paper, brushed with mayonnaise. Bake at 425°F for 20 minutes. Invert pan on towel;

carefully remove wax paper. Cover with combined ham, cheese, and green onion. Roll from narrow end, lifting with towel while rolling.

Sauce: Combine sauce ingredients; mix well.

Serve omelet seam down; top with Mustard Sauce. Garnish with watercress (or parsley) and tomato slices.

DOUBLE ORANGE SCONES WITH ORANGE BUTTER

Scones:

2 cups flour	½ cup mandarin orange
3 + 1 tablespoons sugar	sections, chopped and
2½ teaspoons baking powder	drained
2 teaspoons grated orange peel	¼ cup milk
⅓ cup margarine or butter	1 egg, slightly beaten

Orange Butter:

½ cup butter, softened	2 tablespoons orange
	marmalade

Yield: Makes 8 servings

Note: Lightly spoon flour into measuring cup; level off.

Scones: Preheat oven to 400°F. Lightly grease cookie sheet. In large bowl, combine flour, the 3 tablespoons sugar, baking powder, and orange peel. With fork or pastry blender, cut in margarine until mixture resembles coarse crumbs. Add orange segments, milk, and egg. With fork, stir just until mixture leaves sides of bowl and forms soft dough.

Turn dough out onto floured surface. Knead lightly 10 times. On greased cookie sheet, roll or pat into a 6-inch circle. Sprinkle with the 1 tablespoon sugar. Cut into 8 wedges; separate slightly. Bake at 400°F for 15 to 20 minutes or until golden brown.

Orange Butter: Beat butter in small bowl until light and fluffy; stir in marmalade. Serve with warm scones.

FLUFFY FRENCH TOAST WITH ORANGE SYRUP

French Toast:

8 slices French or Italian bread, 1-inch thick	6 eggs, beaten
	⅛ teaspoon ground cinnamon
1 cups half-and-half	⅛ teaspoon ground nutmeg

Orange Syrup:

¾ cup orange juice	2 teaspoons fresh lemon
1 tablespoon cornstarch	juice
½ cup sugar	1 teaspoon grated
2 tablespoons butter	orange peel

Yield: Makes 8 servings

French Toast: Arrange bread in single layer in pan, fitting closely together. Blend half-and-half, eggs, cinnamon, and nutmeg in medium bowl. Pour egg mixture over bread. Cover pan and refrigerate until bread absorbs mixture, turning once, about 3 hours. (Can be prepared one day ahead. Keep refrigerated.)

Preheat oven to 325°F. Transfer French toast to a generously buttered sheet pan. Bake until tester inserted into center of bread comes out clean, about 30 minutes. Flip over once to check browning on both sides.

Orange Syrup: Stir orange juice and cornstarch in small saucepan until smooth. Add sugar and stir over medium heat until thick, about 8 minutes. Add butter, lemon juice, and orange peel, and stir until butter melts.

Recut French toast into 8 separate slices. Serve with warm syrup.

MAY 10

Sisters are out in Bethany circle picking nosegays of violets and lilies of the valley to give as Mothers' Day greetings. These are two of my mother's favorite flowers; they take me back to the early days of my life and the times I spent with her. One scene in particular comes to mind.

Sunsuit & Pigtails

The sun was hot on my face and bare arms, but a strong breeze tempered the heat of this bright summer day. It was only 11:30, and I was already hungry. I was always hungry after the long climb up Mt. Herman, and we would be here for quite a while longer picking all these blueberries.

I opened my lunch: thick slices of homemade Kulish, a Ukrainian Easter Bread filled with white raisins and citron, thickly spread with real butter, accompanied by hard-boiled eggs straight from the hen that morning, cooked just enough to be firm but not too hard, and a touch of freshly grated horseradish.

The taste of this simple wholesome food and the feeling of sun, wind, and fresh air combined to give me a sense of contentment and well being. I loved the outdoors. It was a good thing I did, because Mama was always taking me on outings like this. In the early spring we made frequent trips to a hillside pasture where we dug dandelions and gathered wild forget-me-nots and watercress that sprang up in and around a clear brook of pure spring water. The chilly stream running across my toes, the soft plush carpet of thick green grass under my bare feet—it was exhilarating!

I understood why humble pastures held such an attraction for Mama. I never tired of hearing her tell of her favorite cow that she tended as a young peasant girl in the old country, and how during a frightening storm she would crouch beneath the cow for protection from the lightning and thunder, holding onto her legs till the storm subsided.

Mama and I spent many hours in the woods, and if there was anything within miles that was edible or transplantable into a garden, my mother found it and we brought it home. Our front yard was filled with mountain laurel, the driveway lined with pale yellow iris and purple phlox against a white picket fence. Our backyard was a virtual flower show, boasting a garden of perennials that rivaled any I have ever seen in all my visits to botanical gardens. Every flower had a story behind it. Most of them had found their way into our yard from one of my mother's explorations of nearby fields and woods.

I was a stocky, sunburnt bundle of energy. I spent most of the summer in a sunsuit and pigtails working in the yard, the garden, and the kitchen, except on Sundays when we almost always went on picnics, usually in the woods by a nice stream. Even though Mama had a strong conviction that Sunday should not be a day of work, we usually returned home with a picking of wild strawberries or blackberries to be made into jam on Monday morning. If you came upon God's gifts while you were in the woods, he wouldn't want you to leave them to go to waste just because you found them on his day.

Mama's chickens were her pride and joy. She treated them with tender loving care, carried on a dialogue with them, and constantly praised them for producing the largest, creamiest eggs of any hens. I was convinced that the more she did this, the more they responded to please her.

In appreciation, she insisted that, like her vegetables, these choice eggs be eaten as soon after gathering as possible, so we had them most mornings, usually soft-boiled or poached just right, never too hard, never too soft. We liked them in other ways as well—scrambled the Greek way with feta cheese, or the Italian way with fried green peppers. These made nice lunches with our crusty rolls.

We often made nice egg drop noodles, too, and had them in our chicken soup, or sometimes just in a bowl of warm milk or with butter for a light meal.

Mama thrived on giving things to people, whether it was a loaf of bread, a blueberry pie, a fistful of flowers, baskets of grapes or tomatoes, or a combination of all of these. She lavished them bountifully on friends as well as perfect strangers, never distinguishing much between the two. It took her no time to become acquainted with someone.

Of course there were those who took advantage of this side of her nature, but never without her being aware of it, and never did this discourage her from continuing to give. She was wise and discerning, and seldom, if ever, was she deceived by anyone.

She had an abundance of good common sense and assumed that most everyone else did. Whenever I would protest that I didn't know how to do something, her response would be, "Just use your head." More than one novice would receive that response from me later in my life.

Mama with grandchildren

When she had a good crop of anything, she would always attribute it to God's goodness. "God blessed my raspberries so much this year," she'd exclaim, smiling at them in her work-worn hands. Her philosophy seemed to be that since God gave them so bountifully, he honored her giving them away, so that she couldn't really lose by giving them, regardless of the attitude of the receiver—a principle that equipped me for much of what I was to do later in my life.

She was very practical about the use of everything, be it time, energy, or money. When you picked berries, you always picked them clean, meaning that no leaves, stems, or bad berries went into your bucket. When you dug dandelions or picked lettuce, you cut off the roots or shook the soil off outdoors to make less dirt and work indoors. When you washed vegetables at the outside faucet, you caught the water and watered the rose bushes and hydrangeas with it. You made the most of everything. God blessed you with bumper crops, but he also expected good stewardship of what he gave.

Rosie DiRocco was a very large, round woman with a thick, braided bun at the back of her head. She lived on the other side of the lot behind our house, and she had a very thin, little husband whom she always referred to as "my man Richard." He was somewhat bald and noticeably quiet. Together they were the embodiment of Jack Sprat and his wife. They had been married for many years but never had any children. Mama wanted me to be born at home in our own house, and Rosie decided she'd be the midwife. From then on I think she somehow considered me her own.

I had to pass her house on the way home from school, and almost always

she would be sitting on her porch swing crocheting. She would call me over, fold me in her big arms, smother me with garlic-scented kisses, then take me into her kitchen and sit me down to have a snack, whether I was hungry or not. It was always something like a bowl of broccoli cooked in olive oil with tomatoes and lots of garlic, or it might be a plate of fried zucchini blossoms, or a dish of pasta. Whatever it happened to be, it was always accompanied by a large glass of milk. She would sit across from me and watch me until I had cleaned my plate. Then marching to the cupboard, she would bring the ritual to a grand finale by pulling out her tin of biscotti. She would wait until I expressed my delight, then with a great flourish, she would remove the lid and thump the tin down in front of me, roughly gesturing to me to help myself, and I knew it was important that I eat more than one.

Some of the neighborhood children were a little afraid of her, but I was comfortable with her and enjoyed my frequent visits to her kitchen. To this day, Italian biscotti remain high on my list of preferred treats. They are wonderful with a cup of tea in the afternoon or dunked in coffee at mid-morning. Keeping a tin of them on hand has stood me in good stead many a time when unexpected visitors have dropped in. They make a nice little gift, pack and travel well, and maintain their freshness indefinitely. Plus they have a special appeal to those who like a not-too-rich sweet.

There are any number of variations of this versatile biscuit. Nuts, candied fruit, even chocolate chips can be added, as well as a frosting, but the way I like them best is simply with a little aniseed for flavoring, just the way Rosie used to make them.

Sunday picnic

Mama felt that too much leisure or idleness was not good for anyone. Besides, there was always so much more to be done. Nevertheless, I did spend a certain amount of time playing with neighborhood schoolmates, especially the McGranagans. They were an Irish family with five children. Mama was always handing vegetables over the back fence to Mrs. McGranagan, who was always hanging up wash on her many clotheslines in their backyard. They had a wonderfully large lawn to play in, but no garden. I suppose this was because Mrs.

McGranagan was always too busy doing laundry to till a garden.

My main memory of her was of her carrying her large wicker baskets of clothes in and out of their house. My other memory was of her standing at the stove, making Shepherd's Pie, which she did without fail every Monday with the leftover lamb from the family's Sunday roast. Every so often she would invite me to stay for dinner with them, and I was always happy when it fell on Shepherd's Pie night. We frequently ate baked, boiled, and roast potatoes at our house, but we seldom had them mashed, and there was something about all those fluffy mashed potatoes piled high on the runny gravy and lamb beneath it that held a special appeal for me—just like the peanut butter sandwiches on fluffy, white, store-bought bread that the McGranagan children so often ate.

I always have a very "homey" feeling eating Shepherd's Pie. I don't know if I associate it with the McGranagan household where I always felt so much at home, or whether it just happens to be one of those "homey" kind of dishes. Perhaps both.

Rosie never knocked when she came to our house. She just pulled the screen door open and bellowed, "Bessie, you home?" Inside the back door was a small entryway, always cluttered with things either going to or coming from the garden, such as Mama's garden shoes, a bucket of compost makings, or a basket of Swiss chard to be washed or of string beans to be snapped. This always annoyed Rosie, whose house was starkly neat, and she would grumble about how difficult it was to get through the narrow space. Nevertheless, the entryway remained cluttered, no matter how often Rosie complained about it.

Every so often Mama and Rosie would have a very loud disagreement about something. Mama always felt she was right and so did Rosie. Whenever this happened, Rosie would not show up for a time, even though she still continued to call me into her house for snacks. After a while, she would come walking across the lot to Mama out in her garden. Reaching a plate to her over the fence she'd say, "I make struffoli today."

After that I knew Rosie would be coming back for visits and lunches again.

Mama did most everything in excess. If we were having company, she never would think of serving only one main dish. There had to be a choice of several so that no one would be disappointed. The extra work involved in doing this was of no consideration. What mattered was that food was prepared as much as possible to a person's liking and that the guests were pleased and satisfied.

Almost always she would include Pierogies or Stuffed Cabbage Rolls as a side dish.

Sometimes I think the saddest loss a "Mediterranean" could suffer would be the loss of tomatoes from his or her diet. Tomatoes can find their way into so many dishes. A simple meal we often had during the peak of tomato season was crusty bread dipped in a sauce of fresh hot peppers slowly simmered together with fresh tomatoes and olive oil. Cooked down to a thick consistency and allowed to sit and season for a few hours, or days for that matter, it was one of the most satisfying lunches we ever ate.

Fresh tomatoes simmered with a little sautéed onion are good to keep on hand to spoon over vegetables such as broccoli, cauliflower, or chopped zucchini. They also make a nice sauce over an omelet.

Every summer Uncle Chris, Aunt Beatrice, and cousin Penny would come to visit. Papa had been responsible for bringing his only sister Beatrice to America and arranging for her to marry Uncle Chris.

Uncle Chris owned a chain of very fine French pastry shops in New York City that catered to a wealthy clientele, including many celebrities. Specializing in hand-dipped chocolates, rich homemade ice cream, and high quality pastries, which were not only beautiful to the eye, but of unspeakable delight to the palate, his business had grown rapidly from one small confectionery to four large, flourishing establishments.

It had become a tradition for Aunt Beatrice to start picking grape leaves on arrival in preparation for her meal of dolmades and moussaka, which she always made with obvious affection for her big brother. This meal was always eaten outdoors under the grape arbor while Papa, Uncle Chris, and Aunt Beatrice reminisced about Tenados, the village they had all come from in Greece. I would always feel as though we were, for that evening, in another country.

Years later, eating a late evening meal under the lemon trees on the island of Crete, I had to excuse myself for missing something in the conversation. I had just taken a mental flight back to the old grape arbor with Uncle Chris and Aunt Beatrice.

DOLMADES
(GREEK STUFFED GRAPE LEAVES)

1 jar grape leaves (about 3 dozen)
1 bunch scallions, finely chopped
2 cloves garlic, crushed
1 tablespoon finely chopped parsley
¾ cup olive oil, divided
¾ cup raw rice
1 tablespoon chopped fresh mint
Salt and pepper
Juice of 2 lemons
2 cups beef broth
1 cup water
Lemon wedges
Chilled yogurt

Yield: Makes about 3 dozen

Remove grape leaves from the jar, scald with hot water, and drain. Cut off the stems from leaves carefully, pat each leaf dry, and place on paper towels with shiny surface down.

In a skillet, sauté scallions, garlic, and parsley in 2 tablespoons hot olive oil; add rice and mint. Season with salt and pepper to taste. Cover and simmer for 15 minutes; let cool.

When cool, place 1 teaspoon of rice mixture in center of each leaf; fold the end of the leaf over to cover the filling; fold up the sides of the leaf and roll over carefully until a cylinder about 2 inches long is formed.

Arrange the rolled grape leaves in layers in a pot; sprinkle each

layer with lemon juice and 2 tablespoons olive oil. Pour beef broth, 1 cup water, and remaining olive oil over all the leaves; place a plate on top to weight the grape leaf rolls; simmer over very low heat for 40 to 50 minutes. Remove, drain, and cool before serving.

To serve, arrange stuffed leaves on a platter garnished with lemon wedges and accompanied by a bowl of chilled yogurt.

MOUSSAKA

1 large eggplant (about 2 pounds)	1 tablespoon snipped parsley
2 tablespoons margarine or butter	2 teaspoons onion salt
	¼ teaspoon pepper
1½ pounds ground lamb or beef	⅔ + ⅓ cup grated Parmesan cheese
1 medium onion, chopped	⅓ + ⅓ cup dry bread crumbs
1 can (15 ounces) tomato sauce	1 egg, beaten
	White sauce (below)
¾ cup red wine or beef broth	Tomato sauce (below)

Yield: Makes 8 servings

Cut unpared eggplant crosswise into ½-inch slices. Cook slices in small amount boiling, salted water (½ teaspoon salt to 1 cup water) until tender, 5 to 8 minutes. Drain.

Heat margarine in 12-inch skillet until melted. Cook and stir lamb and onion until lamb is light brown; drain. Stir in tomato sauce, wine, parsley, onion salt, and pepper. Cook, uncovered, over medium heat until half the liquid is absorbed, about 20 minutes. Prepare white sauce.

Stir ⅔ cup of cheese, ⅓ cup of bread crumbs, and egg into meat mixture; remove from heat. Sprinkle remaining ⅓ cup bread crumbs evenly in greased, oblong baking dish, 13½ x 9 x 2-inches. Arrange half the eggplant slices in baking dish; cover with the meat mixture. Sprinkle 2 tablespoons of remaining cheese over meat mixture; top with remaining eggplant slices. Pour white sauce over mixture; sprinkle with remaining cheese.

Cook uncovered in 375°F oven for 45 minutes. Prepare tomato sauce. Let moussaka stand 20 minutes before serving. Cut into squares; serve with the tomato sauce.

White sauce:

¼ cup margarine or butter	2 cups milk
¼ cup flour	2 eggs, slightly beaten
1 teaspoon onion salt	

Heat margarine over low heat until melted. Blend in flour and salt. Cook over low heat, stirring constantly, until smooth and bubbly; remove from heat. Stir in milk. Heat to boiling, stirring constantly. Boil and stir 1 minute. Gradually stir at least one-fourth of the hot mixture into eggs. Blend into hot mixture in the pan.

Tomato Sauce:

1 medium onion, finely chopped	⅛ teaspoon oregano
	1 teaspoon dried basil leaves
1 clove garlic, finely chopped	½ teaspoon sugar
1 tablespoon olive or vegetable oil	¼ teaspoon pepper
	1 bay leaf, crushed
2 cups chopped ripe tomatoes	½ cup burgundy wine
½ cup water	1 (6-ounce) can tomato paste
1½ teaspoons salt	

Cook and stir onion and garlic in oil in 3-quart saucepan over medium heat until onion is tender. Add remaining ingredients except tomato paste. Heat to boiling, stirring constantly; reduce heat. Simmer, uncovered, until thickened, about 30 minutes. Stir in tomato paste. (Add 2 to 3 tablespoons water, if necessary, for desired consistency.)

KULISH
(UKRAINIAN EASTER BREAD)

2 pkgs. active dry yeast
½ cup warm water
(105° to 115°F)
¾ cup lukewarm milk
(scalded, then cooled)
⅓ cup sugar
1 teaspoon salt
2 eggs
½ cup shortening

½ cup white raisins
1 teaspoon lemon peel,
grated
1 whole orange rind,
grated
3 + 1½ to 2 cups flour
Icing (recipe follows)
½ cup citron (optional)

Yield: Makes 2 loaves

Dissolve yeast in warm water in large bowl. Stir in milk, sugar, salt, eggs, shortening, raisins, citron, lemon peel, and 3 cups of the flour. Beat until smooth. Stir in enough remaining flour to make dough easy to handle.

Turn dough onto lightly floured surface; knead until smooth and elastic, about 5 minutes. Place in greased bowl; turn greased side up. Cover; let rise in warm place until doubled, 1 to 1½ hours. (Dough is ready if indentation remains when touched.)

Punch down dough; divide into halves. Shape each half into round bun-shaped loaf. Place in two well-greased, 3-pound shortening cans. Let rise until doubled, 40 to 50 minutes.

Heat oven to 375°F. Place cans on low rack so that midpoint of each can is in center of oven. Bake until tops are golden brown, 40 to 45 minutes. (If tops brown too quickly, cover loosely with aluminum foil.) Cool 10 minutes; remove from cans. Spoon icing over tops of loaves, allowing some to drizzle down sides. Trim with tiny decorating citron, if desired.

Note: Two 46-ounce cans may be substituted for the 3-pound shortening cans.

Icing:

1 cup confectioners' sugar
1 tablespoon warm water

1 teaspoon vanilla extract

Mix ingredients until smooth. (Icing should be glaze consistency. Add 1 to 2 tablespoons of water if necessary.)

ROSIE'S BISCOTTI

½ cup butter
3 ounces cream cheese
1 cup sugar
4 eggs
3¼ cups flour
1 teaspoon baking powder

½ teaspoon salt
2 teaspoons aniseed
or 1¼ teaspoons
ground anise
or almond or vanilla
flavoring to taste

Yield: Makes 3 dozen

Cream butter and cream cheese together. Add sugar gradually, beating thoroughly after each addition. Beat in eggs one at a time; continue beating until mixture is light and fluffy. Mix together flour, baking powder, and salt, and add this dry mixture to the creamed mixture; mix well. Add flavoring and mix well. Divide dough in half; place on a lightly greased cookie sheet, and form into 2 rolls the length of the baking sheet and 1½ inches wide. Bake at 350°F 30 to 35 minutes, or until light brown. Remove from oven and cut rolls crosswise into slices about ¾ inch thick. Place on cookie sheet cut side down. Return to oven. Bake 10 minutes longer or until toasted and crisp.

SHEPHERD'S PIE

2 cups or more of leftover roast lamb
2 onions, chopped
1 tablespoon onion salt
Pinch of thyme
Pepper
Lamb bone and pan drippings, if any are left
½ cup white wine
Flour
Frozen peas (optional)
4 cups seasoned mashed potatoes

Yield: Makes 8 servings

Put lamb, onions, salt, thyme, pepper, and if available, lamb bone and pan drippings, in a pot or pressure cooker and cover with water. Cook or boil them until the meat and onions are both soft. Boil the liquid down until flavorful. Add wine and thicken with flour. Preheat oven to 350°F. Place lamb mixture in a pie dish (the peas may be added) and top with mashed potatoes. Bake until golden brown and bubbling through, about 30 minutes.

ROSIE'S STRUFFOLI

2 pkgs. active dry yeast
½ cup warm water
1 cup warm milk
¼ cup sugar
1 teaspoon salt
½ teaspoon anise extract
2 eggs, beaten
½ cup butter, melted
3 to 4 cups flour, sifted
Cooking oil
Ground cinnamon
Honey

Yield: Makes 3 dozen

Soften yeast in water. Pour milk into a large bowl; add sugar, salt, and anise extract. Stir in yeast and beaten eggs; add melted butter, and beat well. Add sifted flour, beating continuously until the batter is smooth and thick. Cover and let rise in a warm place for several hours.

Pour 3 to 4 inches of cooking oil into a deep saucepan, and heat until very hot. (The process is like making doughnuts.) Stir batter well. Drop a tablespoonful of batter into the hot oil, and cook until the batter puffs and is golden brown on all sides. Remove, and drain on paper. Place struffoli on a platter in layers, sprinkling each layer lavishly with cinnamon and warm honey diluted with a little water. Serve at once.

EGG DROP NOODLES

2 eggs
½ cup milk
1 cup flour
½ teaspoon salt
Chicken broth or salted water

Yield: Makes 4 servings

Beat the eggs and milk together. Blend in the flour and salt. Drop from tablespoon, in irregular shapes, into boiling broth or salted water. Boil for 1 minute and drain.

PIEROGIES (POLISH NOODLE DUMPLINGS WITH FILLING)

4 cups flour
2 eggs
5 tablespoons sour cream
3 + 3 tablespoons butter, melted
½ teaspoon onion salt

About ¾ cup water
Sautéed onions, if desired
(or melted butter or
softened cream cheese)
Extra sour cream,
if desired.

Yield: Makes about 70 pierogies

Prepare choice of pierogy fillings, below. Lightly flour 2 baking sheets. Sift flour into a large bowl or onto a flat working surface, making a well in the center. Break eggs into the well. Add sour cream, 3 tablespoons of the melted butter and onion salt. Blend ingredients with your fingertips. Gradually add the water, working and kneading the mixture into a smooth, pliable dough.

Divide dough into quarters. Cover 3 portions with a damp cloth. On a lightly floured board, roll remaining dough portion into a ¹⁄₁₆-inch-thick rectangle. Cut into 3½- to 4-inch circles. In the center of 1 dough circle, place 1 heaping tablespoon of the filling. Fold the dough in half over filling. Crimp the resulting edge with fingertips, forming a tight seal. Repeat this process until all remaining dough is used, placing pierogies on a lightly floured baking sheet.

Bring a large saucepan of salted water to a boil, using ½ teaspoon salt per 2 quarts water. Drop 5 pierogies into the boiling water. Stir gently to prevent them from sticking to the bottom. When the water returns to a boil, add 5 more pierogies. Stir carefully. Cover with a tight-fitting lid. Cook savory pierogies over medium heat, 4 to 5 minutes or until they float. Gently remove pierogies from pot; drain in a colander or strainer. Set on lightly greased baking sheets. Repeat this process until all pieces are boiled.

Heat remaining 3 tablespoons butter in a large skillet. Add 10 boiled pierogies; sauté over medium heat until browned on both

sides, 5 to 6 minutes. Place in a large oven-proof serving dish. Keep hot in the oven. Sauté remaining pierogies. Serve hot, garnished with sautéed onions, if desired. Sour cream may be served along with these.

SAUERKRAUT-POTATO FILLING (FOR PIEROGIES)

½ pound sauerkraut
2 tablespoons butter or margarine
1 medium onion, chopped

Pinch of salt
Pinch of freshly ground pepper
1 cup mashed potatoes

Yield: Makes about 4 cups, or enough to fill 40 to 45 pierogies

In a medium saucepan, place sauerkraut and enough water to cover. Simmer, uncovered, over low heat 30 minutes. Drain well. Using a grinder or food processor fitted with a metal blade, process sauerkraut. Do not purée too fine. Melt butter in a large skillet. Add onion; sauté over medium heat until tender. Blend in sauerkraut, salt, pepper, and mashed potatoes. Let cool.

FRESH MUSHROOM FILLING (FOR PIEROGIES)

2 + 2 tablespoons butter or margarine
2 pounds fresh mushrooms, minced
2 medium onions, minced
¼ cup dry bread crumbs

½ teaspoon salt
½ teaspoon freshly ground pepper
2 tablespoons chopped parsley

Yield: Makes about 4 cups or enough to fill 40 to 45 pierogies

Melt 2 tablespoons butter in a large skillet. Add mushrooms; sauté over low heat until tender, stirring occasionally. Place sautéed mushrooms in a medium bowl. Melt remaining 2 tablespoons butter in a skillet. Add onions; sauté over medium heat

98

until tender. Let cool. Stir in bread crumbs. Stir the mixture into sautéed mushrooms. Season mixture with salt and pepper, and mix in chopped parsley.

STUFFED CABBAGE ROLLS

2 medium cabbages or 1 large
½ cup olive oil
1 can (8 ounces) tomato sauce

1 bay leaf, crushed
Salt and pepper
2 cups beef broth

Stuffing:
½ pound ground lamb
½ pound ground beef
1 egg
1 onion, finely chopped
1 garlic clove, minced
½ teaspoon oregano

¾ cup raw rice
2 tablespoons tomato sauce
3 tablespoons olive oil
½ cup white wine
Salt and pepper

Yield: Makes 4 to 6 servings

Leave cabbage whole, but cut around the stem, and parboil for 5 minutes; let steep for another 5 minutes. Remove cabbage from water and drain; separate cabbage leaves. Chop the small inside leaves and the core and use to line a Dutch oven.

Combine all the stuffing ingredients and mix thoroughly. Season with salt and pepper to taste. Place 1 tablespoon stuffing on each of the larger cabbage leaves, fold ends of leaves over the stuffing, and roll leaves.

Arrange the stuffed cabbage leaves in rows in Dutch oven; sprinkle each layer with olive oil, tomato sauce, and crushed bay leaf. Sprinkle lightly with salt and pepper; add remaining tomato sauce, beef broth, and enough water to cover. Place a plate on top of cabbage rolls, and simmer over low heat for 1 hour. Serve the cabbage rolls with the pot sauce poured over them.

ZUCCHINI-STUFFED TOMATOES

4 tomatoes
½ pound yellow squash
½ pound zucchini squash
1 teaspoon salt
1 cup heavy cream

½ cup Swiss cheese, grated
1 tablespoon freshly grated
   Parmesan cheese
⅛ teaspoon ground white pepper

Yield: Makes 4 servings

Cut tops off tomatoes, scoop out pulp, and drain upside down on paper towel or a rack. Grate squash. Mix in salt. Let sit ½ hour; squeeze out liquid. Add cream, cheeses, and white pepper. Cook squash mixture in frying pan until liquid is absorbed and mixture is thickened. Fill tomatoes. Bake at 375°F until hot and golden brown on top. Do not overcook.

MAY 15

Every morning Brother Nicholas collects the chicken eggs and brings them down from the barn. He leaves the Sisters' share of them on the black cookstove just inside the convent Refectory door. And every morning, just like today, I go out that door and as I see those eggs, a wave of affection for the chickens wells up in me and I silently bless them for these, their faithful, constant gifts.

If you've never held a warm, freshly laid chicken egg in your hand, you won't understand what I'm talking about and you'll probably just chalk it up to my being an eccentric old Sister, but if you've had this experience you'll know that there's something about it that just makes you want to stroke the hen and say, "Good girl. Thank you so much."

We are fortunate, I think, to have colored eggs from our hens, in shades of beige and green. Some people prefer plain white ones, but I like the brown speckled ones the best. I love to have a basket of them sitting nearby just to look at.

A while ago a friend of ours celebrated a significant birthday and was given a weekend in Bethany as one of her gifts. She's from the South, with a homespun country background. I know how she feels about these eggs, so as a greeting from the Sisters, we put a little basket of them in her room.

She received some very lovely gifts for this special birthday. I saw many of them and heard about others. But when she thanked us for our little basket, saying what a special gift it was to her, I knew exactly what she meant. I felt the same way about it myself.

JUNE 1

One of the greatest blessings of my life is the many years of close association I had with Mother Cay, especially preparing her meals later in her life. She was a joy to serve because of her gratitude for whatever was done for her and her keen understanding of the effort involved to prepare something properly.

One day I was walking by Henry's Yard, so named years before after Mother Cay's son's poodle. I overheard her reminiscing with Bill about a favorite inn in England where she had enjoyed staying. "Someday," she said, "I'm going to ask Sister Irene to make me an English breakfast like they always served there." I slowed my footsteps and cocked my head in her direction to catch a description of this breakfast that she was hankering for. The next morning, extremely pleased with myself, I showed up with a breakfast tray of grilled lamb kidneys and bacon, baked beans, codfish cakes, broiled tomato halves, and thin, crisp toast with bitter marmalade. Her face broke into a radiant smile, "Sister Irenie," she exclaimed (the use of this affectionate nickname was always an indication that she was either feeling exceptionally good or slightly mischievous, or both), "you are amazing. Only yesterday I was wishing for this very breakfast and here today you have brought me my heart's desire." Beaming with pride, I served her plate and poured her coffee while she went on expressing her delight in each bite. Then with exaggerated soberness, I cleared my throat and said, "Mother Cay, I'm so sorry to do this to you during your breakfast, but I have a serious confession to make and I don't think it should wait."

"Very well," she replied, putting down her fork and looking up into my face, with equal soberness. "Tell me, what is it?"

Hanging my head and lowering my eyes with feigned repentance I blurted out, "I have to confess, I'm guilty of eavesdropping. I listened through the hedge yesterday. That's how I knew what you wanted. It wasn't my own idea at all."

With the same drama she responded, "That is a serious offense indeed. I'm glad you confessed it. I forgive you, but do not let it happen again."

Then together, we both burst into hysterical laughter. She was always such a good sport about going along with a practical joke.

Breakfast over, I cleared the table, cleaned up the kitchen, and was just about to leave when she called me back. "Now, Sister Irenie," she said, "I have a confession to make to *you!*" Puzzled, I looked at her and caught that little twinkle in her eye that told me this joke was not yet over. "This is very serious, and I know it will come as a great shock to you," she continued. "Yesterday when I heard your footsteps approaching Henry's Yard I purposely said what I did, just to see if you were really on your toes, and I must say, you passed the test with flying colors!"

CODFISH CAKES

1 cup shredded salt codfish	1 egg, well beaten
2 cups seasoned mashed potatoes	½ cup fine bread crumbs
1 teaspoon minced onion	Butter

Yield: Makes 6 servings

Scald and drain the codfish. Add the mashed potatoes, minced onion, and egg. Mix well. Form into balls, roll in bread crumbs, and pan-fry in a small amount of butter until golden brown.

JUNE 15

I walked by the Lower Garden this afternoon, and I couldn't resist picking a stem of basil and crushing it between my fingers. Mama always did that to get the flavor out before using it. I do it instinctively now whenever I touch herbs. I never understand when friends tell me they don't enjoy gardening. I have had my hands in soil since I can remember. Those experiences of planting and tending make the sight of any garden all the more precious to me.

Mother Cay loved to travel, and each time she returned from visiting another country she brought something of it back to the Community. The brilliant monument garden that bloomed for so many years at the entrance to the front driveway was patterned after the gardens she enjoyed in France. The intriguing heather garden with the little turns and hills and paths in front of Zion house epitomized Scotland. And the beautiful rose garden beside Bethany was inspired by her many visits to England. Each of these gardens was loved by all of us who lived here as well as those who visited.

One thing very much disappointed her, however. That was the lack of interest shown in the gooseberries she had planted as another lovely remembrance of England, probably her favorite country of all. "No one seems to like them or want to eat them," I told Mother Cay one day. Calling me aside, she then charged me with the weighty responsibility of seeing to it that this changed, and that a love and appreciation for this bush and its fruit was developed and propagated.

Challenged with this new task, I set out to endear the sisterhood, the Community, and the world at large to this hitherto obscure fruit. I hunted up existing recipes, scarce as they were, and tried them out. I concocted my own, and I experimented using the berries in combination with other fruit.

Every single effort paid off. Not only did everyone around become acquainted with gooseberries, but they also began to acquire a taste for them. We discovered how invaluable they are, and we ended up with a number of winning recipes. To this day, Gooseberry Fool remains one of our most popular tea

desserts, bringing more inquiries and compliments than almost any other tea dessert we serve. People are intrigued with the flavor which they cannot quite identify and the touch of English charm this dessert brings to our tea plate.

I currently make a stuffed turkey breast with gooseberry glaze that is quite appealing to those who are conscious of eating less fat. And my favorite fruit cobbler has become a peach-gooseberry combination with blackberry brandy, which is a result of my experimentation. We freeze the berries whole for a rich winter garnish and a tart accent of flavor to some otherwise bland fruit desserts.

A branch of gooseberries, when they are partially ripened and the leaves are just beginning to change color, can transform an otherwise ordinary center-piece or floral arrangement into one of unusual interest and beauty, and goose-berries added to a fall harvest conserve give it a most unforgettable flavor. You know, I sometimes wonder how we ever managed to get along without them.

STUFFED TURKEY BREAST WITH GOOSEBERRY GLAZE

Stuffing:

½ cup chopped onion
¼ cup slivered almonds
½ cup butter or margarine
4 cups herb-seasoned
    bread cubes

1 cup coarsely chopped
    gooseberries or cranberries
3 tablespoons sugar
2 tablespoons grated
    orange peel

Turkey:

5 to 6 pounds fresh or
    frozen whole turkey breast
    with bone, thawed

Gooseberry Glaze:

¼ cup packed brown sugar
¼ cup sugar
¼ cup cider vinegar
    Dash of ground nutmeg

½ cinnamon stick (3 inches)
1 whole clove
1 whole allspice
1 cup canned, fresh, or
    frozen gooseberries

Yield: Makes 10 to 12 servings

Preheat oven to 325°F.

Stuffing: In a large skillet, sauté onion and almonds in butter until onion is tender. Stir in remaining stuffing ingredients.

Turkey: Bone the turkey breast. Spread the back of breast to open pockets. Spoon the stuffing into the pockets and down center of the breast. Fasten with skewers. Place breast, skin side up, in a roasting pan. Bake for 2 to 2½ hours or until the temperature on a meat thermometer inserted into the thickest part of the breast reaches 170°F.

Gooseberry Glaze: In a small saucepan, combine sugars, vinegar, and nutmeg. Place the cinnamon, clove, and allspice in a cheesecloth bag and place bag in the saucepan. Simmer until sugar is dissolved. Add the gooseberries; simmer, uncovered, for 20 to 30 minutes or until mixture is very thick, stirring occasionally. Remove and discard spice bag. Baste the turkey with the glaze for the last 15 to 20 minutes of roasting.

PEACH-GOOSEBERRY COBBLER

Filling:

½ cup gooseberries
4 cups peaches (about 2
    pounds), peeled and cut
    into ½-inch slices

¼ cup tapioca
¾ cup sugar
1 tablespoon brandy
2 tablespoons butter

Topping:

⅓ cup flour
¼ cup sugar
¼ cup packed brown sugar

2½ teaspoons ground
    cinnamon
6 tablespoons butter, chilled
    and cut into pieces

Yield: Makes 6 to 8 servings

Filling: Preheat oven to 400°F. Mix the fruits, tapioca, sugar, and brandy in a bowl; let stand for 15 minutes. Fill a 9-inch pie plate with the fruit mixture. Dot with butter. Cover with topping. Bake for 1 hour or until juices form bubbles that burst slowly. Cool.

Topping: Combine topping ingredients, blending until the mixture resembles coarse meal.

GOOSEBERRY FOOL

1 cup heavy cream
    Sugar
    Vanilla extract
2 + ¼ cups gooseberry juice

¼ cup Grand Marnier®
    Cordon Rouge liqueur
8 gooseberries and
    medium-sized gooseberry
    leaves (colorful ones)

Yield: Makes 8 servings

Whip heavy cream; sweeten to taste with sugar and flavor to taste with vanilla extract. Mix gooseberry juice and liqueur. Fold 2 cups gooseberry juice mixture into the whipped cream, adding more to taste, if necessary. Do not fold thoroughly, but leave in swirls. Fill sorbet glasses. Drizzle a bit of the remaining ¼ cup gooseberry juice mixture on top and garnish with a gooseberry and a leaf.

JUNE 20

I was delighted to sit with the Ashfords tonight at the Diamond Jubilee Dinner. We reminisced about the last time we had seen each other: six years ago on an Aeroflot flight to Siberia when Jim had shared his precious American peanut butter snacks with me because I wasn't feeling up to any more caviar.

Our annual Diamond Jubilee Dinner is given as an expression of thanks and appreciation to our special donors. It is always a lovely event prepared in an elegant manner and accompanied by entertainment presented by one of the performing arts groups from the Community.

Tonight's meal was superb, featuring a Rosemary Rib Roast with Red Wine Mushroom Ragout as the main course. After talking with the Ashfords I realized that I have had the good fortune to travel in twenty-five different countries that I can remember, singing and touring in most of them, visiting in the others, and eating in all of them.

The one meal that stands out in my memory as having left the most favorable impression on me is the one I ate with a village family in Yugoslavia: fresh pan fried trout, plain boiled potatoes, and a salad of green leaf lettuce dressed with oil, vinegar, and scallions.

MINTED CUCUMBER–BUTTERMILK SOUP

1½ pounds of English (hothouse) cucumbers, peeled, quartered, seeded
2 cups buttermilk
¼ cup chopped onion
1 cup sour cream
¾ cup plain low-fat yogurt
2 tablespoons chopped fresh mint
1 tablespoon chopped fresh chives or green onion tops
1 tablespoon fresh lemon juice
2 teaspoons sugar
Pinch of cayenne
Salt and pepper
Fresh mint sprigs

Yield: Makes 6 servings

Purée cucumbers, buttermilk, and chopped onion in a blender until smooth. Transfer mixture to a bowl. Stir in sour cream, yogurt, mint, chives, lemon juice, sugar, and cayenne. Season to taste with salt and pepper. Cover and refrigerate until well chilled. Stir soup and ladle into bowls. Garnish with mint sprigs. (Can be prepared 24 hours in advance.)

ROMAINE AND ROQUEFORT SALAD WITH HERB VINAIGRETTE

¼ cup red wine vinegar
¼ cup fresh chopped basil
2 tablespoons dry red wine
1 tablespoon fresh lemon juice
1 tablespoon minced shallots
1 tablespoon chopped fresh chives or green onions
1 tablespoon chopped fresh parsley
1½ teaspoons dry mustard
1½ teaspoons sugar
1 cup olive oil
Salt and pepper
2 heads romaine lettuce, each quartered through the stem
4 ounces Roquefort cheese, crumbled

Yield: Makes 8 servings

Whisk together in a medium bowl vinegar, basil, wine, lemon juice, shallots, chives, parsley, dry mustard, and sugar. Gradually whisk in the olive oil. Season to taste with salt and pepper. (Dressing can be prepared up to 4 hours ahead. Cover and refrigerate. Bring to room temperature before using.)

Arrange 1 lettuce quarter on each of 8 plates. Drizzle with dressing. Sprinkle salad with cheese and serve.

FILLET OF SOLE WITH CRABMEAT

Filling:

¼ cup finely chopped onion
1 egg, beaten
2 tablespoons mayonnaise
Crumbs from 4 slices bread (with crusts removed) and 6 saltines
1 pound crab meat
¼ cup chopped green pepper
1 egg white, beaten
2 teaspoons prepared mustard
Parsley
Salt and pepper

Fish:

6 fillets of sole

Sauce:

4 egg whites, beaten until thick
1 tablespoon mayonnaise
¼ cup grated white cheddar cheese

Yield: Makes 6 servings

Mix filling ingredients gently and wrap sole around filling. Place stuffed sole in greased baking dish. Bake at 350°F for 12 to 13 minutes or until sole is flaky.

Mix sauce ingredients together, pour over fish, and cook 3 to 4 minutes at 350°F until golden brown on top.

ROSEMARY RIB ROAST WITH RED WINE MUSHROOM RAGOUT

½ cup chopped fresh rosemary
6 tablespoons vegetable oil
6 large garlic cloves, chopped
2 teaspoons onion salt
1 7- to 7½-pound beef rib roast, well-trimmed, boned, and tied

Yield: Makes 12 servings

Grind chopped rosemary, oil, garlic, and onion salt in processor to a chunky paste. Place the beef in roasting pan. Rub rosemary mixture all over roast. Cover; chill 24 hours.

Position rack in the center of oven and preheat to 350°F. Uncover beef and roast until thermometer inserted straight down from the center registers 125°F for rare, about 1 hour 45 minutes. Let stand 30 minutes. Transfer roast to a platter. Scrape pan drippings into a cup; spoon off fat. Add juices to ragout (see recipe below), if desired. Garnish roast with rosemary sprigs. Serve with ragout.

RED WINE MUSHROOM RAGOUT

¼ cup vegetable oil
5 pounds meaty beef neck bones, cut into 2-inch pieces
1 pound onions, sliced
1 + 6 cups water
2 750-ml bottles dry red wine
1 large plum tomato, chopped
⅛ teaspoon ground cloves
¼ cup (½ stick) butter
1 cup chopped shallots
1 clove garlic, minced
1 large fresh rosemary sprig
3 pounds mushrooms, thickly sliced
Degreased pan juices from Rosemary Rib Roast
Salt and pepper

Heat oil in a heavy large pot over high heat. Add the bones and onions and cook until brown, turning mixture over and scraping bottom of the pot frequently, for about 25 minutes. Add the 1 cup water and boil until reduced to a glaze, scraping bottom frequently, about 8 minutes. Add the remaining 6 cups of water, wine, tomato, and cloves. Bring to a boil. Reduce heat and simmer for 4 hours. Strain stock into a bowl, pressing on solids. Chill at least 1 hour. (Can be made up to 4 days ahead.)

Remove fat from surface of stock. Boil the stock in a medium saucepan until reduced to 2 cups, about 30 minutes.

Melt butter in a heavy 14-inch skillet or Dutch oven over high heat. Add shallots, garlic, rosemary, and sauté for 2 minutes. Add the sliced mushrooms and cook until juices are released, stirring frequently, for about 10 minutes. Add stock and boil until sauce coats a spoon lightly, for about 15 minutes. Season to taste with salt and pepper. (Can be made up to 3 days ahead. Refrigerate. Rewarm ragout over low heat.) Add degreased pan juices from roast if desired.

STILTON POTATO GRATIN

2½ pounds russet potatoes (about 5 medium), peeled, thinly sliced
2 ounces onions, thinly sliced
4 + 4 ounces Stilton cheese or other blue cheese, crumbled
1⅓ cups canned chicken broth
2 tablespoons (¼ stick) butter, cut into small pieces
Freshly grated Parmesan cheese
Salt and pepper

Yield: Makes 6 servings

Preheat oven to 350°F. Butter a 13 x 9 x 2-inch glass baking dish. Arrange one-third of the potato slices and one-third of the onions in bottom of the dish, overlapping slightly. Sprinkle 4 ounces cheese over potatoes. Sprinkle with salt and pepper. Arrange half the remaining potato slices and onions over the cheese, overlapping slightly. Sprinkle remaining 4 ounces cheese over this layer. Sprinkle with salt and pepper. Arrange remaining potato slices and onions decoratively over cheese. Pour broth over all. Sprinkle with salt and pepper. Dot top with butter and Parmesan cheese.

Bake until top is golden brown, potatoes are tender, and liquid thickens, tilting the dish occasionally to baste top layer with the broth mixture, about 1 hour and 40 minutes.

Transfer pan to a rack and let stand 5 minutes. Serve hot.

TOASTED COCONUT SOUFFLÉ WITH CHOCOLATE RUM SAUCE

Chocolate Rum Sauce:

8 ounces semisweet chocolate, chopped	¼ cup dark rum
½ cup whipping cream	¼ cup ruby port

Soufflé:

Butter	2 cups milk
Sugar	1½ teaspoons vanilla extract
1 cup + 6 tablespoons sugar, divided	½ cup sweetened, shredded, coconut, toasted
6 large eggs, separated	1½ teaspoons coconut extract
⅓ cup + 1½ tablespoons flour	

Yield: Makes 12 servings

Chocolate Rum Sauce: Stir chocolate and cream in a heavy saucepan over low heat until chocolate melts. Whisk in the rum and port. (Can be made 24 hours ahead; chill.)

Soufflé: Preheat oven to 450 F. Butter and sugar six 1-cup soufflé dishes. Whisk 1 cup plus 2 tablespoons of the sugar, egg yolks, and flour together in a heavy medium saucepan. Gradually stir in milk and vanilla extract. Add coconut and coconut extract and stir to combine. Bring custard to a boil, stirring constantly. Boil until thickened, about 1 minute. Let custard stand until cool but not set.

Beat egg whites to soft peaks in a large bowl. Gradually add the remaining 4 tablespoons sugar and beat until stiff but not dry. Fold the whites into custard. Divide the soufflé mixture among prepared dishes. Place dishes in a baking pan. Add enough hot water to the pan to come halfway up the sides of the soufflé dishes. Bake until soufflés puff and tops are golden brown, about 20 minutes.

Meanwhile, rewarm the sauce until heated through.

Spoon sauce over each soufflé. Serve remaining sauce separately.

PRINCESS LOUISE CAKE

Cake:

4 cups cake flour, sifted	1 (7-ounce) pkg. almond paste, cut into pieces
4 teaspoons baking powder	
1⅓ cups sliced almonds	1¾ + ½ cups sugar
1 cup (2 sticks) butter, room temperature	¾ teaspoon almond extract
	1⅓ cups milk
	9 large egg whites

Almond Frosting:

1¼ cups sugar	1½ cups (3 sticks) butter, cut into pieces, room temperature
8 large egg yolks	
5 tablespoons Cointreau	
1 vanilla bean, split lengthwise	

Filling and Garnishes:

1 cup raspberry jam, stirred	2 (1-pint) baskets strawberries
1½ cups sliced almonds, toasted	

Yield: Makes 16 servings

Cake: Preheat oven to 350°F. Butter and flour three 9-inch-diameter cake pans with 1½-inch-high sides. Mix flour and baking powder in small bowl. Finely grind almonds in processor. Using electric mixer, beat butter and almond paste in large bowl until well blended. Gradually add the 1¾ cups sugar, beating until fluffy.

Beat in almond extract. Stir in flour mixture alternately with milk. Mix in ground nuts (batter will be very thick). Using electric mixer fitted with clean dry beaters, beat whites to medium peaks. Gradually add the remaining ½ cup sugar, beating until stiff but not dry. Fold whites into batter in 2 additions.

Divide batter among prepared pans. Bake until tester inserted into center of cakes comes out clean, about 35 minutes. Cool cakes in pans on racks 10 minutes. Turn out cakes onto racks; cool completely. (Can be made 24 hours ahead. Cover; let stand at room temperature.)

Almond Frosting: Combine sugar, yolks, and Cointreau in top of large double boiler. Scrape in seeds from vanilla bean. Set over simmering water (do not allow bottom of double boiler to touch water). Whisk egg mixture constantly until mixture thickens and candy thermometer registers 160°F, about 8 minutes. Remove from over water. Using electric mixer, beat mixture until cool and thick, about 8 minutes. Gradually add butter 1 piece at a time and beat until fluffy (frosting will be soft). If frosting appears curdled, place top of double boiler over simmering water; whisk until smooth.

To Assemble: Cut 2 cakes horizontally in half. Place 1 cake layer on plate. Spread with 3 tablespoons jam, then ½ cup (scant) frosting. Top with second cake layer. Spread with 3 tablespoons jam, then ½ cup (scant) frosting. Top with third cake layer. Spread with 3 tablespoons jam. Cut out 6 to 6½-inch-diameter round from center of fourth cake layer, leaving 1-inch cake ring (reserve center for another use). Set cake ring atop layered cake, pressing lightly to adhere. Place cake in freezer until beginning to firm, about 30 minutes.

Spoon ¾ cup frosting into pastry bag fitted with small star tip and reserve. Spread remaining frosting over top and sides of cake, leaving center hollow. Press sliced toasted almonds onto sides of cake. Pipe reserved frosting decoratively over ring of cake. Chill 2 hours to set frosting. Cover with plastic wrap. (Can be made 24 hours ahead. Keep chilled. Uncover and let stand 2 hours at room temperature before continuing.)

Set aside 8 whole strawberries. Hull, stem and quarter remaining berries. Fill cake ring with quartered berries. Garnish cake with whole berries.

JULY 1

It's almost time for SSS!

Every summer we celebrate the Fourth of July with what we have chosen to call our Star-Spangled Spectacular (SSS). This is a series of special events that begins with a yard sale in the morning. Originally it was accompanied by a pancake breakfast, but with time the meal has changed to a Western brunch called the "Hearty Hoe Down," run by the young adults.

HAZELNUT-OATMEAL PANCAKES

2 cups buttermilk
1½ cups old-fashioned oats
2 eggs
½ cup flour
1 tablespoon sugar
1 teaspoon baking soda
½ teaspoon salt
½ cup chopped hazelnuts, toasted
Vegetable oil
Pure maple syrup

Yield: Makes 12 servings

Mix buttermilk and oats in large bowl. Set stand 5 minutes. Whisk in eggs. Mix in flour, sugar, baking soda, and salt; stir in hazelnuts.

Heat heavy large skillet over medium-high heat. Brush with oil. Drop batter by ⅓ cupfuls into skillet, leaving space between. Cook until bubbles form on top of the pancakes, about 2 minutes. Turn and cook until bottoms are golden brown, about 2 minutes more. Transfer to plates. Repeat with remaining batter in batches, brushing skillet with oil as necessary. Serve with syrup.

MULTIGRAIN PANCAKES WITH STRAWBERRY–HONEY SAUCE

Pancakes:

⅓ cup old-fashioned or quick-cooking oats	1¼ cups milk
½ cup flour	1 large egg
½ cup whole wheat flour	2 tablespoons dark brown sugar
2 teaspoons baking powder	1 teaspoon vanilla extract
½ teaspoon salt	

Strawberry–Honey Sauce:

⅓ cup honey	1 pint strawberries, hulled, sliced
1 tablespoon fresh lemon juice	

Yield: Makes 6 servings

Pancakes: Place oats in medium skillet; stir over medium heat until golden, about 3 minutes. Transfer to large bowl; cool slightly. Add both flours, baking powder, and salt. In another bowl, whisk milk, egg, brown sugar, and vanilla extract until blended.

Preheat oven to 250°F. Heat large nonstick skillet over medium heat. Working in batches, add scant ¼ cup batter to skillet for each pancake. Cook until top is golden, about 2 minutes. Turn pancakes; cook until bottoms are golden, about 1 minute. Transfer to baking sheet, cover, and keep warm. Repeat with the remaining batter. Serve with topping.

Topping: Mix honey and lemon juice in medium bowl. Add strawberries and toss. Let stand at room temperature at least 1 hour and up to 3 hours.

JULY 4

Tonight's SSS auction with its elegant dinner under the tent for 350 people has a very distinctive atmosphere about it.

Intending to make this meal typical of Cape Cod, we at first served whole steamed lobsters for the occasion; but we found that even though the meal was very enjoyable, the lobster competed for attention with the auctioneer! So we decided to serve the lobster in some other form. With my own preference for plain steamed lobster, I was not too open to this suggestion, but we did come up with a variation that has been very successful.

The Auction Dinner begins with assorted hors d'oeuvres including a fresh fruit plate. This is followed by New England Clam Chowder, then a garden salad with hot rolls. The main course is lobster Newburg. For dessert there is a nice rich cheesecake with a tart Cape Cod cranberry topping. This dinner seems to please everyone, especially the auctioneer, in spite of my reluctance to give up the original one.

SSS culminates in a lively evening that is completely different from any of the others and has a flavor of its own. It begins with our Bayside Chicken Dinner for about 650 people, who eat at tables under the tent. Dinner is followed by a pops concert, attended by additional people who have not come for the meal. The concert ends just as it becomes dark enough to bring the evening to a grand climax with a spectacular extravaganza of fireworks.

Summer band concerts under the tent have grown in popularity over the years. They are informal, old-fashioned, wholesome, fun times. People usually arrive early and take a little time to stroll through the grounds and enjoy the several flower and vegetable gardens adjacent to the common where the evening's program takes place. The tables are bright and colorful with baskets of fresh garden flowers and herbs usually mixed in color—red, white, and blue on the Fourth of July.

The menu alternates weekly between chicken and ribs, both of which are barbecued on-site at our three barbecue pits. They are always accompanied by fresh corn on the cob, tossed garden salad, and herb-buttered French bread. Either ice cream sundaes or watermelon and brownies are served for dessert with coffee and tea. At intermission time, lemonade and popcorn are available.

Many vacationers to the Cape now plan their time here around the concert dates because they find this such an enjoyable way to spend a summer's evening with family and friends.

Dessert and Dinner Theatres are the most recently introduced special events and have been met with enthusiastic interest and attendance. The food tends more toward the elegant or gourmet in style and flavor than do any of the other meals. A typical Dessert Buffet might include Apricot Mousse with Grand Marnier® Sauce, Chocolate Kahlúa Layer Cake, Strawberry Custard Tart, Sour Cream Apple Crunch Kuchen, Mixed Berry Tiramisu, or Fudge Crostata.

Here are several Dinner Theatre menus:

HOT VICHYSSOISE

4 tablespoons butter or margarine	2 cups chicken broth Onion salt and pepper
4 leeks, finely sliced	1 cup half-and-half
4 potatoes, diced	2 cups milk
1 bouquet garni (1 bay leaf, 1 sprig of thyme, and ¼ bunch of parsley tied together)	Fresh parsley or mint leaves for garnish (optional)

Yield: Makes 4 to 6 servings

Melt butter in a large soup kettle. Add leeks and cook over low heat for 5 to 6 minutes, or until tender. Add potatoes, bouquet garni, and chicken broth. Season to taste with onion salt and pepper.

Raise the heat to medium and allow the soup to cook slowly for

25 to 30 minutes. Turn down the heat and simmer the soup for an additional 10 minutes; remove bouquet garni. In a blender purée soup in batches, transferring puréed soup to a large bowl. Add half-and-half and milk, and stir thoroughly. Garnish the soup with finely chopped parsley or mint leaves, if you wish. Serve immediately.

ARTICHOKE AND HEART OF PALM SALAD

2 tablespoons fresh lemon juice
2½ teaspoons Dijon mustard
1 large garlic clove, minced
6 tablespoons olive oil
Salt and pepper

1 (14-ounce) can hearts of palm, drained, sliced into rounds
1 (14-ounce) can artichoke hearts, drained, quartered
1 head butterhead lettuce
12 cherry tomatoes, halved

Yield: Makes 6 servings

Combine lemon juice, mustard, and garlic in a medium bowl. Gradually whisk in olive oil. Season dressing to taste with salt and pepper. Add hearts of palm and artichoke hearts. Let marinate at room temperature at least 20 minutes and up to 4 hours, tossing occasionally.

Line 6 plates with lettuce leaves. Using a slotted spoon, divide hearts of palm and artichoke hearts among plates. Garnish with tomatoes. Spoon remaining dressing over and serve.

BETHANY BOWKNOT ROLLS

1 envelope yeast
1 + 1 tablespoons brown sugar
2 tablespoons lukewarm water
½ cup butter

1 cup scalded milk
2 eggs, beaten
4 cups flour, sifted
1 teaspoon salt

Egg wash:
1 egg

1 tablespoon water

Yield: Makes 2 dozen

Preheat oven to 375°F. Dissolve yeast with 1 tablespoon brown sugar in the lukewarm water. Cream the butter and the remaining tablespoon brown sugar until fluffy and smooth. Cool milk to lukewarm, and combine with yeast and creamed butter and sugar. Beat eggs until very light, and add to mixture. Sift flour, measure, and sift with salt. Stir yeast mixture into flour and beat very hard for 3 to 4 minutes. This dough is too soft to knead. Set the bowl in a pan of very warm water, cover with towel, and let the dough rise until doubled in bulk. Beat down again until spongy and elastic; toss onto a floured board and roll to ⅓-inch thickness.

Form into knots and brush with egg wash. Bake 15 to 18 minutes or until golden at 375°F.

ROAST RACK OF LAMB WITH WALNUT CRUST AND PEAR-BOURBON SAUCE

Pear–Bourbon Sauce:

1 teaspoon olive oil	½ cup (or more) chicken stock or canned broth
2 pears (about 1 pound), peeled, cored, cut into ¾-inch pieces	2 tablespoons pure maple syrup
1 shallot, minced	½ teaspoon ground cinnamon
1 garlic clove, minced	¼ teaspoon ground nutmeg
4 + 1 tablespoons bourbon	Salt and pepper

Lamb:

3 tablespoons coarse-grained prepared mustard	½ teaspoon dried thyme
1 tablespoon pure maple syrup	¼ teaspoon marjoram
1 small shallot, minced	Onion salt and pepper
1 small garlic clove, minced	1 teaspoon olive oil
½ teaspoon dried rosemary	1 1½-pound rack of lamb, trimmed
	⅓ cup finely chopped walnuts

Yield: Makes 2 servings

Pear–Bourbon Sauce: Heat oil in a heavy medium saucepan over medium-low heat. Add pears. Sauté until golden, about 6 minutes. Add shallot and garlic. Sauté until shallot is translucent, about 2 minutes. Remove from heat. Add the 4 tablespoons bourbon. Add ½ cup chicken stock, maple syrup, cinnamon, and nutmeg. Cover pan and cook until pears are soft, stirring occasionally, about 10 minutes. Purée sauce in a food processor until smooth. Return mixture to saucepan. Add the remaining 1 tablespoon of bourbon and thin with more stock, if desired. Season to taste with salt and pepper. (Can be prepared 24 hours ahead. Cover and refrigerate.)

Lamb: Preheat oven to 375°F. Combine mustard, maple syrup, shallot, garlic, rosemary, thyme, and marjoram in a small bowl. Season with onion salt and pepper. Heat the oil in a heavy large skillet over medium-high heat. Add lamb; cook until brown, about 1 minute per side. Remove from heat; pat lamb dry. Brush lamb with the mustard mixture and sprinkle with walnuts; press nuts into lamb.

Place lamb on a rack in a roasting pan. Pour water into roasting pan to ½-inch depth. Cook until a meat thermometer inserted into the thickest part of the lamb registers 130°F for medium-rare, about 25 minutes. Transfer lamb to a platter. Let stand 10 minutes.

Bring sauce to a simmer. Cut lamb between the bones into 4 double chops. Place 2 double chops on each plate and serve with sauce.

POTATO AND WILD MUSHROOM GRATIN

2 large russet potatoes, peeled, cut into ¼-inch-thick slices	Salt and pepper
2 + 2 tablespoons butter	2 tablespoons chopped fresh chives
6 ounces button mushrooms, sliced	4 tablespoons olive oil, divided
6 ounces fresh shiitake mushrooms, stemmed, sliced	6 tablespoons grated Parmesan cheese, divided
	Onion salt

Yield: Makes 4 servings

Bring a large pot of salted water to boil. Add potato slices and blanch for 3 minutes. Drain and cool. Pat potatoes dry on paper towels.

Melt 2 tablespoons butter in a large, heavy skillet over medium-high heat. Add button mushrooms and sauté until tender, about 4 minutes. Transfer to a bowl using a slotted spoon. Melt the remaining 2 tablespoons butter in the same skillet. Add shiitake mushrooms and sauté until tender, about 4 minutes. Transfer to bowl with button mushrooms and cool. Season to taste with salt and pepper. Mix in chives.

Brush a 6-cup soufflé dish with olive oil. Line the bottom with foil or parchment. Brush foil with oil. Overlap one-fourth of the potatoes in bottom of prepared dish, covering completely. Season generously with salt and pepper. Top with one-third of the mushrooms. Sprinkle with 2 tablespoons Parmesan cheese. Drizzle with 1 tablespoon olive oil. Repeat this layering twice with potatoes, salt, pepper, mushroom mixture, Parmesan, and oil, using one-fourth of the potatoes in each layer. Top with remaining potatoes; drizzle with remaining 1 tablespoon oil. Season with onion salt and pepper. Cover with a piece of oiled foil. (Can be prepared up to 6 hours ahead. Cover and chill. Bring to room temperature before continuing.)

Preheat oven to 400°F. Bake gratin until potatoes are tender, pressing down on foil with a spatula every 15 minutes to flatten, about 1 hour.

Remove foil. Turn gratin out onto plate. Remove top piece of foil. Cut into wedges and serve.

ASPARAGUS WITH GLAZED CHERRY TOMATOES

1 bunch asparagus	1 tablespoon vegetable oil
1 teaspoon onion salt	1 teaspoon sugar
10 to 12 cherry tomatoes	

Yield: Makes 3 to 4 servings

Cook asparagus in onion salted water until tender. Keep in a warm oven. Put oil in a pan and sauté tomatoes for about 1 minute. Sprinkle sugar over tomatoes and sauté an additional minute. Do not let tomatoes burst if possible. Serve the tomatoes over the asparagus.

BLACK–BOTTOM CAPPUCINO MOUSSE CAKE

Crust:

9 ounces thin, crisp chocolate wafer cookies	4 tablespoons butter, melted

Ganache:

6 ounces bittersweet chocolate, finely chopped, divided	1 cup heavy cream
	¼ teaspoon vanilla extract

Mousse:

2 tablespoons water	4 large egg yolks
1 pkg. (1/4 oz.) unflavored gelatin	1 large whole egg
1½ cups milk	2 tablespoons instant espresso powder
½ + ½ cup granulated sugar	Ice water
2 cinnamon sticks	1½ cups heavy cream, chilled
½ vanilla bean, split	

Cream and Coffee Topping:

1½ cups heavy cream, chilled	2 tablespoons coffee liqueur
1½ tablespoons confectioners' sugar	½ teaspoon ground cinnamon

Yield: Makes 12 servings

Crust: Preheat oven to 400°F. Grind the cookies in a food processor until fine. Transfer to a bowl and work in the melted butter with your fingers until mixed. Turn the crumbs into a 10 x 2-inch or 3-inch springform pan. Firmly and evenly press the crumbs into the bottom and 1½ inches up the sides of the pan. Freeze the crust for 10 minutes. Put frozen crust in hot oven for about 8 minutes, or until set, but soft when pressed gently on the bottom. Let cool on rack.

Ganache: Melt half the chopped chocolate in the heavy cream in a small saucepan over moderately low heat, stirring constantly. Remove from heat and stir in remaining chocolate until smooth. Let cool completely; stir in vanilla extract. Pour cooled ganache into cookie crust and refrigerate until set, at least 1 hour.

Mousse: Pour 2 tablespoons of water into a small bowl. Sprinkle the gelatin over the water and set aside to soften. In a medium saucepan, combine milk with ½ cup granulated sugar and the cinnamon sticks. Scrape the seeds from the vanilla bean into the milk and add the bean as well. Bring to a boil over moderate heat. Lower the heat and simmer gently for 10 minutes. Meanwhile, using an electric mixer at medium speed, beat the egg yolks with the whole egg and the remaining ½ cup of granulated sugar until thickened and light in color, about 2 minutes.

Whisk espresso powder into hot milk mixture until blended. Using a rubber spatula, gradually stir the hot espresso mixture into the beaten eggs. Return mixture to the saucepan and cook over moderate heat, stirring constantly, until custard coats the back of a spoon and reaches 170° on an instant-read thermometer. Do not let boil. Remove from heat and strain the custard into a large bowl. Stir in the softened gelatin until blended.

Place custard bowl in a larger bowl filled with ice water and stir the custard frequently until chilled, about 10 to 12 minutes. In a separate bowl, beat heavy cream until stiff. Using a rubber spatula, fold the whipped cream into the custard in 2 additions. Scrape the mousse into the cookie crust. Cover lightly pressing waxed paper onto the surface of mousse and refrigerate for at least 6 hours.

Shortly before serving, unmold cake. With a thin, sharp knife, cut around the sides of the cake to loosen crust from the pan. Release the springform latch and remove pan side. Place the cake on a round platter or cake stand.

Cream and Toffee Topping: Beat the heavy cream in a large bowl with the confectioners' sugar until nearly stiff. At low speed, beat in coffee liqueur. Spoon the topping onto the cake and spread in waves with a rubber spatula. Dust with cinnamon just before serving.

FRESH MUSHROOM SOUP

6 + 6 tablespoons butter
3 cups onion, coarsely chopped
3 cups finely chopped celery
4 pounds thinly sliced mushrooms
Juice of 3 lemons
¾ cup flour
1 gallon + 2 cups rich chicken broth
¾ cup sherry
Freshly ground pepper

Yield: Makes 15 servings

Melt 6 tablespoons butter in large saucepan. Add onion and celery. Cook about 2 minutes. Add mushrooms and lemon juice. Stir and cook gently 10 minutes. Sprinkle mushroom mixture with flour, stir to coat. Add broth, stir, and simmer, uncovered, 10 minutes. Pour into food processor, process to fine purée. Return to saucepan and bring to boil. Add the remaining 6 tablespoons butter, sherry, and a generous grinding of pepper.

SCALLOP, SPINACH, AND ORANGE SALAD

2 oranges, peeled, white
  pith removed
1 cup orange juice
3 tablespoons balsamic
  vinegar
2 tablespoons minced shallots
1/4 cup olive oil
12 large sea scallops,
  each cut horizontally
  into thirds
2 tablespoons (1/4 stick)
  butter, melted
1/4 teaspoon paprika
  Salt and pepper
8 cups fresh spinach leaves
  (about 10 oz.)
2 tablespoons sliced
  almonds, toasted
1/4 cup (1/2 stick) chilled
  butter, cut into pieces
1 teaspoon onion salt

Yield: Makes 4 servings

Using a knife, cut between orange membranes to release segments. Mix juice, vinegar, and shallots in bowl. Whisk in oil. Reserve 1/2 cup of the dressing. In a small saucepan, simmer remaining dressing until reduced to 1/4 cup, about 5 minutes.

On baking sheet lined with foil, overlap 9 scallop slices, forming a ring; press to flatten. Repeat with remaining scallops, forming three more rings. Brush scallops with melted butter; season with paprika, salt, and pepper.

Preheat the broiler. Toss spinach with reserved 1/2 cup of dressing. Mound the spinach on salad plates and garnish with orange segments and almonds.

Broil the scallops until cooked through, about 3 minutes.

Bring dressing in saucepan to simmer. Remove from heat. Gradually add chilled butter; whisk just until melted. Season with onion salt and pepper.

Place scallops atop spinach salad. Drizzle sauce over the scallops and serve.

BEEF TENDERLOIN WITH PEPPERCORN CRUST AND WHISKEY SAUCE

Whiskey Sauce:
1 1/4 pounds beef neck bones
4 large shallots,
  coarsely chopped
6 garlic cloves,
  coarsely chopped
2 large carrots,
  coarsely chopped
1 cup whiskey
2 tablespoons tomato paste
4 fresh thyme sprigs
  or 1 teaspoon dried
2 teaspoons whole
  black peppercorns
2 cups chicken broth
2 cups beef broth
  Salt

Beef:
1/4 cup whole black
  peppercorns, lightly crushed
1 tablespoon cornstarch
2 teaspoons chopped
  fresh thyme or 1/2 teaspoon
  dried
1 teaspoon chopped
  fresh oregano or 1/4
  teaspoon dried
1 + 1 tablespoon
  vegetable oil
1 (2-pound) beef
  tenderloin roast

Yield: Makes 6 servings

Whiskey Sauce: Brown beef bones, shallots, garlic, and carrots in a heavy large saucepan over medium heat, stirring occasionally, about 20 minutes. Add the whiskey, increase the heat, and boil until liquid is reduced by half, about 5 minutes. Mix in tomato paste, thyme, and peppercorns. Add broths and boil until the liquid is reduced to 1 cup, about 20 minutes. Strain through a fine sieve into a heavy small saucepan. Season to taste with salt. (Can be prepared 24 hours ahead. Cover and refrigerate.)

Beef: Preheat the oven to 350°F. Mix peppercorns, cornstarch, thyme, and oregano on large plate. Brush 1 tablespoon of the oil over beef. Roll beef in peppercorns, coating completely. Season with salt.

Heat the remaining 1 tablespoon of oil in a heavy large ovenproof skillet over medium-high heat. Add beef and brown on all sides, about 5 minutes. Transfer skillet to the oven and roast until meat thermometer inserted into the center of the beef registers 130°F for rare, about 30 minutes. Let beef stand 10 minutes.

Slice beef and arrange on plates. Bring sauce to simmer; spoon over beef.

BRAISED ORANGE BALSAMIC ONIONS

2 pounds sweet onions
2 tablespoons (¼ stick) butter
2 tablespoons olive oil
6 tablespoons orange juice
6 tablespoons balsamic vinegar
2 tablespoons water
2 teaspoons onion salt

Yield: Makes 6 side-dish servings

Bring a large pot of water to boil. Add onions and cook 2 minutes. Drain and cool the onions. Peel onions and cut off root ends.

Melt butter with the oil in a large nonstick skillet over medium heat. Add onions; sauté until brown and tender, about 10 minutes. Add orange juice, vinegar, and water to skillet. Reduce the heat to medium-low. Simmer until the liquid is reduced to glaze, about 4 minutes. Season with onion salt.

GINGERED SWEET POTATO PURÉE

2 medium sweet potatoes (about ¾ pound)
3 tablespoons milk
1 tablespoon butter
¾ teaspoon peeled, grated fresh gingerroot
1 teaspoon onion salt
Pepper

Yield: Makes 2 servings

Peel potatoes and cut into 1-inch pieces. In a small saucepan boil potatoes in salted water to cover for 15 minutes, or until very tender; drain well in a colander.

In a food processor purée the hot potatoes with milk, butter, and gingerroot until mixture is smooth. Season with onion salt and pepper.

CHOCOLATE TRUFFLE LOAF WITH RASPBERRY–PORT SAUCE

Loaf:
½ + 1½ cups heavy cream
3 egg yolks, slightly beaten
2 pkgs. (8 ounces each) semi-sweet chocolate
½ cup light or dark corn syrup
½ cup butter or margarine
¼ cup confectioners' sugar
1 teaspoon vanilla extract

Raspberry–Port Sauce:
1 pkg. (10 ounces) frozen raspberries, thawed
⅓ cup corn syrup
¼ cup port

Yield: Makes 12 servings

Loaf, Step 1, Stovetop method: Mix the ½ cup cream with the yolks. In a 3-quart saucepan stir the chocolate, corn syrup, and butter over medium heat until melted. Add the egg mixture. Stirring constantly, cook 3 minutes. Cool to room temperature. Continue with step 2.

Loaf, Step 1, Microwave method: In a 3-quart microwavable bowl, mix the chocolate, corn syrup, and butter. Microwave at High, stirring twice, 2 to 2½ minutes or until melted. Stir in egg mixture. Microwave, stirring twice, 3 minutes. Cool to room temperature. Continue with step 2.

Loaf, Step 2: Beat the remaining 1½ cups cream, confectioners' sugar, and vanilla extract until soft peaks form. Fold into the chocolate until no streaks remain.

Step 3: Line 8½ x 4½ x 2½-inch loaf pan with plastic wrap. Pour chocolate mixture into pan. Refrigerate 8-10 hours or chill in the freezer for 3 hours. Remove from pan and cut into 12 slices. Serve on a puddle of sauce.

Raspberry–Port Sauce: In blender, purée raspberries; strain. Stir in corn syrup and port.

NEW ENGLAND CLAM CHOWDER

4½ pounds littleneck or
  cherrystone clams (well
  scrubbed)
½ cup water
¼ cup butter
1 medium onion, minced
1¼ pounds boiling
  potatoes, peeled and
  cut into ½-inch cubes

1¼ to 1½ cups whipping
  cream
½ to ¾ cup milk
Cayenne
Salt and pepper
Minced fresh parsley

Yield: Makes 5 (1-cup) servings

Place clams in large saucepan; add the water. Cover and cook over medium heat just until the shells open, about 10 minutes. Remove opened clams. Cook remaining clams 2 more minutes; discard those that do not open. Drain clams, reserving liquid. Remove clams from shells; chop coarsely. Strain liquid.

Melt butter in heavy large saucepan over medium low heat. Add onion and cook until softened, stirring frequently, about 10 minutes. Mix in reserved clam liquid and potatoes, pushing potatoes into liquid. Cover and simmer over low heat until potatoes are just tender, stirring frequently, 10 to 12 minutes.

Transfer 1½ cups of potatoes to a food processor using a slotted spoon. Add ¾ cup potato cooking liquid, and purée until smooth, about 30 seconds. Return potato mixture to saucepan. (Can be prepared 24 hours ahead. Cover potato mixture and clams separately and refrigerate.)

To assemble: Combine 1¼ cup cream and ½ cup milk. Return potato mixture to simmer, stirring occasionally. Add cream mixture and stir just until heated through; do not boil or mixture will curdle. Reduce heat to low, add clams, and stir just until heated through, about 2 minutes. Thin chowder with the remaining ¼ cup milk and ¼ cup cream, if desired, and stir until heated through. Season to taste with cayenne, salt, and pepper. Ladle into bowls. Garnish with parsley.

SEAFOOD NEWBURG

1 pkg. cocktail shrimp
  (undercooked)
½ pound scallops (if large,
  cut in into halves)
½ pound crab meat
½ pound lobster meat

White wine
Butter
6 tablespoons flour
1 quart light cream
1 bottle clam juice or
  lobster base or sherry

Yield: Makes 8 to 10 servings

Quickly sauté separately all the shellfish. Do not overcook or burn. Render the sauté pan with a little white wine after each type of shellfish and save juices separately. Set shellfish aside in one stainless steel bowl. Add a little butter for each succeeding batch.

To make a roux, melt 7 tablespoons butter in a large sauté pan. Whisk in the flour; let cook on low heat to cook out flour taste; do not brown or burn. Slowly pour in the cream. As the cream sauce thickens, use the clam juice and/or sherry to thin to the proper consistency (dropping from a spoon, not runny). Once the cream sauce is made, cook for 3 minutes at medium heat or lower; do not boil. As the sauce thickens, replace the liquid with the shellfish juices, white wine with pan juices, or more cream.

Put all the seafood into a pot. Fold the sauce to evenly disperse the seafood. (Can be made up to 1 hour ahead; keep on lowest heat; do not brown or boil. Stir often.)

CAPE COD CRANBERRY CHEESECAKE

Crust:

¼ cup butter
1 cup + 2 tablespoons flour

½ cup sugar
¾ teaspoon baking powder
1 egg, well beaten

Cheesecake:

2 pkgs. (8 ounces each) cream cheese, softened
1½ tablespoons flour
1 cup sugar

3 eggs
1 teaspoon vanilla extract
1½ cups milk

Topping:

3 tablespoons + ¾ cup sugar
1 tablespoon cornstarch

1½ cups fresh or frozen cranberries
⅓ cup water
1 tablespoon port

Yield: Makes 12 servings

Crust: Mix all ingredients together and put into a 13 x 9-inch baking pan.

Cheesecake: Mix the cream cheese, flour and sugar. Then add the eggs, vanilla extract, and milk. This will be very thin. Pour into the crust. Bake at 325°F for 50 to 55 minutes.

Topping: Combine the 3 tablespoons sugar and cornstarch in a small bowl. In a medium saucepan over medium heat, combine the cranberries, the ¾ cup sugar, and water. Bring to a boil, stirring until sugar is dissolved; boil 2 minutes, stirring constantly. Stir cornstarch mixture into cranberry mixture. Bring to a boil; boil 1 minute, stirring constantly. Remove from heat and add the port. Cool to room temperature and spoon onto cooled cheesecake.

BARBECUED CHICKEN AND RIBS

¼ cup chopped onion
2 tablespoons vegetable oil
1 cup chili sauce
½ cup tomato juice
¼ cup lemon juice
¼ cup firmly packed brown sugar

2 tablespoons Worcestershire sauce
6 drops hot sauce
3 pounds chicken quarters, or back or country-style pork ribs
Salt and pepper

Yield: Makes 4 servings

Sauté onion until tender in hot oil in a small saucepan. Add chili sauce, tomato juice, lemon juice, brown sugar, Worcestershire sauce, and hot sauce; simmer 20 minutes.

Prepare barbecue grill (low heat).

Cut chicken or ribs into serving-size pieces; season with salt and pepper. Place chicken or ribs on the grill, 5 inches from heat. Grill 45 minutes to 1 hour or until done, turning frequently. Brush with sauce and cook in 250°F to 300°F oven until very tender. Serve with remaining sauce.

APRICOT MOUSSE WITH GRAND MARNIER® SAUCE

Apricot mousse:

6 ounces apricot preserves   ¼ cup confectioners' sugar
1 egg white, room temperature   1 teaspoon vanilla extract
1 cup whipping cream

Grand Marnier® sauce:

2 (10-ounce) pkgs. frozen   3 tablespoons Grand Marnier®
raspberries, sweetened, thawed   Cordon Rouge liqueur

Cookie shells:

1 cup finely ground,   6 tablespoons (¾ stick)
   blanched almonds   butter, melted
½ cup sugar   2 tablespoons (or more) milk
1 tablespoon + 1 teaspoon   ½ cup whipping cream
   flour   Fresh mint sprigs
½ teaspoon salt

Yield: Makes 6 servings

Mousse: Stir the preserves in a medium bowl until pale. Beat the egg white until stiff but not dry. Fold into preserves. Beat the cream, sugar, and vanilla extract until soft peaks form. Fold into apricot mixture. Freeze until ready to use.

Grand Marnier® Sauce: Purée the raspberries in a food processor. Strain through a fine sieve to eliminate seeds. Stir in the liqueur. Cover and chill.

Cookies: Preheat oven to 350°F. Have ready a muffin tin or 12 custard cups placed upside down. Line 2 baking sheets with parchment, cutting each piece into 6 squares. Mix almonds, sugar, flour, and salt. Blend in butter and milk. Spoon about 2 tablespoons batter onto each square. Using a knife, spread into a thin round. Repeat with remaining batter, adding 1 to 2 teaspoons more milk if the batter becomes too stiff to spread. Bake the cookies until golden brown, turning baking sheets once, 12 to 14 minutes. Cool 2 to 3 minutes on paper; mold onto outsides of muffin or custard cups. Let cool completely. Peel parchment paper off cookies.

To Assemble: On a large dessert plate spoon a medium-sized puddle of raspberry sauce to one side. Just before serving, spoon mousse into cookie shell and place on puddle of raspberry sauce. With the whipped cream drizzle an "S" on the raspberry sauce. Swirl through this with a knife a few times to give it lacy "tails." (The cream will hold in the raspberry sauce for about a half hour.) Drizzle a little sauce over the mousse. Garnish with mint sprig on the raspberry puddle.

CHOCOLATE KAHLÚA LAYER CAKE

Cake:

2 cups sugar   2 cups flour
1 stick butter   2 rounded teaspoons
2 eggs   baking soda
3 squares baking chocolate,   1 cup hot water
   unsweetened   2 teaspoons vanilla extract
½ cup sour milk (or add   Kahlúa
   1 tablespoon white vinegar
   to scant ½ cup milk)

Chocolate–Brandy Frosting:

¼ cup brandy   1 pound bittersweet (not
¾ cup whipping cream   unsweetened) or semisweet
6 tablespoons (¾ stick)   chocolate, coarsely chopped
   butter, cut into pieces   (not chocolate chips)
     1½ cups sour cream

Yield: Makes 12 servings

Cake: Cream together sugar and butter. Add all the rest of the ingredients except Kahlúa and mix well.

Grease and flour cake pans (2 or 3 round or one 9 x 13-inch). Line the cake pans with waxed paper; grease and flour. Bake at 350°F until the top will not dent when touched, about 20 to 25 minutes. Cool a few minutes and carefully remove the paper while cake is still warm. The cake layers are delicate, so handle them carefully.

Pierce the layers with a fork and add Kahlúa when the layers are warm; or do the same thing when cool and ready to frost: Start with bottom layer and pierce each layer all around with a fork; drip the Kahlúa into the whole surface of the layer. Frost and add next layer; repeat the process.

Chocolate–Brandy Frosting: Bring the brandy, cream, and butter to simmer in a heavy large saucepan, whisking until the butter melts. Remove from heat. Add chocolate and whisk until melted and smooth. Add sour cream and whisk to blend. Refrigerate frosting until thick enough to spread, stirring occasionally, about 30 minutes.

STRAWBERRY CUSTARD TART

Crust:

1¼ cups flour	2 tablespoons (approx.)
¼ cup confectioners' sugar	beaten egg
½ teaspoon salt	1 teaspoon almond extract
½ cup (1 stick) butter, cut into pieces	

Filling:

1 cup milk	2 tablespoons (¼ stick)
3 large egg yolks	butter
¼ cup sugar	1 tablespoon Cointreau
⅛ cup flour	1½ teaspoons
⅛ cup cornstarch	vanilla extract

Topping:

3 (1-pint) baskets strawberries, hulled	⅓ cup strawberry preserves
	1 tablespoon water

Yield: Makes 8 servings

Crust: Blend flour, sugar, and salt in a food processor. Cut in butter, turning processor on and off alternately, until mixture resembles coarse meal. Again turning processor on and off alternately, add egg and extract until dough just begins to form moist clumps. Gather dough into ball; flatten into a disk. Wrap in plastic and chill 30 minutes. (Can be made up to 3 days ahead. Let stand briefly at room temperature before rolling.)

Preheat oven to 375°F. Roll out dough on lightly floured surface to 12-inch round. Transfer to 9-inch-diameter tart pan with removable bottom. Trim edges to fit. Freeze 15 minutes.

Line crust with foil. Fill with dried beans or pie weights. Bake until sides are set, about 20 minutes. Remove foil and beans; bake crust until golden, piercing with fork if bubbles form, about 15 minutes. Transfer to rack; cool completely.

Filling: Bring milk to simmer in heavy medium saucepan. Whisk yolks, sugar, flour and cornstarch in a medium bowl to blend. Gradually whisk in hot milk. Return the mixture to saucepan. Bring to a boil over medium heat, whisking constantly. Reduce heat to medium-low and cook until thick and smooth, whisking constantly, about 1 minute. Remove from heat. Whisk in butter, Cointreau, and vanilla extract. Transfer to a bowl. Press plastic wrap onto surface. Chill until cold, at least 2 hours.

Spread filling in crust. Place strawberries atop filling, pointed ends up, covering completely the top of the filling. Stir preserves and water in small saucepan over medium-low heat until preserves melt. Brush over berries. (Can be made up to 4 hours ahead. Refrigerate.) Remove from tart pan.

SOUR CREAM–APPLE CRUNCH KUCHEN

Crust:

1¼ cups flour	Pinch of salt
½ cup (1 stick) chilled butter, cut into pieces	4 tablespoons (approx.) ice water
2 tablespoons sugar	

Filling:

1 cup sour cream	⅛ teaspoon salt
1 egg, large, lightly beaten	¼ cup flour
2 teaspoons vanilla extract	2 pounds Granny Smith apples, peeled, cored and thinly sliced
¾ cup sugar	

Topping:

⅓ cup flour	¾ cup walnuts, chopped
¼ cup sugar	6 tablespoons butter, unsalted, chilled and cut into pieces
¼ cup brown sugar, packed	
2½ teaspoons ground cinnamon	

Yield: Makes 6 to 8 servings

Crust: Blend flour, butter, sugar, and salt in a food processor until of consistency of coarse meal. With the machine running, add water by tablespoonfuls until clumps form. Turn out onto a floured surface. Gather dough into a ball. Flatten to a disk. Wrap in plastic; chill until firm, at least 30 minutes.

Preheat oven to 400°F. Roll out dough on a floured surface to a 13-inch round. Transfer to a 9-inch glass pie plate. Trim the edge to ½-inch overhang. Fold edge under and crimp. Freeze for 10 minutes. Line crust with foil; fill with beans or pie weights. Bake until sides are set, about 12 minutes. Remove the foil and beans.

Filling: Combine the sour cream, egg, vanilla extract, sugar, salt, and flour, in a large bowl, stirring until well blended. Stir in apples. Pour into unbaked crust. Bake at 425°F for 10 minutes. Reduce heat to 350°F and bake an additional 30 minutes.

Topping: Combine topping ingredients, blending until the mixture resembles coarse meal. Spoon topping over pie and bake at 350°F for an additional 15 to 20 minutes, or until the filling is bubbly.

MIXED BERRY TIRAMISU

1 (12-ounce) pkg. frozen mixed berries, unsweetened	1 teaspoon almond extract
6 + 6 tablespoons sugar	1 teaspoon vanilla extract
1 (10-ounce) pkg. frozen raspberries in syrup, thawed	1 (1-pint) basket strawberries, hulled
¼ cup raspberry liqueur	2 (½-pint) baskets raspberries
3 (4.40-ounce) pkgs. champagne biscuits (4-inch-long, ladyfinger-like biscuits)	1 (½-pint) basket blueberries
3 (8-ounce) containers mascarpone cheese	

Yield: Makes 10 servings

Cook frozen mixed berries and 6 tablespoons sugar in a heavy medium saucepan over medium heat until mixture resembles jam and is reduced to 1 cup, stirring frequently, about 15 minutes. Cool jam mixture.

Strain syrup from thawed raspberries through sieve set over bowl, pressing gently on solids. Discard solids. Add raspberry liqueur to raspberry syrup in bowl. Using sharp knife, trim 1 biscuit to a 3-inch (approx.) length. Quickly dip biscuit into syrup, turning to coat lightly. Place rounded end up and sugared side against side of 9-inch-diameter springform pan with 2¾-inch-high sides. Repeat with as many biscuits as necessary to cover sides of pan. Dip more biscuits in syrup and arrange on bottom of pan, covering completely and trimming to fit.

In bowl, whisk mascarpone with the remaining 6 tablespoons sugar, and blend in extracts. Thinly slice enough strawberries to measure ½ cup. Gently spread half of jam mixture over biscuits in bottom of pan. Spoon half of mascarpone mixture over jam; smooth top. Sprinkle with sliced strawberries, ½ cup fresh raspberries, and ½ cup blueberries. Dip more biscuits into syrup; arrange over fruit in pan, covering completely and trimming to fit. Gently spread remaining jam mixture over biscuits. Spoon remaining mascarpone mixture over jam; smooth top. Cover; chill at least 4 hours.

Release pan sides. Transfer cake to platter. Arrange remaining fresh berries decoratively atop cake and serve.

FUDGE CROSTATA

Crust:
See recipe for Basic Pie Crust (page 33)

Filling:

6 ounces (1 cup) semi-sweet chocolate chips	⅔ cup sugar
	1 cup ground almonds
2 + 6 tablespoons butter or margarine	1 egg
	1 egg, separated

Yield: Makes 10 to 12 servings

Crust: Prepare a two-crust pie pastry. Use a 10-inch tart pan with removable bottom or a 9-inch pie pan. Place one crust in pan; press in bottom and up sides of the pan. Trim edges if necessary. Preheat oven to 425°F.

Filling: In small sauce pan over low heat, melt chocolate chips and 2 tablespoons butter, stirring constantly until smooth. In medium bowl, beat the remaining 6 tablespoons butter with sugar until light and fluffy. Add almonds, egg, egg yolk, and melted chocolate; blend well. Spread mixture evenly over bottom of pie-crust-lined pan.

Lattice top: Cut remaining crust into ½-inch-wide strips. Arrange strips in lattice design over chocolate mixture. Trim and seal edges. In small bowl, beat egg white until foamy; gently brush over lattice. Bake at 425°F for 10 minutes. Reduce heat to 350°F. Bake an additional 30 to 35 minutes or until crust is golden brown. Cool completely. Cover edge of pie crust with strip of foil the last 10 minutes of baking if necessary to avoid excessive browning.

JULY 15

Last night at dinner, those of us who love to cook were sharing our earliest memories of food. I was never really taught how to cook. I just did it without ever thinking about it. Mama seldom, if ever, followed a recipe. She put things together by taste and feel, so I do likewise. To this day, I use a recipe only as a kind of springboard and adapt it according to what comes naturally.

Two essentials were instilled in me—freshness and flavor. Vegetables were always brought straight from the garden to the sink, to the stove, and then to the table or the freezer.

Seasoning was of prime importance, yet Mama fussed over it very little. She would take an inexpensive cut of pot roast, brown it in a Dutch oven, rub a little fresh crushed garlic, salt, and pepper into it, add a few herbs and vegetables, and leave it to cook itself. She would vary the ingredients from time to time, yet in each instance when it was served or eaten, those who tasted it testified to feeling like Esau, who gladly would have sold his birthright for another serving.

I talked with Sister Lucille a while ago about meals and recipes she used when for a period of time she was in charge of guest and retreat cooking and I was not involved in the kitchen. She has a flair for the more avant-garde and expanded the kitchen's old repertoire of recipes while she had that job.

I was surprised, and yet not so surprised, to hear her say the meals that people seemed to like best and comment on the most were the homier, simpler ones. This observation confirms my own feeling that most people find satisfaction in the familiar and prefer the ordinary even if they have an appreciation for the extraordinary.

I recently had a little experience that I think bears this out. Friends had taken me to dinner at the Ritz where we had enjoyed a superbly elegant meal, followed by a dessert buffet that offered an elaborate selection of the finest caliber desserts. There were at least ten to choose from. After going around the table, I selected a warm bread pudding with which I could not have been more pleased or satisfied. As I was being served, a lady came up alongside me and chuckled, "You've made the best choice. It's what I choose each time I come here." We both laughed, two people happening to share the same biased opinion. But as I made my way back to our table, I realized this simple, old-fashioned dish would not be served here again and again if there weren't those who preferred it over all the other desserts extraordinaire.

BREAD PUDDING

1 large loaf French bread
1 stick butter, melted
9 eggs
1½ cups sugar
  Pinch of salt
4 cups milk

1¼ cups heavy cream
1¼ teaspoons vanilla
  extract
1 teaspoon ground
  cinnamon
½ teaspoon ground nutmeg
  Confectioners' sugar

Yield: Makes 8 servings

Preheat oven to 300°F.

Cut the bread into ¾-inch slices. Brush one side with melted butter and arrange in single layer in greased 9 x 13-inch baking pan, packed tight, butter side up. In a large bowl or blender, mix the eggs, sugar, salt, milk, cream, and vanilla extract. Add cinnamon and nutmeg. Pour over the bread until it floats. (Recipe can be made to this point 24 hours before and refrigerated. If it is made ahead, fill the pan a little fuller, as the bread absorbs some of the custard and the pans will be less full by morning.)

Bake about an hour or until a knife inserted in the center comes out clean and top is golden brown. Sift confectioners' sugar over the top and broil to finish browning. Serve with one of the sauces below.

Bourbon Sauce:

¼ cup butter	2 tablespoons water
½ cup sugar	2 tablespoons bourbon
1 beaten egg yolk	1 teaspoon vanilla extract

Yield: Makes 8 Servings

In a small saucepan melt the butter. Stir in sugar, yolk, and water. Cook and stir constantly over medium-low heat for 5 to 6 minutes or until the sugar dissolves and mixture boils. Remove from heat and stir in bourbon and vanilla extract. Serve warm.

Raspberry Sauce*:

1 (12-ounce) pkg. frozen raspberries	½ cup sugar

Put raspberries and sugar in a small pot. Cook, breaking up the raspberries, until the sugar is dissolved and mixture is hot.

* For the Raspberry Sauce you may substitute fresh, sliced strawberries sprinkled with sugar.

Maple–Pecan Sauce:

2 tablespoons butter, cut into chunks
1 cup maple syrup
½ teaspoon ground nutmeg
½ cup chopped pecans, toasted

Melt butter; stir in syrup and nutmeg. Heat thoroughly and add pecans.

JULY 21

Looking today at the garden, especially the tomato patch, I was reminded that Mama was very big on green tomatoes, as well as ripened red ones. She loved green tomato piccalilli and fried green tomatoes. I often find myself smiling as I think of Mama's special way with piccalilli.

We enjoy sharing the fruits of our garden with those living around us who have not planted gardens. When we came up with the idea of a harvest basket for each of our neighbors, nothing could have been more natural to me. I loved the idea and in no time at all put together a sample one.

Lined with a swatch of fall-colored burlap, the basket was chock-full of tomatoes, carrots, yellow and green summer squash, dark shiny eggplants, apples, grape clusters, and bunches of bright marigolds. They blended together into a rich, colorful expression of the season's bounty—and they pleased and touched each neighbor.

The harvest baskets caught on so well that soon they were going far beyond the immediate neighbors to an ever-enlarging circle of friends and acquaintances. A little basket of fresh produce to people who have no garden of their own can mean more than even I, an avid vegetable lover, ever realized.

GREEN TOMATO PICCALILLI

1 peck green tomatoes	4 pounds brown sugar
12 large onions	2 tablespoons dry mustard
1 cup coarse salt	2 tablespoons whole cloves
3 quarts cider vinegar	2 sticks cinnamon
12 green peppers, sliced thin	2 tablespoons ground ginger
6 sweet red peppers, diced	1 tablespoon salt
12 garlic cloves, minced	1 tablespoon celery seed

Yield: Makes 6 quarts

Wash green tomatoes and cut into thin slices. Peel onions, cut into thin slices, and add to tomatoes. Sprinkle with coarse salt. Let mixture stand for 12 hours.

Wash mixture in clear water and drain. Heat vinegar to boiling point. Seed green and red peppers, remove membranes, and add to vinegar. Add garlic and brown sugar. Add tomato and onion mixture. Tie the 6 spices in a cloth bag and add to pot. Simmer until tomatoes are transparent, about 1 hour. Stir frequently.

Remove bag of spices. Place picalilli in sterile jars and seal. Picalilli may be blended briefly for a finer texture, if desired.

AUGUST 1

Here we are in August, the month for Master Schola.

Master Schola is a week-long symposium designed for choirmasters and organists. As many as sixty-eight attend from all over the United States and abroad. In various courses and seminars, each master gives instruction on the different aspects of singing, playing, and conducting sacred music.

This year focused on the works of Schubert, Brahms, and Mendelssohn in honor of the anniversary of their birth or death. The week culminated with a Sunday afternoon public performance of Schubert's *Mass in E-flat* and Brahms's *Ein Deutsches Requiem*. A chicken basket dinner, similar to the pops concert meal, was served for three hundred during intermission.

Sisters do most of the cooking, with some assistance from the Brothers and the Community. The serving is shared by different groups from the whole Community.

Throughout the week, meals for those attending the Schola itself are served either under an outdoor tent or in the Fellowship Room. During this week creativity flourishes, expressing itself in the cooking and decorations, with different themes each evening. It has become traditional to have a Cape Cod evening that features New England clam chowder and cod. Sometimes the Brothers, dressed in slickers or fishermen's garb, serve this meal and entertain the group with a barbershop sea chantey here and there.

This year we prepared a German meal in honor of Brahms, with knockwurst, sauerkraut, and apple strudel. We often have a Western barbecue with ribs, corn, and black-eyed peas, and always, by popular demand, we repeat an Italian night with a ludicrous singing of "O Schola Mia."

Because the gardens are then at their peak, and these folks are so partial to our salad bars, we include at least three of these during the week for lunches. We cater to the goodly number of vegetarians by providing innovative combinations of grains, lentils, and beans, with lots of home-baked breads and a variety of sandwiches. These always meet with praise and applause.

Every evening a little remembrance of Cape Cod is placed on each pillow: a jar of beach plum jam, a shell plaque, a lavender or pine sachet, and always without fail, a bag of Sisters' granola to which every true musician develops an addiction after a week at Master Schola.

TYPICAL SCHOLA LUNCHES

NEW POTATO AND CUCUMBER SALAD WITH FRESH HERBS

2¼ pounds red skinned potatoes

2 medium cucumbers, peeled, seeded, and diced

½ cup chopped red onions

1 cup plain low-fat yogurt

6 tablespoons chopped fresh dill

2 teaspoons minced garlic Salt and pepper

1 teaspoon chopped fresh parsley

Yield: Makes 8 servings

Cook potatoes in large pot of boiling salted water until tender, about 18 minutes. Drain potatoes and cool; peel. Cut into ¾-inch cubes and place in a large bowl. Add cucumbers and onions. Whisk yogurt, dill, and garlic in a small bowl. Add to potatoes and season with salt, pepper, and parsley. (Can be made up to 8 hours ahead and chilled.)

Note: This recipe works well with any combination of yogurt, mayonnaise, or sour cream. Green onions may be used in place of red.

BLACK-EYED PEA AND BARLEY SOUP

8 ounces dried black-eyed peas
6 cups water
¾ cup pearl barley
4 cups water
2 tablespoons olive oil
2 medium onions, chopped
1 smoked ham hock (about 12 ounces)
1 tablespoon chopped garlic
2 bay leaves
1½ teaspoons ground allspice
8 cups chicken broth, or more
Salt and freshly ground pepper
¼ cup fresh lime juice
¼ cup chopped parsley
4 ripe plum tomatoes, seeded, diced into ¼-inch cubes

Yield: Makes 8 servings

Pick through the peas, discarding any stones, and rinse. Place peas in a bowl, cover with 6 cups water, and soak 8-10 hours. Drain and rinse.

Place barley in a medium-size saucepan and cover with 4 cups water. Bring to a boil over high heat, reduce the heat to medium, and simmer uncovered until tender but not mushy, 45 minutes. Drain the barley if necessary.

Heat oil in a large, heavy pot over low heat. Add onions and cook until wilted, 5 to 7 minutes. Add peas, ham hock, garlic, bay leaves, allspice, and chicken broth. Bring to a boil, reduce the heat to medium, and simmer uncovered until peas are tender, 40 to 45 minutes, occasionally skimming off foam that rises to the surface. Add a bit more broth if peas seem dry.

Remove ham hock and let stand until cool enough to handle. Shred any meat from the bones and return to peas.

Add barley, season with salt and pepper, and stir gently to combine.

Before serving, heat through and fold in the lime juice and parsley. Serve in bowls and garnish with diced tomatoes. This soup may be served hot or cold. Store covered in refrigerator for up to 2 days.

GREEK TORTELLINI SALAD

Salad:

2 9-ounce plain or tricolored refrigerated cheese tortellini, cooked and drained
1 red or green sweet pepper (or combination), cut into thin strips (1 cup)
1 small red onion, thinly sliced
1 medium tomato, chopped
¼ cup sliced, pitted ripe olives
1 cup crumbled feta cheese

Dressing:

½ cup rice wine vinegar or white vinegar
½ cup olive oil
1½ tablespoon chopped fresh parsley
1½ tablespoon oregano
3 tablespoons lemon juice
2 tablespoons dry sherry
1½ teaspoons onion salt
⅛ to ¼ teaspoon crushed red pepper
1 teaspoon pepper

Yield: Makes 12 to 14 side dish servings

Salad: In a large bowl, combine cooked tortellini, sweet peppers, onion, tomato, and olives.

Dressing: Combine vinegar, oil, parsley, oregano, lemon juice, sherry, onion salt, red pepper, and pepper. Pour over salad and toss to coat.

Cover. Chill for 4 to 24 hours. Stir in cheese. Use a slotted spoon to serve.

CHICKPEA SALAD

6 tbsp. + ¼ cup olive oil
1 cup finely chopped onion
4 cloves garlic, minced
1 teaspoon aniseed
1 (19-ounce) can chickpeas
   (garbanzo beans), drained

2 tablespoons dry white wine
   Onion salt and freshly
   ground pepper
2 tablespoons parsley
3 tablespoons wine vinegar
   Lettuce leaves

Yield: Makes 6 servings

Warm the 6 tablespoons olive oil in a large nonstick skillet over medium-low heat. Add onion, garlic, and aniseed. Cook, stirring occasionally, until vegetables are very tender, about 15 minutes.

Add the chickpeas, white wine, onion salt, and pepper. Cook, stirring, over medium-low heat until most of the liquid is absorbed and the flavors blend together, 6 to 8 minutes. Stir in parsley.

Add the remaining ¼ cup olive oil and wine vinegar. Toss and serve over lettuce leaves.

GREEK PORK PITA POCKETS

1 pound boneless pork loin
4 tablespoons olive oil
4 tablespoons lemon juice
1 tablespoon prepared mustard
2 cloves garlic, minced
1 teaspoon dried oregano
1 cup plain yogurt

1 cucumber, chopped,
   peeled
½ teaspoon crushed garlic
½ teaspoon dill weed
2 tablespoons chopped
   fresh mint
2 pita rounds
   Red onion, chopped

Yield: Makes 4 servings

Cut the pork loin into thin strips and place in a shallow dish. Combine olive oil, lemon juice, prepared mustard, minced garlic, and dried oregano. Pour the marinade over pork. Refrigerate for 1 to 8 hours.

Stir together the yogurt, cucumber, crushed garlic, dill weed,

and mint. Cover mixture and refrigerate.

Remove pork from the marinade; stir-fry in a nonstick pan over medium heat for 2 to 3 minutes. Halve pitas and open to form a pocket. Fill pockets with pork. Top with cucumber mixture. Garnish with chopped red onion.

OPEN-FACE TURKEY REUBENS

1 tablespoon oil
1 pound uncooked turkey
   breast slices
4 slices pumpernickel
   bread, toasted
4 tablespoons Thousand
   Island dressing

½ cup sauerkraut, drained
1 onion, thinly sliced,
   slightly sautéed
1 medium tomato, sliced
1 cup (4 ounces) Swiss
   cheese, shredded

Yield: Makes 4 sandwiches

Heat oil in a skillet over medium heat. Add turkey slices and cook 2 to 3 minutes on each side or until the turkey is no longer pink. Drain. Spread each toast slice with 1 tablespoon of the dressing. Top with turkey, sauerkraut, onion, tomato, and cheese. Place on an ungreased cookie sheet. Broil 4 to 6 inches from heat for 1 to 2 minutes or until cheese is melted.

FOCACCIA WITH OLIVES AND ROSEMARY

2 cups warm water (105°F to 115°F)
2 teaspoons dry yeast
4½ cups flour or more
2 teaspoons salt
1 + 2 tablespoons olive oil
24 black or green brine-cured olives (such as kalamata or Greek), pitted, halved
1 tablespoon chopped fresh rosemary, or 1½ teaspoons dried
Grated Parmesan cheese

Yield: Makes 8 servings

Place warm water in a large bowl. Sprinkle dry yeast over; stir with a fork. Let stand until yeast dissolves, about 10 minutes.

Add the 4¼ cups flour and salt to yeast mixture, and stir to blend well (dough will be sticky). Knead dough on a floured surface until it is smooth and elastic, adding more flour by tablespoonfuls if dough is sticky, about 10 minutes. Form dough into a ball. Oil a large bowl; add dough, turning to coat. Cover with plastic wrap and let rise in a warm area until doubled, about 1½ hours.

Punch down dough; knead into ball and return to same bowl. Cover with plastic wrap and let rise in a warm area until doubled, about 45 minutes.

Coat a 15 x 10-inch baking sheet with 1 tablespoon oil. Punch dough down. Transfer to prepared sheet. Using fingertips, press out dough to 13 x 10-inch rectangle. Let dough rest for 10 minutes. Drizzle the remaining 2 tablespoons of oil over dough. Sprinkle evenly with olives and rosemary. Sprinkle generously with Parmesan cheese. Let the dough rise uncovered in a warm area until puffy, about 25 minutes.

Preheat the oven to 475°F. Press fingertips all over the dough, forming indentations. Bake bread until brown and crusty, about 20 minutes. Serve the bread warm or at room temperature.

VEGETABLE CROWN SANDWICH WITH BASIL PESTO

2 (1½-pound) round loaves of rye, pumpernickel, or sourdough bread

Vegetables:
4 tomatoes
½ cup spinach leaves
6 red bell peppers
4 small zucchini
1 medium eggplant
1 head broccoli
12 thin red onion rings
¼ cup olive oil
Onion salt and pepper

Basil pesto:
1 cup olive oil
4 cups fresh basil
2 cloves garlic
¼ cup grated Parmesan cheese

Vinaigrette:
½ cup olive oil
¼ cup balsamic vinegar
Onion salt and pepper

Yield: Makes 12 servings

Vegetables: Slice peppers into 1-inch-wide chunks. Cut the zucchini and eggplant into ¼ inch slices. Slice tomatoes thinly. Brush peppers, eggplant, and zucchini with oil and season with onion salt and pepper. Roast in a 400°F oven for about 20 minutes, or until tender. Turn halfway through baking time. Cut broccoli into small florets. Steam florets until tender.

Basil Pesto: Place all the pesto ingredients in a food processor and blend until well mixed.

Vinaigrette: Mix the oil and vinegar to make a vinaigrette. Season with onion salt and pepper. Sprinkle over the zucchini and eggplant and peppers.

To Assemble: Using a serrated knife, cut the top off the round loaves and set aside. Remove the insides of the bread leaving a ½-inch shell. Spread pesto thinly in each of the bread rounds. Then layer each of the vegetables, including spinach and onion, in the loaves and place the bread tops on the loaves. Wrap tightly in plastic wrap and refrigerate for at least 4 hours. Slice each loaf into 6 sandwiches to serve.

COLD ZUCCHINI SOUP

- 4 medium zucchini, quartered and sliced
- 2 (15-ounce) cans chicken broth
- 1 bunch of green onions, chopped
- 1 teaspoon onion salt
- 1 teaspoon pepper
- Dill weed
- 2 (8-ounce) pkgs. cream cheese
- 1 cup sour cream with chives (½ pint)
- Chopped chives, or paprika

Yield: Makes 6 to 8 servings

In a saucepan, combine zucchini, chicken broth, onions, salt, and pepper. Season to taste with dill. Cook mixture until soft, approximately 20 to 30 minutes. Blend cream cheese and sour cream in a blender until smooth. Blend in zucchini mixture, a portion at a time, until smooth. Chill 8 to 10 hours or until very cold. Garnish with chopped chives or paprika.

VEAL SCALLOPS WITH CAPERS, VERMOUTH, AND DILL

- ½ cup flour
- Onion salt and pepper
- 1 pound veal scallops (about ¼ inch thick)
- 2 + 3 tablespoons butter
- 1 tablespoon olive oil
- 2 tablespoons dry vermouth
- 3 tablespoons drained capers
- ⅓ cup chopped fresh dill

Yield: Makes 4 servings

Place flour in a pie pan. Season with onion salt and pepper. Coat veal with flour mixture, shaking off excess. Melt 2 tablespoons of butter with the oil in a heavy large skillet over medium-high heat. Working in batches, add veal and cook until light brown, about 1 minute per side. Transfer to a platter. Add the remaining 3 tablespoons of butter to the skillet and melt, scraping up any browned bits. Add vermouth and capers; bring to a boil. Sprinkle with the dill. Season with onion salt and pepper and pour over the veal.

GRILLED BEEF TENDERLOIN WITH MARSALA– MUSHROOM SAUCE

Marsala–Mushroom Sauce:

2 + 2 tablespoons butter
1 cup leek, chopped (white and pale green parts only)
1 garlic clove, crushed

4 cups mixed, fresh, wild mushrooms, sliced (such as oyster, stemmed portobello, and stemmed shiitake)
⅔ cup dry Marsala wine
⅔ cup beef stock or broth

Steaks:

4 8-ounce beef tenderloin steaks

Olive oil
Onion salt and pepper

Yield: Makes 4 servings

Marsala–Mushroom sauce: Melt 2 tablespoons butter in a heavy large skillet over medium-low heat. Add leek and garlic and sauté until almost tender, about 5 minutes. Increase heat to medium-high. Add mushrooms and sauté until golden brown, about 6 minutes. Add Marsala wine and stock and boil until the liquid is reduced by half, about 4 minutes. Strain sauce, reserving the mushrooms. Cover strained sauce and mushrooms.

Steaks: Brush steaks with olive oil. Sprinkle with onion salt and pepper. Grill to desired doneness, about 4 minutes per side for medium-rare. Transfer to a platter and tent with foil.

Bring sauce to a simmer in a heavy large skillet. Remove skillet from heat. Gradually whisk in the remaining 2 tablespoons butter. Add reserved mushrooms and stir over low heat until mushrooms are heated through, about 2 minutes. Season to taste with onion salt and pepper.

Place steaks on plates. Spoon sauce over them and serve.

PORK TENDERLOIN WITH CARAMELIZED PEARS

1¼ pounds pork tenderloin, trimmed, cut crosswise into 1-inch-thick slices
2 + 1 + 1 tablespoons butter
4 large Anjou pears, firm but ripe, peeled, halved, cored, cut into ⅓-inch-thick wedges

1 teaspoon sugar
Salt and pepper
½ cup chopped shallots
1 teaspoon dried thyme
¼ cup pear schnapps
1 cup whipping cream
⅓ cup pear nectar
Onion salt

Yield: Makes 4 servings

Place pork slices between plastic wrap. Using a meat mallet, pound pork slices to ¼-inch thickness.

Melt 2 tablespoons butter in a large nonstick skillet over high heat. Add pears and sugar; sauté until pears are tender and deep golden, about 8 minutes.

Melt 1 tablespoon butter in another large nonstick skillet over high heat. Season pork with salt and pepper. Working in batches, add pork to the skillet; sauté just until cooked through, about 2 minutes per side. Transfer to a plate. Cover. Reduce heat to medium. Melt the remaining 1 tablespoon butter in the same skillet. Add shallots and thyme; sauté 2 minutes. Add schnapps and boil until reduced to a glaze, scraping up any browned bits, about 2 minutes. Add cream and pear nectar; boil until thickened to sauce consistency, about 5 minutes. Season with onion salt and pepper.

CREAMED SPINACH WITH CHÈVRE

3 cups fresh spinach, steamed and well drained
½ cup water
½ cup whipping cream
2 ounces soft, fresh goat cheese (such as Montrachet)
1 large shallot, minced
½ teaspoon grated lemon peel
Salt and pepper

Yield: Makes 4 servings

Preheat oven to 250°F. Put cooked and drained spinach on an ovenproof platter in oven to keep warm. Put the water in a medium skillet. Add cream, goat cheese, shallot, and lemon peel. Stir over medium-high heat until sauce is thick and reduced to ⅔ cup, about 6 minutes. Season with salt and pepper.

Pour sauce evenly over spinach. Serve immediately.

TYPICAL SCHOLA DESSERTS

FRENCH APPLE–ALMOND TART

Crust:
2 large egg yolks
2 tablespoons Calvados or brandy
1¼ cups flour
2 tablespoons sugar
¼ teaspoon salt
¼ teaspoon ground nutmeg
9 tablespoons (1 stick + 1 tablespoon) chilled butter, cut into ½-inch pieces.

Filling:
1¼ cups slivered almonds, blanched
¾ cup + 1 + 1 tablespoons sugar
2 large eggs
1 + 1 tablespoons Calvados or brandy
1 teaspoon vanilla extract
½ teaspoon almond extract
¼ teaspoon salt
4 + 2 tablespoons (¾ stick) butter, room temperature
3 tart green apples, peeled, quartered, cored, cut into ⅛-inch-thick wedges

Topping:
¼ cup apricot preserves
1 tablespoon Calvados or brandy

Yield: Makes 10 to 12 servings

Crust: Stir the egg yolks and Calvados in a small bowl to blend. Combine flour, sugar, salt, and nutmeg in a food processor. Add the butter; cut in, turning processor alternately on and off, until butter is the size of small peas. With the processor running, add the yolk mixture. Process until large moist clumps form.

Turn out dough on a lightly floured surface. Gather the dough into a ball; flatten it into a disk. Wrap the dough in plastic; refrigerate until cold, about 1 hour. (Can be made 24 hours ahead. Keep chilled. Let soften slightly before rolling out.)

Roll out dough on a lightly floured surface to a 14-inch round. Transfer to an 11-inch-diameter tart pan with a removable bottom. Fold the overhang in and press, forming double-thick sides. Chill while making filling.

Filling: Combine the almonds, ¾ cup sugar, eggs, 1 tablespoon Calvados, extracts, and salt in a food processor. Blend until soft paste forms. Add 4 tablespoons butter; blend 10 seconds. Spread this mixture in the crust. Chill until firm, about 45 minutes. Stir apples, the remaining 1 tablespoon Calvados, and 1 tablespoon sugar in a large bowl. Let stand 30 minutes.

Preheat oven to 400°F. Drain apples; overlap in concentric circles atop filling. Melt the remaining 2 tablespoons butter; brush over apples. Sprinkle with the remaining 1 tablespoon sugar.

Bake tart for 15 minutes. Reduce temperature to 350°F. Bake until the apples are tender, about 45 minutes. Transfer pan to a rack.

Topping: Stir preserves and 1 tablespoon Calvados in a small saucepan over low heat until preserves melt. Strain into a small bowl; brush over apples. Cool. (Can be made up to 8 hours ahead. Let stand at room temperature.)

PINEAPPLE-COCONUT NAPOLEONS

Coconut tuiles:

Nonstick vegetable oil spray
2 cups (about 5 ounces) shredded coconut
¼ cup flour
1 cup sugar
2 tablespoons + 1 teaspoon butter, room temperature
¾ cup egg whites (about 6 large)

Pineapple syrup:

3 cups canned, unsweetened pineapple juice
½ cup sugar
2 teaspoons cardamom
1 teaspoon black peppercorns
2 whole cloves
1 cinnamon stick
½ jalapeño chili with seeds
1 large pineapple, peeled, cored, cut into 12 rounds (each about ⅓ inch thick)

Mascarpone cream:

12 ounces mascarpone cheese (about 1 cup + 2 tablespoons)
1¼ cups whipping cream, chilled
¼ cup sugar
1 tablespoon dark rum

Garnish:

1 pint strawberries, hulled, sliced

Yield: Makes 6 servings

Coconut tuiles: Preheat oven to 300°F. Coat large nonstick baking sheet with vegetable oil spray. Mix coconut and flour in a small bowl. Using an electric mixer, beat the sugar and butter in a large bowl until blended. Gradually add egg whites and beat until mixture thickens slightly. Stir in coconut mixture.

Form 2 tuiles by spooning 1 very generous tablespoonful batter for each tuile onto prepared baking sheet, spacing them 4 inches apart. Using a small metal spatula or the back of a spoon, spread the batter to thin 3-inch to 3½-inch rounds. Bake until tuiles are golden, about 22 minutes. Working quickly and using the metal spatula, transfer tuiles to racks. Return baking sheet to the oven briefly if the tuiles harden and stick slightly to the sheet. Working in batches, repeat with remaining batter, coating the baking sheet with vegetable oil spray before each batch. Cool completely.

Pineapple syrup: Boil juice, sugar, cardamom, peppercorns, cloves, cinnamon, and jalepeño in a heavy large pot until the liquid is reduced to 2½ cups, about 4 minutes. Arrange the pineapple rounds in layers in the pot. Reduce heat to medium; cover and cook until the pineapple is tender and translucent, turning the rounds occasionally, about 20 minutes. Using a slotted spoon, transfer the pineapple rounds to a large baking sheet. Cool. Strain the pineapple cooking liquid; return to same pot. Boil until syrup is reduced to ½ cup, about 5 minutes. Transfer to a bowl and cool. (Tuiles, pineapple, and syrup can be prepared 24 hours ahead. Store the tuiles in an airtight container. Cover and refrigerate pineapple and syrup separately. Bring to room temperature before assembling.)

Mascarpone cream: Beat mascarpone, cream, and sugar in a large bowl until firm peaks form. Beat in rum.

To assemble: Place 1 tuile on each of 6 plates. Place 1 pineapple round atop each. Spread 3 tablespoons mascarpone cream atop pineapple. Top with another tuile, 3 tablespoons mascarpone cream, then 1 pineapple round. Spoon remaining mascarpone cream into pastry bag fitted with medium star tip. Pipe rosettes in center of pineapple rounds. Drizzle pineapple syrup around Napoleon. Surround with strawberry slices and serve.

COFFEE HAZELNUT RASPBERRY TORTE

Filling:

1 cup unsweetened, frozen raspberries, thawed, drained	1 cup raspberry jam

White Chocolate–Coffee Frosting:

¾ + 1¾ cups chilled whipping cream	3 tablespoons + 1 teaspoon instant coffee crystals
10 ounces good-quality white chocolate, chopped	

Cake:

1 cup hazelnuts, toasted, husked	6 large eggs, separated
1 cup sifted flour	¼ cup water or hazelnut coffee
1¼ cups sugar, divided	1 teaspoon vanilla extract
1 teaspoon instant coffee crystals	½ teaspoon almond extract
¼ teaspoon salt	Fresh raspberries (optional)

Yield: Makes 8 to 10 servings

Filling: Press raspberries through a fine sieve into a small bowl. Press the jam through the same sieve into the raspberry purée; discard the seeds. Stir to blend well. Cover the bowl and chill 8 to 10 hours.

White Chocolate–Coffee Frosting: Combine ¾ cup cream, white chocolate, and coffee crystals in a heavy medium saucepan. Stir over low heat just until the chocolate melts, the coffee dissolves, and the mixture is smooth. Remove from heat. Let stand until cool and thick, whisking occasionally, about 1½ hours.

Using an electric mixer, beat the remaining 1¾ cups cream in a large bowl until firm peaks form. Fold a large spoonful of the whipped cream into the chocolate mixture. Then fold the chocolate mixture into the whipped cream in 4 additions. Cover and refrigerate frosting until very firm, about 6 hours. (Can be prepared 24 hours ahead; keep chilled.)

Cake: Preheat oven to 350°F. Line three 9-inch-diameter cake pans with 1½-inch-high sides with parchment. Butter and flour the parchment. Combine nuts, flour, ¼ cup of the sugar, coffee crystals, and salt in a food processor. Blend until nuts are finely ground.

Using an electric mixer, beat the egg yolks and ½ cup of the sugar in a large bowl until very thick, about 5 minutes. Beat in the water and vanilla extract. Stir in the flour mixture. Using clean dry beaters, beat the egg whites in a large bowl until soft peaks form. Gradually add the remaining ½ cup sugar, beating until stiff but not dry. Fold into yolk mixture in 3 additions.

Transfer the batter to the prepared pans. Bake the cakes until tester inserted into center comes out clean, about 18 minutes. Cool cakes in the pans on racks. Cut around the pan sides to loosen the cakes. Turn the cakes out; peel off parchment.

Place 1 cake on a platter and a second cake on a piece of foil. Spread ⅓ cup of the filling over each; let stand 20 minutes to set up. Spread 1 cup frosting over each. Lift cake off foil; place atop the cake on platter. Top with the third cake. Spread remaining frosting over the sides and top of the torte. (Can be prepared 24 hours ahead. Cover with cake dome and refrigerate.)

Garnish torte with fresh berries, if desired. Cut into wedges and serve.

AUGUST 10

The cucumbers and tomatoes are now at their peak! Since Saturday is "Make Your Own" lunch day, I'm going to make a sandwich like the ones I used to eat years ago with Mama and Rosie. I called it our summertime sandwich.

It was made on Mama's crusty homemade rolls. It began with a thick spreading of homemade mayonnaise, then leafy green lettuce, lengthwise slices of cucumber, very red ripe tomatoes, tender green scallions, and sprigs of fresh dill. The combination was marvelous! What gave it its mouthwatering flavor was, of course, the zesty mayonnaise, but equally important was the warmth of the ingredients. There is a definite place for chilled tomatoes and cool cucumbers, but nothing equals the flavor of sun-ripened tomatoes and cucumbers at their natural temperature as they come from the vine.

HOMEMADE MAYONNAISE

½ teaspoon dry mustard	2 egg yolks
1 teaspoon onion salt	2 tablespoons vinegar
¼ teaspoon sugar	or lemon juice
¼ teaspoon paprika	2 cups salad oil
(optional)	
⅛ teaspoon ground red pepper	

Yield: Makes about 2 cups

In a small mixer bowl combine mustard, onion salt, paprika if desired, and red pepper. Add yolks and vinegar or lemon juice. Beat with an electric mixer on medium speed until combined.

With the mixer running, add the oil, 1 teaspoon at a time, until 2 tablespoons of oil have been added. Add the remaining oil in a thin, steady stream. (This should take about 5 minutes.) Cover and store in the refrigerator up to 2 weeks.

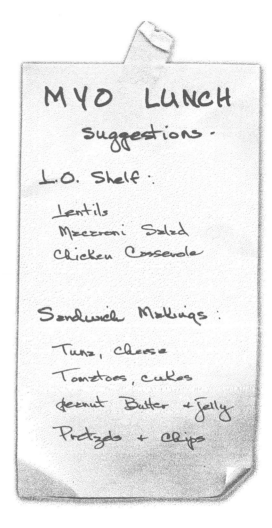

MYO LUNCH
suggestions.

L.O. Shelf:

Lentils
Macaroni Salad
Chicken Casserole

Sandwich Makings:

Tuna, Cheese
Tomatoes, cukes
Peanut Butter & Jelly
Pretzels + Chips

MAMA'S CRUSTY BREAD

2 tablespoons yeast	2 teaspoons salt
1/3 cup warm water	1 1/4 cups water
3 1/2 cups flour	

Yield: Makes 2 loaves

Stir yeast into the 1/3 cup water and allow to dissolve.

Mix flour and salt together in a large bowl and add the 1 1/4 cups water; stir together. Add the yeast and water mixture to the flour mixture and mix thoroughly.

Turn the dough out onto a lightly floured surface and knead until elastic, 8 to 10 minutes. Put the dough into a clean bowl and allow to double at room temperature, about 2 to 3 hours. Punch down dough and allow to double again, about 1 1/2 hours. Punch down dough and divide in two. Form loaves and put on a baking pan to rise again for 30 to 40 minutes.

Pre-heat the oven to 450°F and move rack to the bottom of oven. Mist loaves with a spray bottle of water just as you put them in the oven. Mist again at 8 minutes and at 15 minutes. The bread should be done in 20 to 25 minutes. Allow to cool or serve warm. Best served on the day you bake it.

AUGUST 18

"What do you do all day, Sister Irene?" someone asked me a few days ago. I find this difficult to answer on the spot because no two days are ever alike, though all of them contain some of the same basic ingredients.

"Well, then, suppose you give an example of a typical day in your life," the person suggested. So I decided to describe one as best I can.

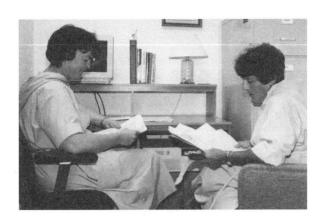

I open my eyes and glance at the clock. Almost five o'clock. Time to get up. I thank God for the night's rest and for his grace for whatever the new day holds. I quietly make my bed, dress, and prepare for the day. As I start down the dimly lit hall, Elijah, with his distinctively Siamese voice, sometimes meets me, making loud noises and rubbing up against my leg to let me know that he hasn't had anything to eat since the night before. On the landing, Sunshine barely stirs, opens one eye, and reaches a limp paw out to me from her bed. Alfie, in the hall below, nervously jumps down from the sofa on which he's not supposed to sleep, wagging his tail in an overly friendly gesture designed to ward off any early morning correction.

I get my mug full of coffee and go off with my Bible for a quiet time of reading, meditating, and listening in preparation for the day ahead. Then I check my mail and read through the notes that Sisters have turned in, checking especially to see if there is anything urgent that particularly needs to be prayed about in the morning services. Whatever time remains, I spend writing.

Matins begins at 7:00. This service is sung in Gregorian chant by the Brothers and Sisters with some Community members and often a guest or two joining us. In the brief time between Matins and morning communion, I read through my list of current prayer intentions so that I can be remembering these needs during the Eucharist service. By this time, the entire Community has arrived for our daily Eucharist, the one time during the day when we all worship together as a family before going our separate ways for the day.

Breakfast follows, eaten in silence. Both the Friary and the Convent observe silence from after Compline the evening before through Lauds the next morning.

Lauds is sung by the Brothers and Sisters after breakfast. It is in this service that I pray individually for each of our sixty-four Sisters, and six novices, as well as our twenty-five Brothers. When this service is over the day's work begins.

Sister Rachel and I begin our work by going over the matters at hand for the day. We must answer questions and either make certain decisions or take them to the Sisters' council for their consideration, or to the Prioress. And there are a number of Sisters who are asking to talk with us.

Sister Alyn, an extern nursing Sister, wants to give us a report on a visit from her parents, and talk with us about a home nursing situation that is giving her reason to consider leaving one job for another.

Donna needs to talk to us about personnel problems in the Art Room, suggesting some changes and presenting a need for more help there.

Sister Louise is concerned about another Sister who seems to be dealing with the added pressure of new responsibilities by becoming short-tempered with those around her. After mentioning this to the Sister with no results, Sister Louise is asking us to talk to her together.

The budget Sister wants to discuss how to handle recent requests for money to pay for music lessons that are being recommended for several Sisters by the band director.

Two Sisters from another community are coming to spend several days with us and are asking to participate in our daily life in a way that they can most freely experience it. We need to plan this with the guestmistress.

Sister Linda has just returned from her trip to Turkey. She wants to tell us about it and the effect it has had on her.

While we are waiting for her to show up, I casually ask Sister Jane—who is once again registering a complaint about how a certain matter is being handled—if she is still feeling as strongly about it or has changed her mind. She assures me that she has not and then goes on to reiterate her reasons. The intensity of her emotions reveals that this is not the real issue, although she adamantly insists that it is. Time is slipping by, we are already behind schedule, and Linda is waiting, so we end the conversation with Jane. She feels she is not understood or being listened to, not a good note on which to leave things.

After Sister Linda has finished talking with us, I know we need to circle back

to Jane or a bad situation will only turn into one that is much worse. As we start all over again, we let her repeat everything she has already said several times. This time her story is accompanied with such wrenching sobs and tears that after a while she herself admits that the whole thing matters way too much even if she should have some valid ground for complaint. Her sense of unfairness and lack of recognition is way out of proportion to the facts. We suggest to her that this may have something to do with her place in her family. Something clicks and somewhere this registers as true, and much of her intensity is suddenly diffused.

The phone rings and it is a long distance call from Madeleine. She is a young woman who left the sisterhood some years ago but keeps in touch with us regularly and counts on our prayers and support. It is not unusual for her to call just to chat about what is going on with her or with us, but it is unusual for her to be calling at this time of day. When I take the phone she tells me that she has just received word about a tragedy in her family. Her sister's nephew, a young man, has burned to death, leaving a young wife and four small children. She is making arrangements to go to the wake and feels she needs to talk about her own feelings as well as those of the family members she will soon be with, and her concern as to how she can be a support and blessing to them in the face of such devastation. After spending some time on the phone with her, I promise her we will let the Sisters know about this need so that she can be assured of our prayers.

I come away from the call sobered and saddened for all concerned, but at the same time grateful for the maturity evidenced in Madeleine and for the strong bond of love between her and us. I am assured that her presence will be a comfort to this family.

It is now 11:00 AM. I have just enough time to clean my four toilets, vacuum my room, and stop by the infirmary for a little visit with a Sister who is recovering from surgery. At 11:45 it is time for the Sext/None service, which lasts until noon—lunchtime.

After lunch I pick up my mail, check the computer for new messages, and prepare for study time from 1:00 to 2:30, a quiet period of the Sisters' day set aside for spiritual reading, meditation, prayer, and studying. I plan to prepare for a class on prayer that I am scheduled to teach the novices, and to select the readings I need to do for Matins next week.

A message comes that there is an urgent fax in the mailroom from the Sisters in Canada. On my way to pick it up, I see Ethel, a fairly new Community member, but a faithful friend of many years. I know she feels somewhat down with both her own birthday and the anniversary of her husband's recent death approaching. The Sisters are planning a surprise tea for her tomorrow but I cannot remember if her birthday is today or tomorrow, so before greeting her, I poke my head into the switchboard room to see if the operator can tell me. As I do, she exclaims, "Oh, it's Sister Irene. She's right here," and hands me the phone.

On the other end is Simone calling from Albania, her third day after arriving there. "Oh, Sister Irene, it's so good to hear your voice. I miss you so much. I can't tell you how much I miss you." She goes on at length telling me how much everyone at home means to her, describes her new situation, her surroundings, and the orphanage where she will be working, and finally ends the conversation by telling me once again how much she loves me. She is so effusive in expressing her affection that it would be amusing if one did not know the history behind this.

For her, the past several years have been a period of coming to grips with profound feelings of rejection by her father, who walked out on her and her mother when she was only a child. The intense rage and hatred she felt inside had to come out against someone, so those closest to her became the main target for her hostility—not an easy situation for any involved. There was good reason to wonder if she would make it or whether she would eventually resort to a life of overt rebellion.

It has been a long haul over a painful period of time. However, with the wise direction of the Prioress, sensitive counseling from a clergyman, and patience on the part of the Sisters, Simone is now on an even keel, genuinely sorry for having been so difficult to live with and ready to throw herself into something she has long wanted to do. When she tells me she loves me and that she misses all of us, I know this is more than a severe case of homesickness and separation from all that is familiar and secure. I know this means that a tremendous work

has been accomplished within her, and that gladdens my heart.

It is 2:30 as I sit down at my desk. I need to write Helen Cheberenchick, a devout eighty-one-year-old Byzantine Catholic woman. She requests prayer for numerous people, because, as she puts it, she "knows God listens to us." Her letters are always such a joy as she enumerates the many ways her prayer requests have been answered. I like to make sure each of these people receive some little word of encouragement and assurance that they are being prayed for.

I promised Madeleine that I would write to the parents and wife of the young man who died so tragically. I am long overdue writing to Magda, a young girl I met six years ago on the street in Poland, who helped me find my way to a gift shop. We have kept in touch ever since, and now she is asking me serious questions about her faith and wants prayer regarding a decision about whether to marry someone of a different religious background. I also want to get a little note off to Belinda, a young mother suffering from depression.

Summaries for our weekly report to the Prioress are due. I have to contact Nancy about some behavioral problems with the children in the nursery school. The Sisters in Bermuda are waiting for some answers to questions. But before settling down to that, I want to find Sister Lois and see how she is doing. Tonight this adopted twenty-eight-year-old Sister will meet her birth mother. After a year of searching, and many years of wrestling with anger over the circumstances of her birth, she will finally meet the mother she has desperately wanted to find.

Although this is what Lois has longed for, and although years of regular, consistent counseling have been preparing her for this moment, she faces it with conflicting emotions. She knows the entire sisterhood is praying for her, and she has two Sisters to talk to daily as well as a psychologist when needed, but it is important for her to feel our support also.

While talking to Sister Lois it occurs to me that someone else may be having some emotions about this meeting of mother and daughter. That is Sister Jennifer, another adopted Sister who for a longer period of time has been trying to get in touch with her birth mother, but hasn't succeeded. I think it would be wise to see what state she is in. Lois at one point struggled with jealousy of Jennifer, who seemed to be making so much more headway in finding her mother. Now the

tables have turned, with Lois's mother appearing almost effortlessly out of the blue, eager to find her daughter. Jennifer still must wait to hear from the adoption agency, wondering if her own mother is going to want to respond to her inquiry. This situation is not easy for her, and once again I remind her that God knows what is best for her and will grant it in the right time.

I remember that I promised to meet with Sister Adele who wants some input regarding a proposed menu for the out-of-town guests coming next month to the groundbreaking ceremony for our new church building. After talking about the menu, I go to see Sister Nancy, who is in charge of the natural crafts department for the Christmas Fair. She wants me to look at some sample items and tells me about some new ideas she has for this year.

Tomorrow is my night of the week to cook and serve dinner to the Zion household. Since tomorrow at 4:00 PM I will be at a meeting that will go almost until dinner time, I need to do some food preparation today. I'm planning a New England boiled dinner, most of which can be cooked in advance.

After getting everything cooking on the stove and putting my pumpkin pudding into the oven to bake, I grab my windbreaker and head for the tidal flats to walk while the tide is still out. Crossing through the backyard of the Convent over favorite patches of moss, I take the little road to the harbor. No sooner do I step up into the beach grass than a gull swoops down from overhead, and I turn my gaze to the broad expanse of sea and sky. Fiddler crabs scurry across the moist, winding path through the beach heather, and as I come onto the flats a sandpiper runs ahead of me, leaving his tracks in the shifting patterns of sand. Friendly creatures these are, all welcoming me to their world with its pressure-free pace and restful rhythm.

Being in this wide-open space clears my mind and helps me collect my thoughts and get some perspective on the rest of the day. I breathe in the salt air like a restorative tonic as I walk along the shore. I could be tempted to linger here indefinitely, but the scruffy little pine at the edge of the dune tells me when I have reached my measured mile and it is time to turn around.

I pick up a hand full of scallop shells before starting back and as I do, a quahog—a hardshell clam—spits up a little geyser of salt water, mischievously squirting me in the shin, a happy little finale to this all-too-brief respite.

Returning, I quicken my pace past Nineveh Garden in order to get to Vespers on time, and I hear my name being called. Sister Barbara, running to catch up with me, is asking if Sister Rachel and I are busy during dinner. It so happens that we have a council meeting tonight because several Sisters have to be out of town at its regularly scheduled time. I ask the reason for her question and she tells me that today in the office where she works there has been a problem that has left her upset. "I need some help," she says with tears welling up in her eyes, "to see where I'm responsible for what's happened." She is obviously very emotional about it, so I promise her we will get in touch with her after dinner as soon as the meeting is over.

The meeting runs longer than usual tonight. When Sister Rachel and I try to locate Sister Barbara as we promised to do, we find she has left word that she has had to go to a rehearsal that will take up the rest of her evening, and she will get in touch with us first thing tomorrow.

That being the case, I go back to the kitchen to wash dishes and clean up from the cooking I did earlier. While I'm doing this, some of the kitchen Sisters start reviewing their day, and we laugh about the number of unfinished matters remaining on each of our "to-do lists."

"Shouldn't something be said to Brother Lawrence about all those big choice ripe tomatoes he's using for spaghetti sauce rather than the small, less perfect ones?" Sister Evelyn adds.

"You mean that's where all the nice tomatoes have disappeared the last few days?" queries Sister Sue. "While we've been trying so hard to save them for slicing and use the little rejects for cooking?" By this time everyone is rather slaphappy and tired and everything feels out of control. It seems best just to laugh about it all. At this very moment in walks Brother Lawrence with a big grin. "What could possibly be so funny?" he asks, "I could hear you laughing way back in the mailroom."

"It's you and the tomatoes," I reply in jest, intending in lighthearted spirit simply to discuss together how best to use the tomatoes. Not knowing what had preceded his entrance, my answer registers something other than I intended. Another Sister tries in vain to explain. Hurt and angry, Brother Lawrence now becomes very heated and emotional. We all love this Brother and we are sorry that we haven't been more sensitive to how he must have felt walking into the situation as he did, but there's no point in trying to talk any further. We drop the matter for the moment and he leaves, very upset.

It's now 7:30 and I return to my desk to read through the evening mail and to complete as much unfinished business from the afternoon as possible. Sister Rachel calls to tell me that Sister Gloria's CAT scan report has come back showing some suspicious spots in her lungs and Dr. Williamson is on his way over to tell her about the report. She is sure that Sister Gloria will want to talk with us after he leaves. With a history of cancer in her family and already having had a mastectomy, she has reason to be concerned.

When we finish talking with Sister Gloria it is 8:45. Just a half hour till Compline and I know I need to talk with Brother Lawrence before the night is over. By this time he has had a chance to think things over and to talk with a couple of the Brothers about his reactions. I apologize for not being more considerate of him. He is sorry for his anger. We end up more than agreeing about the future use of tomatoes, and we go off to Compline reconciled and at peace with each other.

After Compline, I straighten things up, put things away, feed Hosanna for the night, check my mailbox for new messages and answer any that need immediate replies, then prepare for bed. Pulling the covers up around my ears, I give God thanks for his grace and blessings on the day, commit myself and each Sister, Community member, and loved one to him and praise him for whatever he has in store for tomorrow.

AUGUST 31

Today is the last Harborside Tea of the summer season, and as always, when this day arrives, I feel a certain sadness about there being no more until the Christmas Season.

You would think that after more than ten years, some of the charm and fascination of doing these Harborside Teas would wear off, but so far it has not. Each Friday afternoon during the summer, I feel that same sense of excitement and anticipation as 3:00 PM approaches. Each week when I step into Bethany dining room, the sight of the fresh flowers, embroidered linens, and delicate china blends together in a picture of loveliness that simply takes my breath away.

No two tables are alike. Each is uniquely different from the other in size, shape, linens, china, silver, flowers, and place cards; yet all are in harmony with each of the others. The room is filled with heirlooms. The silver service on the sideboard belonged to Mother Cay when Bethany was still her home; it had been her grandmother's. Indeed, there is a story behind each set of china and silver.

An elderly lady donated one of the loveliest sets; it was a floral pattern of French Haviland and had been her mother's wedding gift china. This former professional cellist had to move into a retirement home, but because she treasured this china she wanted to provide it with a home where it could be appreciated, used, and enjoyed by many. She could think of no place where she would be happier to have it than Bethany. Now she is a fast friend of the Sisters, especially those who also play the cello, and we sometimes invite her and her musician friends for tea at off-season times—a convenient excuse to use the china set and to keep in touch with her during the winter months.

Some of the tables in the dining room were inherited by different Sisters and given to be used in Bethany. This is also true of much of the silver.

Many of the cloths are old family treasures, most of which when given to us were yellowed and stained with age. Hours of patient, tedious work have restored them to their present beauty. Each is carefully laundered and ironed by hand. Some are less antique than others, but each has an interesting history.

There is a lovely one of lace we picked out when we were in Venice and went to see the lacemakers on the island of Burano. Another beautifully embroidered cut-work cloth we brought back from Czechoslovakia.

Now as I make my way around the room, pinning a corsage on each guest, I see a lady at the Limoges table fingering with obvious pleasure her place card with its hand-drawn calligraphy. When I hear her say, "I don't know anything quite like this anywhere else," I find myself agreeing with her. When her friend adds, "We've just come from a flower show and nothing there equals the beauty of what I see here," I don't even feel flattered. I simply believe her, because each Friday, I too am amazed at the fresh new beauty of the flower arrangements, always different each week, and always having a kind of "anointing" about them.

At the Rose Chintz table in the center of the room, I find a happy family from Connecticut celebrating a ten-year-old girl's birthday. She tells me with great enthusiasm how she dried and saved her corsage from last year, and that the one thing she wanted more than anything else for her birthday was to come again to a Harborside Tea at Bethany.

Mr. Whitecomb, a widowed violinist, smiles at me from the Thistle table by the fireplace, where he sits every week so he can best hear the chamber ensemble. I think back over the painful year following the loss of his wife, and I thank God for the tender way in which he touched this lonely man. As a result of several visits by some of the Sisters, he came to tea and was able to enjoy the kind of music he loved and shared with his wife. Now we see him regularly, and he considers us his adopted family.

A waitress passes me with a tea plate; today's sandwiches include a ribbon—one of ham, Swiss cheese, and cucumber on multigrain bread with Dijonnaise™ and accented with a sprig of fresh oregano; a round, open-faced crabmeat salad with a twist of lemon zest; and a miniature orange-cranberry muffin filled with smoked turkey, fresh cranberry relish, and alfalfa sprouts. There's a bright cherry tomato and fresh parsley garnish on the plate and an individual fresh fruit meringue filled with whipped cream, strawberries, and nectarine and kiwi slices centered with a bit of mint—beautiful and full of color.

Laughter out on the patio tells me that the annual busload from a nearby

retirement home has arrived. For these elderly folks, the Harborside Teas have become a favorite event. They eagerly look forward to them and never can fully express their joy and delight at being able to attend.

In the corner of the sun parlor I come upon a pair of young honeymooners from Los Angeles, who have just stumbled upon us while exploring the harbor. They cannot believe they have discovered something so unexpectedly delightful, and they are full of questions as to what type of place this is. They sum up their feelings by saying that sitting in atmosphere like this, experiencing what they feel here, is more than enough, even without food and drink.

I think of these many different types of people who have come: the interior decorator from California, so intrigued with the needlepoint chairs and wanting to be put on our mailing list; the group of nurses having a reunion and making plans to return again for the Christmas Tea and English Carol Concert; the sophisticated lady from Ohio, smiling at me through tears and saying, "Each time I come here I never want to leave." I ask myself, "What makes these people feel this way?"

I think the answer may be, at least in part, that the amount of time, effort, and special attention that goes into the preparations—whether of the table settings, the food, the corsages and flower arrangements, the hand-painted place cards, or the music—gives people an extraordinary sense of being cared for. As one lady expressed, "I simply have no words for all of this." It's obvious that those who prepare the teas have a love for them.

Each of our special events has its own special appeal to me. But it's no secret which of them is my favorite. These teas are to me like an exquisite little gem scintillating with rare beauty and loveliness, capturing and preserving some of the charm and excellence of the past. One does not often come across such gems in this modern age.

Regardless of the event, whether it be one of elegance and delicacy such as a tea, or a casual, rather rough-and-tumble barbecue, we always emphasize preparing and serving it with care and attention to detail, along with consideration for the individual being served.

154

SOME FAVORITE TEA FOODS

STUFFED CHERRY TOMATOES

12 large cherry tomatoes

Bacon–cheese filling:

1 cup white cheddar cheese
7 slices crisp bacon, finely chopped

2½ tablespoons finely chopped green pepper
3 tablespoons mayonnaise
Small basil leaves

Chicken salad filling:

1 cup chicken, finely diced
¼ cup celery, finely diced
¼ cup mayonnaise

Onion salt
Paprika
Parsley

Yield: Makes 12 servings

Wash cherry tomatoes. Take stems off and turn upside down (they stand up better). Cut a cross on the top of each tomato.

Mix together ingredients for either the bacon-cheese filling or the chicken salad filling. Using a teaspoon, carefully fill each tomato, trying to keep the outside of the tomato from getting messy. Wipe off fingers before handling the next one. Garnish with small basil leaf for bacon-cheese-filled tomato, or with paprika and parsley for chicken salad-filled tomato.

Chicken salad filling is also nice served in a miniature cream puff shell or as a tea sandwich, using white and whole-wheat bread. Make a sandwich with one side of each kind of bread, spread with mayonnaise, and cut off crusts. Cut sandwich in four dainty squares, or cut into triangles and serve standing on edge.

SLICED SMOKED TURKEY IN ORANGE MUFFINS

1 cup sugar
½ cup (1 stick) butter
2 eggs
1 teaspoon baking soda
2 cups flour
½ teaspoon salt
1 cup buttermilk

1 cup raisins
Zest and juice of 1 orange
¼ pound smoked turkey breast, thinly sliced
⅜ cup Cranberry-Orange Relish (see recipe p. 155)
Alfalfa sprouts

Yield: Makes 6 to 8 servings

Orange Muffins: Preheat oven to 400°F; grease small muffin tins.

With an electric mixer, cream the sugar and butter until smooth. Add eggs and beat until fluffy. Add baking soda to buttermilk. Sift flour and salt together, and add to the sugar-butter mixture alternately with the buttermilk. Stir until well mixed.

In a food processor, grind the raisins and orange zest. Add to the batter and combine. Spoon the batter into the prepared muffin tins and bake until golden brown and firm to the touch, about 12 minutes. Remove the tins to a baking rack and set close together. Brush the tops of the muffins with the orange juice while still warm. After 5 minutes, turn out from the pans. Cool completely, cut 1 to 2 muffins per person in half crosswise. Freeze the extra for use another time. Spread mayonnaise on bottom half of each muffin. (This recipe makes 30 muffins.)

Turkey: Cut turkey into small pieces and put small amount on bottom half of each muffin. Top turkey with ½ teaspoon of Cranberry-Orange relish and alfalfa sprouts, cover with muffin top, and serve.

CRANBERRY–ORANGE RELISH

2 cups cranberries   1 cup sugar
½ orange

Grind cranberries. Remove seeds from the orange and grind. (You may prefer to use only the yellow portion of the orange skin, as the white is often bitter.) Stir ground orange into cranberries, and add sugar. Place ingredients in covered jars in refrigerator. Let ripen for 2 days before using.

HOT CRABMEAT BUNDLES

11 ounces cream cheese
1 (6½-ounce) can crabmeat
3 to 4 tablespoons finely
    chopped onion
½ to 1 teaspoon fresh
    lemon juice

3 tablespoons sherry
6 frozen phyllo pastry
    sheets, thawed
¼ cup margarine or butter,
    melted
Dried dill weed

Yield: Makes 40 appetizers

Preheat oven to 350°F. Soften cream cheese. Mix in crabmeat, onion, lemon juice, and sherry; cook 1 to 2 minutes or until heated though. Unroll phyllo sheets; cover with plastic wrap or towel. Place one sheet on work area; brush with margarine. Layer with 2 more sheets, brushing each layer with margarine. With a sharp knife, cut through all layers of phyllo to make 20 rectangles.

Place a heaping teaspoonful of the crab mixture in the center of each rectangle. Bring up edges of the pastry; twist together with a circular motion. Place on ungreased cookie sheets. Repeat with the remaining 3 phyllo sheets and the remaining filling. Sprinkle bundles with dill weed. Bake for 18 to 20 minutes or until a golden brown.

INDIVIDUAL PAVLOVAS

Meringues:
4 egg whites   1 cup sugar
½ teaspoon cream of tartar

Custard filling:
¼ cup sugar   1 cup milk
1 tablespoon cornstarch   Vanilla extract
1 egg yolk, beaten   Butter

Whipped cream   Assorted fresh fruits,
Fresh mint sprigs for garnish   such as strawberries, kiwi,
                                 and nectarine slices

Yield: Makes 6 servings

Meringues: Preheat oven to 275°F. Line a cookie sheet with parchment paper. In a large bowl, beat egg whites and cream of tartar at medium speed until soft peaks form. Add sugar, 2 tablespoons at a time, beating at high speed until stiff and glossy peaks form and sugar is dissolved. Spoon meringue onto parchment-lined cookie sheet. Shape into 6 indented rounds, 3 inches in diameter. Bake for 35 minutes. For softer meringues, remove the pan from the oven immediately. Cool on a wire rack. For dry, crisp meringues, turn oven off and leave the meringues in the oven with the door closed for 2 to 10 hours. Carefully remove meringues from the parchment; place on serving plates.

Custard filling: Combine sugar, cornstarch, egg yolk, and milk in a medium saucepan. Bring to a boil, stirring constantly. Cool. Add small amount vanilla extract and a little butter.

Pavlovas: Fill center of meringues with custard and frost with whipped cream. Decorate with assorted fresh fruits such as strawberries, kiwis, and nectarine slices; add fresh mint sprigs for garnish.

BRANDY SNAPS

½ cup margarine or butter
½ cup dark corn syrup
⅓ cup packed brown sugar
2 teaspoons + 1 tablespoon
  brandy
¾ cup flour

½ teaspoon ground
  ginger
1 to 2 cups whipping
  cream, chilled
2 tablespoons
  confectioners' sugar

Yield: Makes approximately 30 cookies

Preheat the oven to 350°F. Heat margarine, corn syrup, and brown sugar to boiling in a 1½-quart saucepan, stirring frequently. Remove from heat. Stir in the 2 teaspoons brandy. Mix flour and ginger together and gradually stir into the syrup mixture.

Drop the dough by teaspoonfuls about 5 inches apart onto lightly greased cookie sheets. Bake until cookies have spread into 3-inch to 4-inch rounds and are golden brown, 6 to 8 minutes.

Cool the cookies 1 to 3 minutes before removing from cookie sheets. Working quickly, roll each cookie on the greased handle of a wooden spoon, slip from spoon, and place on wire racks. If cookies become too crisp to roll, return to oven to soften, about 1 minute.

Beat whipping cream and confectioners' sugar in a chilled bowl until stiff. Fold in the remaining 1 tablespoon of brandy. Using a decorators' tube with a plain tip, pipe whipped cream into each end of the cookies.

Unfilled cookies should be stored in an airtight container.

LEMON CURD TART WITH FRESH RASPBERRIES

Phyllo squares:
  6 fresh phyllo pastry sheets
    or frozen, thawed

6 teaspoons sugar or more
2 tablespoons butter, melted

Lemon curd:
  3 cups sugar
  3 eggs

Juice of 3 lemons
5 tablespoons butter

Lemon cream:
  ½ cup chilled whipping
    cream
  1½ teaspoons confectioners'
    sugar or more

½ teaspoon vanilla extract
¼ cup lemon curd

  2 half-pint baskets fresh raspberries
    or 2 cups frozen unsweetened,
    thawed, drained
  Whipped cream for garnish

Yield: Makes 6 servings

Phyllo squares: Preheat oven to 375°F. Lightly oil 2 large baking sheets. Stack phyllo sheets on a work surface. Trim the sheets to 10½-inch squares (reserve scraps for another use). Place 1 phyllo square on the work surface (cover remaining phyllo with plastic wrap and damp kitchen towel). Sprinkle with 1 teaspoon of the sugar. Top with second phyllo square. Brush lightly with melted butter. Sprinkle with another teaspoon sugar. Top with third phyllo square. Sprinkle with a teaspoon sugar. Cut phyllo stack into 9 equal stacked squares. Arrange stacked phyllo sheets on a prepared baking sheet. Repeat layering and cutting with remaining 3 phyllo sheets, sugar, and butter, making a total of 18 stacked phyllo squares. Bake until phyllo is golden, about 10 minutes. Transfer baking sheets to racks and cool completely.

Lemon curd: Place sugar in mixing bowl and add eggs, one at a time, beating well after each addition. Stir in lemon juice; pour the mixture into the top pan of a double boiler set over simmering water. Add the butter, 1 tablespoon at a time, stirring constantly until butter melts. When mixture is thick enough to coat a metal spoon, remove from heat and cool completely before using. (Keeps in refrigerator for several weeks.)

Lemon cream: Beat cream, 1½ teaspoons of the confectioners' sugar, and vanilla extract in a large bowl until medium peaks form. Whisk lemon curd in another medium bowl until smooth; add to cream mixture. Beat to stiff peaks.

Spread 1 generous tablespoon lemon cream on each phyllo square. Top each with 6 raspberries and layer 3 stacks, one on the other. Top each with 1 phyllo square. Sift confectioners' sugar over desserts. (Can be prepared up to 8 hours ahead. Cover loosely and refrigerate). Garnish with fresh berries and a dollop of whipped cream.

FRESH STRAWBERRY PRESERVES

1¾ cups fresh strawberries, crushed	½ of a 6-ounce bottle liquid fruit pectin
4 cups sugar	2 tablespoons lemon juice

Yield: Makes 4 half-pints

In a bowl combine berries with sugar. Let stand 10 minutes.

Combine pectin and lemon juice. Add to berry mixture; stir for 3 minutes.

Ladle at once into jars or freezer containers, leaving ½-inch headspace. Seal; label. Let stand at room temperature about 2 hours or until jam is set. Store up to 3 weeks in refrigerator or 1 year in freezer.

CODDLED CREAM AND BISCUITS

Biscuits:

4 cups flour	⅔ cup vegetable shortening
1 teaspoon salt	2 eggs, well beaten
8 teaspoons baking powder	1¼ cups milk
2 tablespoons sugar	

Coddled Cream:

1 quart cream	12 ounces cream cheese

Fresh Strawberry Preserves (see previous recipe)

Yield: Makes 50 servings

Biscuits: Preheat oven to 425°F. Sift together flour, salt, baking powder, and sugar; cut in the shortening until the mixture resembles coarse crumbs. Add eggs and milk, mixing just until moistened. Turn out on a lightly floured surface. Pat the dough 1 inch thick and, with a floured biscuit cutter, make rounds the size of a silver dollar. Bake for about 20 minutes or until light brown. (Can be stored in freezer and then warmed before serving.) Split and serve each biscuit with generous spreading of preserves and a dollop of coddled cream.

Coddled Cream: Whip the cream and stir in the softened cream cheese. Mix well.

HONEY-PEACH TARTS

Crust:

1¼ cups flour
⅔ cup confectioners' sugar
½ teaspoon salt
10 tablespoons (1¼ sticks)
   butter, chilled, cut into pieces

2 large egg yolks
1 tablespoon cold water

Filling:

2 + 1 tablespoons sugar
2 tablespoons flour
2 tablespoons honey
2 tablespoons (¼ stick) butter,
   melted, cooled

1¼ pounds fresh ripe
   peaches (about 5 medium)
   halved, pitted, thinly sliced

Yield: Makes 8 servings

Crust: Preheat oven to 400°F. Mix the flour, sugar, and salt in a processor. Add butter; process until the mixture resembles coarse meal. Mix egg yolks and the water in a small bowl. Add to flour mixture and process until moist clumps form. Turn out onto a floured work surface. Gather the dough into a ball. Roll out the tart crust to 13-inch round. Slide a 10-inch diameter springform pan under the dough.

Filling: Mix 2 tablespoons sugar and the flour in a small bowl. Sprinkle over the tart crust leaving a 2-inch border. Arrange the sliced peaches in concentric circles atop the sugar mixture in the crust, leaving a 2-inch border. Drizzle peaches with honey. Gently fold pastry edges up around peaches. Brush edges of crust with melted butter. Sprinkle crust and peaches with the remaining 1 tablespoon sugar.

Leaving the tart on pan bottom, place on a heavy large baking sheet with a rim. Bake tart until crust is golden and peaches are tender, about 35 minutes. Transfer baking sheet to a rack. Using a pastry brush, brush any juices from center of the tart over the peaches and the crust. Cool for about 20 minutes. Transfer to a platter; cut into wedges.

SEPTEMBER 5

I was out on the tidal flats this morning taking in the changes of the season. The beach grass is now of varying shades of gold and bronze, reflecting the light of the morning sun. Stronger, increased winds have blown in clumps of seaweed and driven deep ridges into the sand, exaggerating its gentle pattern of the summer months.

Most of the friendly little creatures, so present in warmer days, are now absent or have gone somewhere below. Except for one large raucous conference of gulls, and a lone one meditating here and there, the scene is almost desolate. Not in a sad or forlorn way, just noticeably minus the summer populace.

Mother Cay used to say she could tell without looking at a calendar when it was the day after Labor Day because of a certain peace that comes over Cape Cod at that point once the visitors and tourists have evacuated. Likewise, the flats reflect this peace. No squealing children trying to catch wiggling little fish or poking at horseshoe crabs. No sun bathers. Just one quiet, retired, resident couple steadily digging quahogs (hardshell clams). They said it was slim pickings today, but they had gathered a half bucket in twenty minutes, and that sounded pretty good to me. I've been threatening not to have our shellfish licenses renewed next year if Sister Sue doesn't get some Sisters out digging soon. It has been too long since we've had a good quahog chowder.

SEPTEMBER 10

*Yesterday on my flat walk, I picked up a clam, brought it home,
and gave it to Sue as a reminder that there are others out
there just waiting to be found.*

Today I found the little steamer clam I had given her yesterday on the counter in the kitchen. I assumed she wasn't interested in him, so while I was preparing Zion's dinner I dropped him into a little pot and steamed him open. Oh, what flavor—nothing like it! But that little one only whetted my appetite for more.

Later Sue was looking all around the kitchen for her little steamer. Had I seen him anywhere? Well, as a matter of fact, I had, and I'd eaten him as well. "So sorry, but I can tell you where you can find lots more."

SEPTEMBER 14

As I crunched my granola at breakfast this morning, the very texture of it made me happy for some reason. I love the variety of it, and how basic it seems, how healthful. Such a simple thing, really, but complex at the same time.

Over the years we have tried many different combinations of ingredients to make a granola that would be wholesome and cost less than the granola we could buy. We have now come up with a recipe that satisfies us. Not only do we all like it, but so does most everyone else who tastes it. It combines oats, sunflower seeds, raisins, cinnamon, nutmeg, a little oil, and corn syrup.

Sisters love it for breakfast with yogurt or milk, or for a midday or bedtime snack, as do many of our Bethany guests. We give it to our families and relatives for gifts, take it as a "thank you" when we visit friends' homes, add it to our harvest baskets that we prepare each fall, and sell lots of it at our annual Christmas Fair. There is always a "good market" for Sisters' Granola, and keeping enough of it on hand is quite a trick.

We roast it on large, flat baking sheets, and after cooling it, store it in big, empty see-through pretzel barrels. Seeing a good supply of it on the storeroom shelves gives every Sister a nice feeling of security.

SISTERS' GRANOLA

5 cups old-fashioned oats	5 tablespoons + 1 teaspoon
1 cup sunflower seeds	melted margarine
½ cup brown sugar,	⅔ cup corn syrup
packed	2 teaspoons vanilla extract
2 teaspoons ground cinnamon	½ cup raisins
1 teaspoon ground nutmeg	

Yield: Makes one 34-ounce batch

Preheat oven to 275°F. Combine all ingredients except the raisins. Break up the brown sugar so there are no clumps, and mix well so that oats are evenly coated. Spread granola onto a baking sheet. Bake for 45 minutes or longer, stirring occasionally. Test granola for doneness by taking a sample piece and letting it cool; it should be golden and crispy. Immediately stir granola when it first comes out of the oven; otherwise it will be difficult to break up once cooled. When granola has cooled, add raisins and store in an airtight container.

SEPTEMBER 20

Today's mail brought me an alumni letter from my alma mater, Valley Forge Christian College (VFCC), where I received my training when I was seriously considering becoming a missionary.

Last year at VFCC

I have two very strong remembrances of VFCC. One was the deep spiritual influence it had on my life, and the other was the old-fashioned, hot apple dumplings that were always served for special occasions. It was my first introduction to this flaky-crusted, syrupy, spice-filled wonder, and it was love at first bite!

As a result I came up with my own recipe for them, one which I have repeatedly used over the years, especially for men's retreats.

OLD FASHIONED APPLE DUMPLINGS

Syrup:

1 cup sugar	⅛ teaspoon ground allspice
¼ teaspoon ground cinnamon	1¾ cups water
¼ teaspoon ground nutmeg	2 tablespoons butter

Pastry:

2¼ cups flour	6 to 8 tablespoons water
¼ teaspoon salt	6 small apples
⅔ cup shortening	Ice cream, optional

Topping:

¼ cup sugar	¼ teaspoon ground nutmeg
¼ teaspoon ground cinnamon	⅛ teaspoon ground allspice

Yield: Makes 6 servings

Syrup: In a heavy medium saucepan, mix sugar, cinnamon, nutmeg, allspice, and water. Bring to boiling; reduce heat. Simmer for 5 minutes. Remove from heat; stir in the butter.

Pastry: In a mixing bowl, combine flour and salt. Cut in shortening until coarse crumbs form. Add water, a little at a time, mixing until moistened. Form into a ball. Roll into an 18 x 12-inch rectangle; cut into six 6-inch squares.

Peel and core apples; place one on each pastry square.

Topping: Combine sugar, cinnamon, nutmeg, and allspice.

Sprinkle topping over fruit. Moisten edges of pastry; fold corners to center atop fruit. Pinch to seal. Place in an 11 x 7 x 1½-inch baking pan. Pour syrup over. Bake in a 375°F oven about 45 minutes or until fruit is tender and pastry is brown. Serve with ice cream, if desired.

SEPTEMBER 25

I just sent a fax to four of our novices who are part of a group of twenty-five Community young people making a three-week spiritual pilgrimage through Spain, France, and Italy. Today they are in France, and it just occurs to me that since our novices are responsible for Sunday night Convent dinners, we can be sure to expect some French cuisine in the near future.

We have a really neat class of novices, six young women all with differing personalities, each exceptionally gifted in her own way. It is such a joy to me to see these young women, every one of whom could easily be successful in any number of walks of life, seriously considering committing themselves to the life of a Sister. Honestly wrestling with the issues at stake, counting the cost, they are forthright about their struggles with what they have to gain and what they will lose. I feel privileged to be included in their lives on such a personal level, and I have a special love for each of them.

Sometimes we get together as a group just to talk about whatever is most on their hearts at the time, how they're getting along with each other in living together, and what problems they face. They examine where they feel they've succeeded or failed of late. When I can, I like to make a dessert to eat with them. My meetings with them are special times to me. Somehow, I always come away feeling nourished, with or without a dessert.

WHIPPED CREAM ROLLS

1 cup flour	2 tablespoons butter
1 teaspoon baking powder	1 teaspoon vanilla extract
2 eggs	Whipped cream,
1 cup sugar	sweetened
½ cup milk	Confectioners' sugar
	Fresh strawberries, sliced
	(optional)

Yield: Makes 9 servings

Sponge Cake: Combine flour and baking powder. In a bowl beat eggs with an electric mixer on high speed about 4 minutes or until thick. Gradually add sugar; beat at medium speed for 4 to 5 minutes or until light and fluffy. Add the flour mixture; beat at low to medium speed just until combined. In a saucepan heat and stir the milk and butter until butter melts; remove from heat and add vanilla extract. Add milk mixture to the batter, beating until combined. Pour into a greased, wax-papered jelly roll pan. Bake at 350°F for 15 minutes or until golden but not dry.

To assemble: Cool and cut into 4½-inch squares. Spread with sweetened whipped cream. Roll up and sprinkle with confectioners' sugar. Wrap tightly in waxed paper and refrigerate until serving. May be served with fresh, sliced strawberries and a dollop of whipped cream alongside.

APPLE TARTLETS

½ pkg. (17¼ ounce) frozen puff pastry (one 9¾ x 9¼-inch sheet), thawed	½ teaspoon ground cinnamon
	⅛ teaspoon ground nutmeg
2 to 3 small baking apples (such as Golden Delicious, Granny Smith, or Jonathan)	⅛ teaspoon ground allspice
	2 tablespoons butter, melted
4 tablespoons sugar	¼ cup apple jelly

Yield: Makes 6 servings

On a lightly floured surface, roll the pastry to a 13½ x 10-inch rectangle. With a sharp knife, cut dough into 6 (5 x 4½-inch) rectangles. Starting with one of the rectangles, cut a ½-inch square of pastry from each corner and discard (this makes folding the pastry easier). With a pastry brush or your finger, dampen each side of the rectangle with water. Fold each edge over, forming a ⅛- to ¼-inch border. Dampen border and fold again, forming a thicker border. Crimp the border lightly with the tines of a fork and seal the corners.

Place shaped pastry on a greased baking sheet. Repeat with remaining pastry rectangles, working quickly so dough doesn't dry out. Cover with plastic wrap and chill till needed—up to 2 hours.

Peel apples and halve lengthwise. Use a melon baller to scoop out cores. Thinly slice each apple half. In a small bowl, combine sugar and spices. Sprinkle half the sugar mixture on top of the dough rectangles. Overlap the apple slices on top. Brush the apples with butter. Sprinkle with remaining sugar mixture.

Adjust oven rack to the upper middle of oven. Bake the tartlets for 25 to 30 minutes at 375°F or till the pastry is golden and apples are fork tender. Transfer the baking sheet to a wire rack and cool.

Meanwhile, in a small saucepan, melt jelly, stirring occasionally. Brush the jelly on top of tarts. Serve at room temperature.

OCTOBER 10

Fall is really upon us. The bittersweet is bursting open, the leaves are turning. These sights take me back to Vermont, where I made some lasting friendships and some big decisions in my life.

The Flower Pot, a rustic little flower shop and greenhouse at the summit of the hill in Winooski, Vermont, was every bit as charming as the name it bore. A winding flagstone path, thickly bordered with vivid shades of portulaca, led from the split-rail fence along the road to the entrance of the shop. Out the front door one viewed the formal beauty of the campus of St. Michael's College, and out the back window of the workroom, the natural, brilliant panorama of the Vermont mountains, including a gorge and a waterfall. I already felt at home.

The side door opened and the owners, two sisters, French Canadian in background, entered. The one tiny in stature was Marion, rather timid and apologetic. She constantly deferred to her older sister, Vina, who, by contrast, was very large, aggressive, and self-assertive. Marion ran the shop, but there was no question that Vina was in charge. They both were unmarried and lived together in the large family house across the drive from the shop. The Flower Pot seemed almost like an annex, and a cozy one at that. I was sure I was going to like working here.

Vina had four obvious loves, which she pursued continually. She loved to eat, to cook, to feed people, and to complain. We made friends in no time. One of her most frequent complaints was that her recently developed heart condition kept her from spending time in the shop where she dearly longed to be. It did not, however, keep her from the kitchen, where she was daily cooking up something.

Ed was a kind-hearted, rather sad widower, still mourning the loss of his wife some years before. Dick, a thin, wiry, hyper, nineteen-year-old rock music enthusiast who wore a headset night and day, more than compensated for Ed's quietness. Both worked in the greenhouse and did the delivering and the heavy work around the shop. Marion and I arranged the flowers. We were an unusual combination, but we had good times together.

Most every afternoon around 4:00 PM, Vina would come out with a preview of the night's dinner or something sweet she had just baked. Her specialties included Coq au Vin, Pork Chow Mein, Spicy Apple Twists, and a great Grape-Nuts Bread, all of which I have emulated over the years.

I worked at the Flower Pot during the day and was involved in some church activity almost every night of the week and, of course, on Sunday. Quite a number of friends or members of the church were shut-ins, and I visited them regularly, often with Queenie Krekarian, another young woman from the church who became one of my best friends.

One fall, I improvised an autumn preserve that combined oranges, peaches, cranberries, and pineapple into a colorful jam. Decorated with a swish of talisman-colored ribbon and a few mums, a jar of this jam made a cheerful gift. Each of the shut-ins were thrilled to receive it in anticipation of the upcoming holiday season.

I chose this combination of fruits for their color, but I was so pleased with the taste that I continued to use the recipe long afterwards for many other occasions. A jar of it adds a bright sparkle to a harvest basket.

When I made my decision to go to Boston, Queenie put me in touch with her brother's family who lived in Chelsea, just outside of Boston. The Krekarians were a warm, friendly Armenian family who took me under their wing as if I were a blood relative. They were a tremendous help to me during this transition, and after I was settled in my new job and living quarters, I made frequent visits to their home on the weekends and spent my first Thanksgiving in Boston with them and all of their relatives.

Nick Krekarian always cooked the Sunday meal. As in the McGranagan family, Sunday dinner was always roast lamb, but unlike Mrs. McGranagan who turned the leftover lamb into shepherd's pie, Nick turned it into an Armenian stew. He took such obvious pleasure in preparing this dish, that I found it entertaining to watch him. First he would slice onions and sauté them in olive oil. Then he would chop fresh tomatoes and add them, along with fresh green beans, to the onions, stirring them with care. Finally he would put in the leftover lamb and a few seasonings, cover the pot, and leave everything to slowly simmer on low heat for most of the afternoon. He would check it periodically until the beans were soft and had absorbed most of the juice from the tomatoes, and the lamb had fallen off the bone.

We would always have this stew for the evening meal served with hot rice, and it would always remind me of something Papa might have cooked.

STUFFED SHOULDER OF LAMB WITH OREGANO ROAST POTATOES

1 small eggplant (about 1 pound)	1 shoulder of lamb, boned (about 4 pounds)
Salt and pepper	½ + ½ cup white wine
1 cup + 2 tablespoons + ¼ cup olive oil	Juice of 1 lemon (reserve rind)
1 onion, grated	8 small potatoes, peeled and parboiled
1 garlic clove, mashed	Oregano
¼ cup finely chopped fresh mint	½ cup bread crumbs
1 teaspoon chopped parsley	

Yield: Makes 4 servings

Peel eggplant and cut into thin slices. Season eggplant with salt and pepper, and lightly brown in 1 cup olive oil until almost, but not quite, tender; place on paper to drain.

In another skillet, lightly brown onion, garlic, mint, and parsley in 2 tablespoons olive oil. Lay out shoulder of lamb flat and spread the sautéed onion mixture over the inside of the meat. Season with salt and pepper and arrange the eggplant on top.

Roll and tie the lamb; place in a roasting pan; pour ½ cup wine over roast. Brown the rolled lamb in the oven preheated to 450°F for 15 minutes; then reduce heat to 300°F and roast for 1 hour 45 minutes for pink lamb; 2 hours 15 minutes for well done. Combine the remaining ¼ cup olive oil with lemon juice and baste lamb frequently with this mixture, using the lemon rind half pierced with a fork to baste.

One half hour before lamb is done, add potatoes to the roasting pan; sprinkle lightly with salt, pepper, and oregano; baste with pan juices; continue cooking.

When lamb is cooked, remove roast to a warm platter, and skim the fat from the pan juices. Add the remaining ½ cup wine. Season with salt and pepper to taste, and simmer sauce for several minutes. Cut the lamb roll in 1-inch-thick slices; place slices on platter surrounded with Oregano Roast Potatoes. Serve with pan gravy.

AUTUMN JAM

2 cups fresh or canned peaches
1 whole orange
1 cup fresh or canned pineapple chunks
1 cup gooseberries or cranberries (fresh or frozen)
1 1¾-ounce pkg. powdered fruit pectin
5½ cups sugar

Yield: Makes 7 half-pints

Cut the peaches and orange into bite-size pieces. In an 8- or 10-quart kettle combine fruits and pectin. Bring to a full rolling boil, stirring constantly. Stir in sugar.

Return to a full rolling boil. Boil hard for 1 minute, stirring constantly. Remove from heat; quickly skim off foam with a metal spoon. Ladle at once into hot, sterilized half-pint jars, leaving ¼-inch headspace. Adjust lids. Process in boiling-water canner for 5 minutes.

COQ AU VIN

2 to 2½ pounds meaty chicken pieces (breasts, thighs, and drumsticks)
2 tablespoons cooking oil
Onion salt and pepper
10 quartered onions
1¼ cups burgundy
1 cup whole fresh mushrooms
1 tablespoon snipped parsley
2 cloves garlic, minced
½ teaspoon dried marjoram, crushed
½ teaspoon dried thyme, crushed
1 bay leaf
2 tablespoons flour
2 tablespoons softened butter or margarine
2 slices bacon, crisp-cooked, drained and crumbled
Snipped parsley (optional)
2 cups hot cooked noodles

Yield: Makes 6 servings

Skin chicken, if desired. Rinse and pat dry. In a 12-inch skillet cook chicken pieces in hot oil 15 minutes or until lightly browned, turning to brown evenly. Sprinkle with onion salt and pepper. Add onions, burgundy, mushrooms, the 1 tablespoon parsley, garlic, marjoram, thyme, and bay leaf. Bring to boiling; reduce heat. Cover and simmer 35 to 40 minutes or until the chicken is tender and no longer pink.

Transfer chicken and vegetables to a serving platter. Cover and keep warm. Discard the bay leaf. In a bowl stir together the flour and softened butter to make a smooth paste. Stir into burgundy mixture in the skillet. Cook and stir 1 minute more.

Pour burgundy mixture over chicken and vegetables. Sprinkle with bacon and, if desired, additional parsley. Serve with hot noodles.

VINA'S LIMA BEANS WITH MUSTARD AND HONEY

4 cups dried lima beans	½ cup honey
2 onions	2 tablespoons cider
2 ribs celery	vinegar
1 cup salt pork or bacon,	1 tablespoon prepared
chopped	mustard
½ cup brown sugar	2 tablespoons onion salt

Yield: Makes 6 servings

Soak lima beans 8 to 12 hours in water to cover.

Chop onions and celery. Drain lima beans. Combine all ingredients with lima beans in a casserole, adding water to cover, and bake in a slow oven (250°F) for 2 hours or until beans are soft and have absorbed all the liquid. Add additional water as needed during cooking.

SPICY APPLE TWISTS

Crust:

1½ cups flour	½ cup butter
½ cup vegetable shortening	1 teaspoon salt

Filling:

1 teaspoon ground cinnamon	6 large apples (Cortland)
¼ teaspoon ground nutmeg	Butter
1 cup sugar	½ cup apple cider

Yield: Makes 24 twists

Make pie crust dough by working ingredients together lightly and then rolling out into thin strips 6 x ½ inches.

Mix the cinnamon, nutmeg, and sugar together in a medium bowl.

Cut apples into quarters, peel, and remove seeds. Dip each apple quarter into sugar mixture. Twist a ½-inch strip pie crust around each apple quarter, starting at one end and going to the other, leaving a slight opening between each twist so the apple slice is seen. Place twists in a 9 x 12-inch glass baking dish. Sprinkle remaining sugar mixture over all. Dot with butter. Bake at 350°F for 30 minutes or until crust is golden and apples are soft. Add apple cider to bottom of pan as needed, so that pan does not dry out, but twists end up in a light syrup.

GRAPE-NUTS® BREAD

1 cup Grape-Nuts®	1 egg, beaten
1 cup sour milk	1 teaspoon baking soda
1 cup sugar	2 teaspoons baking powder
	2 cups flour

Yield: Makes 1 loaf

Heat oven to 350°F. Mix together Grape-Nuts®, sour milk, and sugar. Let stand for ten minutes. Add the remaining ingredients and blend. Pour into a greased bread pan and bake for 45 minutes. Transfer to a wire rack to cool.

OCTOBER 15

They're picking the pumpkins today and piling them up into a huge pyramid on top of wooden flats. This sight always makes me so happy. I want to carve out a jack-o'-lantern, or fill a pumpkin with mums and colored leaves to put on the table. I want to gather bitter-sweet and Virginia creeper to twine around it with a few acorns. I want to cook up a savory harvest beef stew and serve it piping hot out of one of the big beauties hollowed out into a sturdy soup tureen.

The round, chubby shapes of pumpkins please me greatly and stir up autumn childhood memories, such as picking the last stalwart tomatoes stubbornly clinging to their vines and helping Mama cover others with burlap to protect them from the predicted frost. Such as baking gingery, spice-laden pumpkin pies and puddings, and moist pumpkin breads and muffins.

Yesterday, Sister Adele had Novice Tonya try out that new recipe for Pumpkin Gingerbread Squares with Caramel Sauce—so zippy and alive with flavor. No need for caramel sauce. It really hit the spot with a hot cup of tea. Pumpkins have a way of turning themselves into so many wonderful things. Pumpkins make me so happy!

PUMPKIN GINGERBREAD SQUARES WITH CARAMEL SAUCE

Gingerbread:

2¼ cups flour	¼ teaspoon salt
¼ cup sugar	¼ teaspoon ground cloves
¼ cup brown sugar	¾ cup buttermilk
⅔ cup butter	½ cup light molasses
1½ teaspoons ground ginger	½ cup cooked, mashed
1 teaspoon baking soda	pumpkin
½ teaspoon ground cinnamon	1 egg

Caramel sauce:

½ cup butter or margarine	½ cup whipping cream
1¼ cups firmly packed	Ice cream, optional
brown sugar	Chopped pecans, optional
2 tablespoons light corn syrup	

Yield: Makes 12 servings

Gingerbread: Preheat oven to 350°F. In a large bowl, combine flour and sugars. Using a pastry blender or fork, cut in butter until mixture resembles fine crumbs. Press 1¼ cups crumb mixture into bottom of an ungreased 9-inch square pan. To the remaining mixture, add ginger, baking soda, cinnamon, salt, cloves, buttermilk, molasses, pumpkin, and egg; mix well. Pour evenly over base. Bake at 350°F for 40 to 50 minutes or until toothpick inserted in center comes out clean.

Sauce: In a medium saucepan, melt butter; stir in brown sugar and corn syrup. Bring mixture to a boil; cook until sugar is dissolved, about 1 minute, stirring constantly. Stir in whipping cream; return to a boil. Remove pan from heat. Serve sauce over warm gingerbread topped with a scoop of ice cream (optional). Garnish with chopped pecans, if desired.

GOLDEN HARVEST MUFFINS

2 cups flour	1 cup carrots, shredded
2 cups whole wheat flour	1 cup shredded coconut
2 cups sugar	1 cup raisins
4 teaspoons baking soda	1 cup walnuts or pecans,
4 teaspoons ground cinnamon	chopped
1 teaspoon salt	1½ cups oil
½ teaspoon ground cloves	½ cup milk
4 cups (5 medium) apples,	4 teaspoons vanilla extract
peeled, shredded	3 eggs, beaten

Yield: Makes 36 muffins

Preheat to 350°F. Grease 36 muffin cups or line with muffin papers. In 4-quart bowl, combine flours, sugar, baking soda, cinnamon, salt, and cloves. Add apples, carrots, coconut, raisins, and walnuts; mix well. Add oil, milk, vanilla extract, and eggs; stir until just moistened. Fill lined or greased muffin cups ¾ full. Bake for 20 to 25 minutes, or until toothpick inserted in center comes out clean. Immediately remove from pans.

GINGERY APPLE BETTY

5 cups coarsely cubed bread
¼ pound + 2 tablespoons unsalted butter, melted
⅓ cup sugar
2 teaspoons ground cinnamon
¼ teaspoon ground nutmeg

2 teaspoons ground ginger
1½ pounds baking apples, such as Cortland, peeled, cored and thinly sliced
Whipped cream or vanilla ice cream as accompaniment

Yield: Makes 6 servings

Generously butter a 6-cup charlotte mold or soufflé dish.

Place the bread cubes in a large bowl and drizzle with melted butter while tossing with a fork to moisten.

In another large bowl, combine the sugar, cinnamon, nutmeg, and ginger. Add apple slices and toss to coat evenly.

Mix in 1½ cups of the bread cubes with apple mixture. Put mixture in mold. Top with remaining bread crumbs.

Preheat oven to 375°F. Bake until top is browned, about 50 to 55 minutes.

Let stand at room temperature 5 minutes; serve warm with cream or ice cream.

OCTOBER 21

This is such a wonderfully crisp, nippy fall day. Coming from morning communion across the common through the cold air into the warm Refectory to be greeted by a breakfast of hot, spicy, baked apples, stuffed with buttery bread cubes all golden and crusty, their syrup juice spooned over them—I just know this is going to be a great day. Elijah agrees with me, making his loud noises as he heads for the door, eager to get out into the fresh fall air.

I don't know of any other aroma that can arouse such warm, comforting, homespun feelings more than a baked apple dessert, be it a pie, dumplings, a crisp, a cobbler, or just plain old baked apples lazily bubbling away in their own spiced syrupy sweetness—unless, of course, it might be the smell of old-fashioned homemade chili sauce like the one Mrs. Nicol, our next-door neighbor, used to make. Everyone on the whole block knew when. One by one each of her five children would appear with a slice of soft, white Wonder Bread spread with butter and the thick, warm, freshly made sauce, and I, watching from our kitchen window, would have given almost anything for one of those mouth-watering, open-faced treats. I think I'll tell the kitchen Sisters to be sure to make a batch or two of chili sauce when they have time before all the garden tomatoes are used up.

Ever since the first apple picking, the kitchen Sisters have been itching to make cider. So today they, along with some of the Brothers, are finally doing it. They have the cider press set up at the barbecue pit with buckets of apples surrounding it. A fire is burning under one of the grills. Hot chocolate is simmering in the big black cast-iron pot, and Sunshine is hovering around, begging. Next to carrots, apples are one of her most favorite legal snacks. She is reveling in this activity, wagging her tail and squinting her eyes in her most endearing manner.

While I am there, Brother Ben empties out the press from the first run, and the crushed apples, all matted together, form a striking mosaic of gorgeous, var-

ied colors and hues. I want to gather them up and preserve them in some way for something else, but Sister Evelyn says that she and some other Sisters have promised the apples to Duchess for an afternoon snack. These same five Sisters take turns milking her every morning, so they are becoming quite attuned to her appetites and cravings and see to it that they are met. She has been giving us so much good rich milk, we want to keep her contented. Already we have a dozen or more Gouda cheeses curing for Christmas gifts, thanks to our dear Duchess.

Yesterday's clear, crisp fall day was great, but today's raw, wet, blustery one is equally as enjoyable to me because it gives me a certain zest. Wet falling leaves, blown from the trees, stick all over me, wind and rain are on my face, my nose and fingers are numb with the cold. I love it! But now I'm ready to go in and soak up a little warmth.

Pushing the door open, I am met with the comforting smell of ginger and molasses. Someone is baking spicy cookies, and someone has lit a fire in the fireplace. I strip off my wet rain gear and go to make a cup of hot tea. Someone, sensing the yearning of my heart, hands me a warm, sugar-sprinkled, plump, but crunchy Ginger Molasses Cookie. I sit down on the hearth and savor every bite and sip of this scrumptious treat which I have had the good fortune to come upon. A bit of heaven on earth.

GINGER–MOLASSES COOKIES

1 cup sugar
¾ cup shortening
1 egg, beaten
4 tablespoons molasses
½ teaspoon ground ginger

½ teaspoon ground cloves
1 teaspoon ground cinnamon
½ teaspoon salt
2 teaspoons baking soda
2 cups flour
Sugar for rolling

Yield: Makes 23 large cookies

Combine ingredients and form into 1-inch balls; roll in sugar and place on greased cookie sheet. Bake in 325° to 350°F oven for 10 minutes.

APPLE–CRANBERRY CRISP WITH VARIATIONS

Topping:
1 cup packed brown sugar
⅛ cup rolled oats
⅛ cup flour
6 teaspoons ground cinnamon

2 teaspoons ground nutmeg
1 cup (2 sticks) chilled butter, cut into pieces
1 cup coarsely chopped pecan halves

Filling:
5 pounds large Granny Smith apples, peeled, cored, cut into ⅓-inch-thick wedges
2 cups fresh or frozen, thawed, cranberries or blackberries
⅛ cup sugar

4 tablespoons fresh lemon juice
½ teaspoon grated lemon peel
1 teaspoon ground cardamom
½ teaspoon ground nutmeg
1 teaspoon ground cinnamon

Yield: Makes 8 servings

Topping: Mix brown sugar, oats, flour, cinnamon, nutmeg, and nuts in bowl. Add butter and rub in with fingertips until mixture begins to clump together. (Can be made 1 day ahead; chill.)

Filling: Preheat oven to 375°F. Butter 10-inch-diameter glass dish. Place apples in large bowl. Mix in cranberries, sugar, lemon juice, lemon peel, cardamom, nutmeg, and cinnamon. Transfer to prepared dish, mounding slightly in center. Sprinkle topping over apples. Bake until apples are tender, about 45 minutes. Cool on rack until lukewarm, about 20 minutes. Serve with Apple Custard Sauce (recipe follows).

APPLE CUSTARD SAUCE

6 large egg yolks
⅓ cup sugar
1½ cups milk

3 tablespoons frozen apple juice concentrate, thawed
½ teaspoon vanilla extract

Yield: Makes about 2 cups

Whisk yolks and sugar in medium bowl to blend. Bring milk to simmer in medium saucepan. Gradually whisk milk into yolk mixture. Return mixture to saucepan. Stir over medium-low heat until custard thickens and leaves path on back of spoon when finger is drawn across, about 5 minutes (do not boil). Strain into bowl. Whisk in apple juice concentrate and vanilla extract. Chill until cold, about 3 hours. (Can be made 24 hours ahead. Cover and keep chilled.)

OCTOBER 29

Yesterday, when I sat down at my computer, I found a little basket containing a tin of carmelitas, a copy of Mother Teresa's latest book, and a card with a note of encouragement from one of the Brothers, ending with a P.S. that said, "Go easy on me, this is my first attempt at carmelitas." I was touched and cheered. I opened the tin, bit into a carmelita, and thumbed through the book. I could hardly believe that my eyes fell on these particular words: "It is very compelling that before Jesus explained God's words, before he explained the beatitudes to the crowd, he fed them. Only after they were fed did he start to teach them."

Sister Lynn enjoys telling this story about carmelitas: After graduation from high school, she was uncertain about what she was supposed to do, but concerned that she make some progress in her spiritual life, so she decided to spend a period of time living with the Sisters. This is something young girls just out of high school often do until they feel they have a definite direction about their future.

During this time she stayed in a small, one-room cottage called "The Little House" and worked with the Sisters during the day. Because there were no novices or postulants at that time she spent her mealtimes and evenings alone. Having grown up in a large family, she was used to being surrounded by people all the time, and she found these times alone very difficult. One night after a particularly hard day, in which she felt she had done everything wrong, she felt so lonely that all she could do was cry.

Turning to me, she continues the story: "Suddenly there was a knock on the door, and you walked in holding a plate of warm, fresh-baked carmelitas. 'These are for you,' you said with a half smile that reminded me of my grandmother. Then you were gone. I burst into tears, crying even harder than before, but no longer were they tears of loneliness. I knew I was loved."

NOVEMBER 1

Saturday was groundbreaking day for our new church building, and the weather forecast went from 90 percent chance of rain on Friday afternoon to 100 percent by Friday evening. Saturday morning, after communion, the ladies gathered in the Retreat Kitchen to work on food preparations for the afternoon teas and evening dinner. Ham, Swiss cheese, and chutney sandwiches were at one end of the kitchen, cucumber sandwiches were at another, and egg salad was on the table. Out back, the Fall Fruit Stuffing for the pork roast was in process.

"Sister Irene, would you please pray?" Sister Rose said, turning to me. "It's a little bit confusing here right now."

"Sure," I replied, heading back to the cucumbers until I realized that everyone was gathering around me and that she had meant "out loud." After an initial moment of feeling tongue-tied, I opened my mouth and asked God's blessing on the work at hand, the service, and the entire day, and I was just about to say "amen" when a Sister behind me whispered, "The weather."

"Oh yes, Lord," I added, "the weather, that's your business. Make it what you want it to be. Amen."

At 3:00 PM it was raining. The service was held in the Chapel. Then we all processed out to the site, where the presenters each dug up a shovel full of soil—or should I say mud?—in the rain. From there we went to several locations for tea. Within minutes after we left the site, the wind picked up and torrents of driving rain came beating down for the remainder of the afternoon and evening.

Why had I not prayed for clear skies? It was not that I had anything against sunshine or didn't believe God could give it. It just didn't seem the right thing for me to ask. Some rain or adversity almost seemed fitting for this occasion. Mother Cay, with her old Yankee spirit, used to say that it wouldn't be good for us if life were always too easy, that real satisfaction comes only from accomplishing difficult tasks.

As I mingled with the visiting oblates in the Friary—dry, warm, cozy, and enjoying my tea and sandwiches—we talked about everything that had just preceded and what a very moving experience it had been. "I just felt so blessed," Lucy said. Standing there with the others looking out the window at the relentless sheets of rain now coming down on the site, I couldn't help thinking how good we had had it just a few minutes ago. I agreed with Lucy. I too felt blessed. As one elderly lady used to say, "Just too blessed to complain."

CREAM OF BUTTERNUT SQUASH SOUP

5 pounds butternut squash, peeled and diced
1 quart + 1 cup chicken broth
1 pint heavy cream
3 cups light cream
1 ounce chicken bouillon

¾ cup maple syrup
½ teaspoon ground white pepper
Ground cinnamon and/or
Ground allspice and/or
Ground ginger

Yield: Makes 15 one-cup servings

Boil squash in chicken broth until tender. Purée and return to medium heat. Add heavy cream, light cream, bouillon, syrup, and white pepper. Heat slowly; do not boil. Stir frequently until slightly thick. Add cinnamon, and/or allspice, and/or ginger if desired for additional flavor.

ROAST PORK WITH FALL FRUIT STUFFING

Fall Fruit Stuffing:

- ¾ cup + 3 cups (or more) chicken stock
- ½ cup dried prunes
- ⅓ cup dried apricots, diced into ¼-inch cubes
- 2 tablespoons dried currants

- 2 + 1 tablespoons butter
- ½ cup chopped shallots
- ½ cup fresh bread crumbs
- ¾ teaspoon dried thyme
- ¾ teaspoon dried rubbed sage

Pork:

- 4 pork tenderloins (about 14 oz. each), fat trimmed
- Salt and pepper
- 1 tablespoon vegetable oil
- 1 cup dry white wine
- ½ cup apricot fruit spread or apricot preserves

- 2 tablespoons cornstarch dissolved in 2 tablespoons water
- Fresh thyme and sage sprigs

Yield: Makes 10 servings

Fall Fruit Stuffing: Bring ¾ cup stock to boil in a heavy medium saucepan. Add the fruits. Remove pan from heat and let stand for 20 minutes. Strain fruit mixture through a sieve set over a bowl, pressing down on the fruit with the back of a spoon to extract as much liquid as possible. Transfer the fruit to a bowl and reserve the liquid.

Melt 2 tablespoons butter in a heavy large skillet over medium heat. Add shallots and sauté for 3 minutes. Add bread crumbs, thyme, and sage, and sauté for 1 minute. Add to the fruit mixture.

Pork: Place pork on a work surface. Using a sharp knife, make a cut lengthwise down the center of one tenderloin, cutting two-thirds of the way through. Open as for a book and make a cut lengthwise down the center of each flap, cutting ⅓ inch deep. Using a meat mallet or rolling pin, pound the pork to ¼-inch thickness. Season with salt and pepper. Repeat this procedure with the remaining three tenderloins. (These can be prepared up to 4 hours ahead. Cover pork and refrigerate. Let stuffing and fruit-soaking liquid stand at room temperature.)

Preheat the oven to 350°F. Spread one-fourth of the stuffing over one pork tenderloin, leaving a ½-inch border on all sides. Starting at one long side, roll up the meat in a jelly roll style. Tie the pork with string at 1½-inch intervals to hold shape. Repeat with remaining pork and filling.

Melt the remaining 1 tablespoon of butter with the 1 tablespoon of oil in a heavy large roasting pan over medium-high heat. Add the pork and brown on all sides, about 7 minutes. Remove pork from the pan; do not clean the pan. Set pork on a rack in the same roasting pan. Mix reserved fruit-soaking liquid and the 3 cups of stock. Pour mixture over pork and roast until meat thermometer inserted into the center of the pork registers 150°F, basting every 10 minutes with pan juices, about 35 minutes. Transfer the pork to a platter and make a foil tent over pork to keep warm.

Strain liquid from the roasting pan into a measuring cup. Add more stock if necessary to measure 2 cups. Place roasting pan over medium-high heat. Add wine and 2 cups of the cooking liquid, and bring to a boil, scraping up browned bits. Boil until reduced to 2 cups, about 15 minutes. Mix in apricot spread. Add cornstarch mixture and bring to a boil, stirring constantly. Season with salt and pepper.

Remove strings from the pork; slice and overlap on a platter. Spoon some of the sauce over the pork. Garnish with thyme and sage sprigs. Serve, passing remaining sauce separately.

NOVEMBER 10

*Today Sister Adele and I have been discussing a proposed
Christmas Tea menu as part of the Christmas Fair, which is
only six weeks away. I've been keeping my paints, brushes,
and place cards handy so that when we sit talking for periods
of time, I can be painting the cards for the tea.
I need to make three hundred of them.*

It is never too early to decide on the dessert cart, a very important aspect of the Christmas Fair Tea. We must, without question, have our traditional English Trifle, generously laced with sherry, which is consistently the most popular of all the Christmas desserts. There has to be a good rich chocolate dessert, and as we always have a goodly number of lemon lovers we should probably consider making a lemon dessert. Sister Adele especially wants to try a tall, layered, fresh coconut cake with a lime curd filling and covered with wide strips of fresh coconut. Worth a try, but it looks like a lot of work to me.

We both like the looks and sounds of a Christmas pudding that has dried fruits, including cranberries and figs, in it. It is a lovely old English shaped pudding served with a hard sauce. I can't wait to put it into the oven for a trial so that I can sample it later this afternoon.

There is a definite pre-Advent, pre-Christmas spirit in the air. While we've been discussing desserts, Brother Lawrence has appeared and has made a bee-line toward one of the crates of fresh cranberries. "These are gorgeous," he exclaims, picking up a handful and letting them run through his fingers. I see I'm not the only one captivated by these beautiful jewels. "Careful, keep your mitts off our cranberries," I tease him.

"Your cranberries?" he retorts. "I'm seeing Christmas Fair as I look at these, and we are doing Christmas Fair together," he reminds me, and he is right. This year the Brothers and Sisters together are doing a monastic house of baked goods and foodstuffs. He has already turned out close to one hundred jars of a Cranberry Citrus Marmalade, his very own creation. Now we have to be thinking about all the other goods—cookies, shortbread, fudge, a variety of breads and jams, Sisters' Granola, and fruitcakes—and plan the baking schedule. We've got a lot to do. . . .

ENGLISH CHRISTMAS PUDDING

1 cup flour
1 teaspoon ground cinnamon
1 teaspoon ground ginger
¾ teaspoon baking powder
½ teaspoon salt
½ teaspoon ground cloves
½ teaspoon ground nutmeg
4 cups candied fruit
½ cup citron
4 cups fresh white French
   bread crumbs
1 cup packed brown sugar
3 large eggs
½ cup (1 stick) butter, melted

⅓ cup pure maple syrup
¼ cup Grand Marnier®
   Cordon Rouge or
   other orange liqueur
¼ cup dark rum
1 tablespoon grated
   tangerine or orange peel
2 teaspoons vanilla extract
   Tangerine or orange peel
   twists (optional)
   Fresh cranberries rolled
   in sugar (optional)

   Brown Sugar Hard Sauce
   (see recipe below)

Yield: Makes 12 servings

Generously butter a 2½-quart charlotte mold, pudding mold, or thick heatproof glass bowl. Sift flour, cinnamon, ginger, baking powder, salt, cloves, and nutmeg into a large mixing bowl. Add candied fruit and citron and toss to coat. Mix in crumbs. Whisk brown sugar, eggs, butter, maple syrup, liqueur, rum, grated tangerine peel, and vanilla extract in a medium bowl to blend. Pour over dry ingredients and stir until well combined (batter will be thick).

Spoon batter into prepared mold; smooth top. Cover the mold tightly with a double thickness of foil. Place a rack in a large pot. Set pudding on rack. Pour enough hot water into the pot to come halfway up the sides of the mold. Cover pot. Bring water to a simmer over medium-low heat. Steam the pudding, adding more boiling water to pot as necessary, until a wooden skewer inserted into the center comes out clean, about 5 hours.

Transfer the mold to a cooling rack; uncover and cool 30 minutes. (Can be made up to 2 months ahead. Remove pudding from mold; cool completely. Wrap tightly in plastic and refrigerate. To reheat pudding, unwrap and return to a buttered mold; cover. Place mold on a rack in a large pot. Pour enough hot water into the pot to come halfway up the sides of the mold. Cover pot; steam pudding over medium-low heat until heated through, about 1 hour. Transfer to a cooling rack. Let stand 30 minutes.)

Turn warm pudding out onto a platter. Garnish with tangerine peel twists and fresh cranberries rolled in sugar, if desired. Serve with Brown Sugar Hard Sauce.

BROWN SUGAR HARD SAUCE

⅓ cup brown sugar, packed
3 + 1 tablespoons dark rum
1 tablespoon grated
   tangerine or orange peel

1 cup (2 sticks) butter,
   room temperature
½ cup confectioners' sugar

Yield: Makes about 1¼ cups

Stir together brown sugar and 3 tablespoons rum in a heavy small saucepan over medium-low heat until sugar dissolves. Mix in tangerine peel. Cool to room temperature.

Using an electric mixer, beat the butter in a medium bowl until light. Add the remaining 1 tablespoon rum, brown sugar mixture, and confectioners' sugar; beat until well blended and smooth. (Can be prepared up to 1 week ahead. Cover and refrigerate. Bring to room temperature before serving.)

LIME CURD COCONUT CAKE

Cake:

3 cups cake flour
1 tablespoon baking powder
1 teaspoon salt
1 cup whole milk
½ cup fresh coconut liquid
   (from about 3 coconuts)
   or water

1 teaspoon coconut extract
1½ teaspoons vanilla extract
2½ sticks (1¼ cups) butter,
   softened
1¾ cups sugar
5 large eggs

Lime curd:

6 large egg yolks
¾ cup sugar
½ cup fresh lime juice
3 tablespoons heavy cream

¾ stick (6 tablespoons) cold
   butter, cut into pieces
2 teaspoons lime zest, freshly
   grated

½ + ½ cup fresh coconut,
   shredded, or sweetened
   coconut, flaked

Lime Frosting:

2 large egg whites
1½ cups sugar
½ cup water

1 tablespoon light corn syrup
1 teaspoon freshly grated
   lime zest
1 teaspoon fresh lime juice

4 cups fresh coconut, shaved,
   or 2½ cups sweetened
   coconut, flaked

Yield: Makes 1 cake

Preheat oven to 350°F. Line bottoms of three buttered 9 x 2-inch round cake pans with rounds of wax paper or parchment paper and butter the paper. Dust pans with flour, shaking out the excess.

Cake: Whisk together the flour, baking powder, and salt in a bowl. In a glass measure, stir together milk, coconut liquid or water, and extracts. In a large bowl, with an electric mixer beat butter on medium speed 1 minute and add sugar in a slow stream. Beat mixture, scraping bowl occasionally, until light and fluffy, about 2 minutes. Beat in eggs, 1 at a time, beating well after each addition. Reduce speed to low and beat in flour mixture in 4 batches alternately with milk mixture, beginning and ending with flour mixture and scraping bowl occasionally, until batter is just combined (do not overbeat).

Divide the batter among pans, smoothing tops and tapping pans on counter to allow any air bubbles to escape. Bake cake layers in middle and lower thirds of the oven (arrange pans so they overlap only slightly) until a tester inserted in the center comes out clean, about 30 minutes. Run a thin knife around the edges of the pans and invert cake layers onto cooling racks. Remove the wax paper carefully and cool cake layers completely. (Cake layers may be made 24 hours ahead and kept, wrapped in plastic wrap, in an airtight container in a cool dry place.)

Lime curd: Whisk together yolks, sugar, lime juice, cream, and butter in a heavy saucepan and cook over moderately low heat, whisking constantly, 5 to 7 minutes, or until mixture just reaches a boil (do not let boil). Strain curd through a fine sieve into a bowl and stir in zest. Cool curd, surface covered with plastic wrap, and chill at least 4 hours and up to 2 days.

To assemble cake layers and lime curd: Put 1 cake layer on a cake plate and spread evenly with about half the lime curd. Sprinkle with ½ cup coconut and chill 15 minutes. Repeat layering in same manner with another cake layer, remaining lime curd, and remaining ½ cup coconut, and top with remaining cake layer. Chill cake 15 minutes.

Lime Frosting: Beat together frosting ingredients until combined in the top of a double boiler (unheated) or in a large metal bowl, with a hand-held electric mixer. In a double boiler or in a bowl set over a saucepan of boiling water, beat on high speed until mixture holds stiff glossy peaks, about 7 minutes.

(Depending on mixer and weather, this may take longer.) Remove top of double boiler or bowl from heat and beat frosting until cool and spreadable.

Frost the cake and coat with coconut.

CRANBERRY–CITRUS MARMALADE

2 grapefruits	6 pounds (14 cups) sugar
3 lemons	2 tablespoons molasses
4 oranges	4 cups cranberries
15 cups water	1 cup cranberry juice

Yield: Makes 4 quarts

Combine all the fruits except the cranberries, slicing to whatever thickness you like. Place them in a pan with water and soak overnight. (This soaks the skins.)

The next day, cook over medium heat for 2 hours or until the skins are tender. Add cranberries. Add the sugar, molasses, and cranberry juice, and boil for approximately 2 hours, or until setting point. Pour into sterilized jars.

NOVEMBER 20

*Suitcases and gift bags of early Christmas presents are appearing
in the halls as many Sisters prepare to visit their families for
Thanksgiving. Most of them are taking along a Gouda cheese made
from Duchess's milk.*

For the first Thanksgiving in our Chapel we felt the decorating should express our thanks for all the blessings we had experienced through the year. Where should we start? The gardens, of course. We brought in pumpkins, squash, apples, potatoes, and everything that still remained fresh from the fall harvesting. These we heaped into a bountiful pile. Then we collected the canned and preserved fruits and vegetables, jars of honey from our bees, jellies and jams from our beach plums, grapes, relishes, and pickles. Remembering the chickens, we added fresh eggs; and we couldn't leave out the goats, so we used their tin milk cans to represent them. The Chapel was still unfinished inside, and the open beams and rafters gave a very barnlike appearance and made a perfect setting for the displays.

A creative work is seldom completed until the very last minute. A half hour before the Thanksgiving service, we added freshly picked fall leaves, bittersweet, and loaves of home-baked bread. We were happy with this representation of the material gifts we had received. "But there's just one thing missing," Rick said. "There's no fish. Too bad." "Well, I have a big frozen bass down in the chest freezer," I said jokingly—or was it a joke?

Within minutes the fish was out of the freezer and ensconced in a bed of white linen next to the loaves of bread. With his tail frozen in a flipped up position from being forced into limited freezer space, he looked as if he were swimming; he could not have been frozen into a better position if we had planned it on purpose. He was the finishing touch to the display and the conversation piece of everyone attending church that day. For years after, it became traditional to freeze a big bass or bluefish specifically for this purpose, and everyone looked forward to its appearance in our Thanksgiving bounty decoration.

Mother Cay selected the Thanksgiving dinner menu for the whole Community family. It was an old-fashioned meal:

Carrot and Celery Sticks and Pickles, with Homemade Rolls and Butter
Roast Stuffed Turkey with Mashed Potatoes and Gravy
Butternut Squash and Turnips
Creamed Onions and Cranberry Sauce and Relish
Homemade Apple and Pumpkin Pies and Indian Pudding

She put three of us in charge of cooking and serving the entire meal. She was of the opinion that the fewer people on a job, the more responsibility each assumed, and the more efficiently it would be done.

The whole Community family gathered in the Fellowship Room for this meal. While dessert was being served, everyone who wished to, young and old, spoke of whatever they were most grateful for that year. This was a very deeply moving and inspiring time for all of us. While the sharing was taking place, the turkey carcasses were simmering away in the kitchen. Then while everyone helped clean up and wash dishes, Gordie made soup for the evening meal, which was make-your-own turkey sandwiches and soup.

DECEMBER 1

*We're already one week into Advent. I remember the Advent almost
fifteen years ago when I was assigned to cook meals for ten men in
one of the Community houses.*

I can't remember the reason for the combination of men in that house during that period of time, but I do remember who they were and the enormous appetites they had.

Five of them were novices to the Brotherhood, all big fellows, one 6' 5", another 6' 3", the rest, though not as tall, stocky and large-framed. They were all young, hearty eaters. Among the other men, one was a diabetic and another was allergic to many foods. In addition to the men there was Grandma Rose, a wiry eighty-three-year-old, sharp as a tack and keenly aware of everything and everyone and every move they made.

The first meal was a blueberry pancake breakfast at 7:00 AM, to be cooked, served, and eaten in time for all of them to be in chapel by 7:30. From experience, I knew that each of the novices would easily eat six pancakes apiece and the other men probably three or four. To be safe, I needed to make about fifty pancakes and thirty sausages, plus boiled eggs and toast for the diabetic, and special rice pancakes for the one who was allergic. Someone had given Harry a gift of chicken livers that needed to be cooked soon, and he would love to have them as a side dish if I didn't mind. There would be blueberry sauce as well as regular syrup to heat. Working in an unfamiliar and smaller kitchen than I was used to, I was going to have to start early and plan well the night before.

This I began to do, getting out pots for eggs and sauce and syrup, frying pans for sausages and livers, electric grill and skillets for pancakes. Every burner was reserved. Every electric appliance that showed any possibility of producing a pancake was set out. While I was making all these calculations and preparations, Grandma Rose was nervously wringing her hands and pacing back and forth behind me questioning whether this was going to work, reminding me that George liked a certain coffee mug, that Mark drank only herb tea, that Carl had to have lactose-free milk and no sugar, and that Joe always wanted early coffee before breakfast.

I looked at the kitchen counter lined with appliances and started to laugh. I said good night to Grandma, took the house key, and left. The only way to have this breakfast ready by 7:00 was to get myself over there by 5:00 AM. Even then I would be allowing only about a minute per pancake, plus everything else that needed to be done, but by starting before Grandma was up and around I'd be able to concentrate and accomplish more.

The next morning, I made my way in the dark over to the house and quietly let myself in. I was surprised to see lights on as I entered. Had they been left on all night? Was someone ill? I had been told rising time was 6:00 AM. I stepped into the kitchen and found Grandma Rose perched on a stool beside the counter where all my fast action was going to have to take place. Biting my tongue, I managed a somewhat civil response to her tense "Mornin'." How was this ever going to work? I was fit to be tied.

"You remembering that Joe wants his coffee early?" she began.

"Yes, Grandma."

"You know Carl has to have special milk?"

"Yes, I do, Grandma."

One by one she reiterated each concern she had called to my attention the night before, adding others to the list. I mixed my batter with a vengeance and began to plead with God to help me. Could this be how I often made insecure kitchen Sisters feel? That fleeting thought helped my heart to soften a bit and yield to having her there.

The warm oven was holding the sausages and plates. Juice was mixed and ready to be poured. Sauce and syrup were heating. Eggs and liver were set out. Coffee urn was ready to go. It was now 6:00 AM, time to start the pancakes. I plugged in all my cords and finished setting the table. When I was ready to pour the batter, I found all the griddles and pans stone cold. "Something wrong?" asked Grandma. "Not heating up? No one ever uses those, you know," she added. Of course not, no one ever was foolish enough to try to make this many pancakes in this little time. I wiggled wires, flipped switches on and off. No results. Every minute was counting. Should I quickly cook up a pot of oatmeal? Was there even any oatmeal in the house? Maybe cold cereal was the answer.

"Fuse blown?" questioned Grandma. Of course, that was it! Why hadn't I thought of it? All those electrical things were plugged into one outlet.

"God bless you, Grandma. You've got it." But where to find the fuse box? I headed to the cellar with no idea where to look. It was only 6:15, but this nightmare felt as though it had been going on for hours. And then, still wet from the shower where Grandma had gone to fetch him, Harry came to the rescue. With a flip of a switch we were back in business.

No one ever had hotter pancakes, straight from the griddle to the plate. I just kept flipping them over as the men kept filing by again and again to snatch them away. At 7:25 everyone hurried off to the chapel, well-fed, and commenting on the great breakfast.

And it really was one of the best I had ever turned out—thanks to Grandma Rose. I never could have done it without her.

BLUEBERRY–RICOTTA PANCAKES WITH BLUEBERRY SYRUP

Pancakes:

4 eggs, separated, room temperature	2 teaspoons baking powder
1 cup ricotta cheese	⅛ teaspoon salt
⅓ cup sour cream	¾ cup milk
¼ cup sugar	2 cups fresh blueberries
⅔ cup flour	Melted butter

Blueberry Syrup:

1 + 1 cup fresh blueberries	1 teaspoon fresh lemon juice
½ cup sugar	1 teaspoon vanilla extract
½ cup water	1 tablespoon cornstarch

Yield: Makes 20 (3-inch) pancakes

Pancakes: Thoroughly combine egg yolks, ricotta, sour cream, and sugar in large bowl. Sift flour with baking powder and salt over cheese mixture and stir until smooth. Mix in milk. Fold in blueberries. Beat egg whites until stiff but not dry. Gently fold one-fourth of the egg whites into batter; fold in remainder.

Heat griddle or heavy large skillet over medium heat; brush lightly with melted butter. Ladle batter onto griddle by 3 table-spoonfuls. Cook until bubbles begin to appear on surface of pan-cakes, 2 to 3 minutes. Turn and cook until bottoms are golden brown and pancakes are cooked through, 1 to 1½ minutes. Transfer to heated platter. Repeat with remaining batter, brushing griddle occasionally with melted butter. Divide pancakes among plates. Serve immediately accompanied by warm Blueberry Syrup.

Blueberry Syrup: Cook 1 cup berries, sugar, water, lemon juice, and vanilla extract in heavy medium saucepan, stirring until sugar dissolves. Increase heat and bring to boil. Reduce heat and sim-mer until mixture turns to syrup, stirring occasionally. Thicken with cornstarch. Add remaining 1 cup berries and cook until soft, stirring occasionally, about 5 minutes. (Can be prepared up to 2 days ahead. Reheat before serving.)

DECEMBER 4

*Reservations are steadily rising for the weekend's events. Three teas
are completely sold out; only a few places are left at the other two.*

This year a winter wonderland is planned for the children in the Friary's shop and refectory. Instead of a set time for a party as in past years, there are continuous events all day, including tea and a visit to the pub with Mr. and Mrs. Beaver, gift grab bags, puppet shows, face painting, an obstacle course, a penny candy store, a visit from the Snowman, and a quiet corner for kids.

Saturday the boutiques are open for shopping, the Christmas Village Deli serves lunch, the Yankee Christmas Banquet follows the Vespers service, and the Gloriæ Dei Brass and Bell Ringers give a concert in the evening.

Sunday after church, a Holiday Brunch is served, and in the afternoon the Christmas Garland is presented—a performance of music, theater, and dance.

Six decorated homes this year feature themes and customs from Finland, France, and Canada, as well as a 1797 Bicentennial House, a Doll House, and a Gingerbread House, and of course the Monastic Bake Shop run by the Brothers and the Sisters.

ST. LUCIA BREAD

2 pkgs. (or 5 scant teaspoons) active dry yeast	⅛ teaspoon ground saffron
	3 eggs, slightly beaten
¼ cup warm water	8 cups flour or more
1¾ cups milk	4 teaspoons lemon peel, dried
½ cup vegetable oil	1 cup candied citron, chopped
½ cup sugar	1 cup blanched almonds
½ teaspoon salt	1 egg, well-beaten
	1 tablespoon water

Frosting:

8 cups confectioners' sugar	Water
4 teaspoons almond extract	

Maraschino cherries

Yield: Makes 2 loaves

Soften yeast in the warm water. Heat the milk until warm. Add oil and sugar and stir to dissolve. Stir in softened yeast, salt, and saffron. Add the 3 slightly beaten eggs; blend well. Combine 8 cups flour, lemon peel, citron, and almonds in an electric mixing bowl. Add the liquid ingredients, stirring at low speed (use a bread hook attachment or a wooden spoon) until the mixture has formed a ball. Add more flour if necessary. Turn the dough onto a floured board and knead for 5 minutes or until dough becomes smooth and elastic; add flour as necessary.

Place the dough in a greased bowl, cover, and let rise in a warm place until almost doubled in size, about 1 hour. Punch down and refrigerate dough for at least 3 hours. (The dough can be kept well wrapped up to 4 days in the refrigerator.)

Take the dough out of the refrigerator an hour or so before you plan to work with it. This helps to make it more workable. At this point you can make either 2 large braided ring loaves, 4 small loaves, or buns in the traditional "S" shape.

Preheat oven to 325°F. Have 2 large cookie sheets greased or covered with parchment paper. For the larger rings, cut the dough into 2 equal parts. Cover one of the pieces. The other piece can be cut into 3 equal parts. Knead each one and roll into a long, snake-like shape about 24 inches long. Braid the 3 pieces together and form into a wreath shape, being sure to tuck under the ends very well. Place the braid onto a cookie sheet; cover and let rise in a warm place until doubled. Combine the 1 well-beaten egg and the 1 tablespoon water to form egg wash. Brush the braid with egg wash and bake for about 20 to 25 minutes. Cool on a cookie sheet or a cooling rack. If you plan to freeze braid to decorate at a later time, do so immediately after baking (leave unwrapped). Wrap in plastic when chilled.

For decorating, mix the frosting ingredients, adding water a tablespoon at a time until of desired consistency. Cut the cherries into halves or quarters and decorate for a festive look.

In keeping with the tradition of celebrating the Feast of Lights on St. Lucia's Day, candles may also be used as a decoration. This is one of our most popular Christmas Fair items.

CARDAMOM COOKIES

2 cups sugar
1 cup margarine or butter,
  softened
2 eggs
½ teaspoon almond extract

3½ cups flour
  2 teaspoons baking powder
  2 teaspoons ground
    cardamom
  1 cup half-and-half

Yield: Makes 4 dozen

Note: Lightly spoon flour into measuring cup; level off.

Preheat oven to 350°F. Grease 13 x 9-inch pan. In large bowl, beat sugar and margarine until light and fluffy. Add eggs and almond extract; beat well. Combine flour, baking powder, and cardamom. Alternately add flour mixture and half-and-half to sugar mixture, beating well after each addition. Spread batter in prepared pan. Bake at 350°F for 40 to 50 minutes or until tooth-pick inserted in center comes out clean. Cool completely.

Cut cake crosswise into four 3-inch strips. (Cake can be frozen in strips overnight and then cut and toasted the next day.) Remove one strip at a time from pan. Cut strips into ¼-inch slices; place on an ungreased cookie sheet. Bake at 250°F for 45 minutes or until crisp but not brown.

DECEMBER 6

*When I stepped out into the hall this morning there was a big
wooden shoe there. I knew this meant that it was Saint Nicholas
Day, and I knew that our Dutch sister must be responsible. In
Holland, it is traditional for children to set their shoes out on Saint
Nicholas Eve before they go to bed. When they wake up in the
morning, they find them filled with Dutch chocolates and licorice.
In my case, the shoe was filled with fresh kale and spinach!*

One of the challenges we face each Christmas, as Sisters, is how to come up with an appropriate Christmas gift for family or relatives and each Community household. Always we give something we make ourselves, such as a Christmas tree skirt, a table runner, place mats, pottery mugs, personalized stationery, or a calendar. Often we give a food gift.

One year, we gave each household a little basket of fresh eggs and bagfuls of fresh bean sprouts. Another year, we gave a basket of assorted preserves or an apple basket made up of apple jelly, applesauce, apple butter, applesauce bread, and a decorative but edible apple wreath. Most recently and probably most popular was a spaghetti dinner basket containing sauce we had made with our own garden tomatoes and seasonings, homemade bread sticks, and a bottle of herb vinegar. Coming during the busy holiday season when few people have extra time to prepare meals, this basket was warmly welcomed and received rave reviews.

Increasing numbers of people used to look forward to our annual Christmas Carol and Bell Concert with its festive buffet dinner. This gala meal took place in the Fellowship Room, which had been transformed into a merry old English banquet hall laden with fresh evergreens, pine cones, holly, mistletoe, and poinsettias.

The meal began with a Cranberry Jewel Salad on curly endive with a piped dressing, hot rolls, and butter. The buffet offered Turkey Noël in a rich sherry sauce served over hot puff-pastry shells, petite green peas and little pearl onions, duchess potatoes, gravy, and a splendid roast steamship round of beef at the carving station. Dessert was often a rich chocolate frosted yule log or a cranberry cheesecake.

In more recent years, this meal has been replaced with what we call a New England Yankee dinner. This dinner begins with a crock of blended cheese and assorted crackers. This is followed by salad and rolls, squash and apple soup, sliced pork with stuffing, roast beef, roast potatoes, Brussels sprouts, and baked acorn squash. Dessert is an old-fashioned apple crisp topped with whipped cream.

Both meals seem to be equally as popular and effective in kindling a Christmas spirit in the hearts of those who attend.

CRANBERRY JEWEL SALAD

1 6-ounce pkg. strawberry gelatin	¾ cup chopped walnuts
2½ cups boiling water	¾ cup finely chopped celery
2 cups fresh Cranberry-Orange Relish (see recipe p. 155)	Non-stick cooking spray

Yield: Makes 6 servings

Blend gelatin and boiling water, stirring to dissolve. Stir in Cranberry-Orange Relish. Spray a mold or a 9 x 9-inch pan with cooking spray, and pour in gelatin mixture. Refrigerate. When mixture begins to thicken (to consistency of raw egg whites), add chopped nuts and celery. Stir well. Refrigerate until firm.

TURKEY NOËL

¼ cup margarine or butter
⅓ cup flour
½ teaspoon salt
¼ teaspoon pepper
1¾ cups milk
1 cup chicken broth

Mushrooms (optional)
2 cups cooked, cubed turkey
¼ cup chopped pimiento
2 tablespoons dry sherry
4 patty shells, baked

Yield: Makes 4 servings

In a saucepan melt the margarine. Stir in flour, salt, and pepper. Add milk and chicken broth all at once. Cook and stir until thickened and bubbly. Cook and stir 1 minute more. Add mushrooms, if desired. Stir in turkey, pimiento, and sherry. Heat through. Spoon over patty shells.

DECEMBER 17

*There is an interesting old custom that we still observe during the
week preceding Christmas. It is based on a practice that originated
in the parish and cathedral churches around the fourteenth century.*

In the Vespers service, the Magnificat is always chanted after the appointed psalms for the day. The antiphon, or introduction, is intoned by the cantor and then chanted by all participating in the service. Each antiphon during the eight days leading up to Christmas refers to an Old Testament name given to Christ and is preceded by the interjection "O"—for example, O Emmanuel, O Adonai, and O Radix. Thus, these are referred to as the "O" Antiphons.

It was customary in those early days to be invited to the home of the village canon who intoned the antiphon that evening, in order to celebrate the anticipation of the coming of the Christ Child with a glass of sherry. Over the years this tradition has evolved into what is currently referred to as an "O" Antiphon party, which amounts to a little spread of holiday refreshments as a kind of appetizer preceding dinner. (Often, however, it grows into a mini-banquet.) Generally it includes something like a hot wassail, cheese and crackers, fruit, nuts, tiny meatballs, assorted Christmas cookies, or fruitcake. The cantor intoning the antiphon always hosts the part and briefly shares with the group some thoughts regarding the particular antiphon of the evening.

The first year I was assigned to be the cantor and prepare the food for this party, I was one of the last in the series and tried to think of something that would not repeat what was served by those who had preceded me. The Sister in charge of the kitchen at the time, having so many holiday menus to be concerned about, jokingly said to me, "Why don't you do something monastic so you won't have to fuss with any more fancy little goodies. Just give everyone a crust of bread."

We both laughed, but as I walked away my mind's wheels began to turn. "Crusts of bread?" This might be one of the best suggestions yet.

The result was an "O" Antiphon party served from the black woodstove in our Refectory by a robed monastic.

The menu was Toasted Cloister Crusts, Subiaco Sausage, Benedictine Barley Broth, Gaudete (Joy) Pudding, and Creamy Rice Pudding Laced with Sherry.

The crusts were of toasted, herb-buttered bread. The broth ladled out of a soup pot into thick brown mugs had a wonderfully rich flavor, having been simmered from the bone of the huge steamship round served at the Carol Concert Buffet, with just a bit of wine and barley added. The sausage was a coil of kielbasa broiled and served in a cast-iron fry pan, with each person cutting off a piece to his own liking. The final treat was a sweet, warm rice pudding laced with sherry.

The whole experience was refreshingly different in its simplicity and seemed to capture a spirit probably a bit closer to what had originally been intended. Because it was so effective, we later planned an entire Master Schola dinner and evening around this monastic theme, a nice contrast to some of the more lavish, richer meals we often prepare for Schola.

Above my desk hangs a picture of a golden Himalayan cat with large amber eyes and a pushed-in nose, a Christmas stocking cap on his long-haired head. There's a story behind this picture. It was given to me by a woman who fell in love both with Hosanna, the subject of the photo, and with Bethany Retreat House both at the same time.

"Ho," as he is known to most of us, was a gift to me from the Mothers fourteen years ago. The vet said at his last visit, "He's in good shape for an old boy." That was a bittersweet statement for me. To hear that he was in good shape pleased me and did not really surprise me because, as Sister Agatha says, "He hasn't had a hard life." But to hear him referred to as an old boy pained me for obvious reasons. This fat-footed, furry fellow, as I often refer to him, has been a dear faithful companion with whom I am not looking forward to parting.

Unlike Elijah, who is a hunter and loves the wild outdoors, Ho hardly knows what to do with a mosquito on the wall, other than to be fascinated and amused by it. He has a very sweet, sensitive spirit (except when he's being groomed) that is, at times, a source of unexpected blessing. He lives in the Watchroom up the hall from Bethany Kitchen. This room was so named by Mother Cay because it is where guests can always reach a Sister at anytime during the night.

One evening after attending the Christmas Carol Concert, two women from out of town started to drive home and ran into a blinding snowstorm that turned into sleet and rain. Afraid they would not be able to make it home, they decided to turn around and take their chances on being able to stay at Bethany. It was quite late when they finally inched their way into the driveway after having crept along the slippery highway at a snail's pace to return.

It so happened a room was available and while one Sister went up to turn down beds and find some nightclothes, robes, toothbrushes, and other essentials for the two women, another one made hot cocoa and rekindled the fire in the dining room fireplace. Both women were tense and exhausted. Jane, the driver, was particularly distraught emotionally. I sat with them while they described their treacherous trip back, and after a while they both began to relax and unwind.

While we talked, "Ho" made his way down the hall to the dining room as he is often wont to do. Jane spotted him before I did and let out a cry, "Oh, you gorgeous creature." Making his way into the room with that silent roll-step that he does so perfectly, my boy walked right up to her as though he knew her and let her pick him up. Her eyes filled with tears as she took him in her arms, holding him close to herself.

Finally she spoke, explaining that she had had to have her own cat put to sleep a few days before, and it had been so hard for her at night going home to an empty house. All this time Ho remained docile in her arms. When she finished talking, he did something he occasionally does to me, but never to a stranger. He turned his head and licked her on the cheek, then hopped off her lap and roll-stepped out of the room. It seemed to all of us that it was time to go to bed.

Rested, refreshed, and chipper, Jane and Marge left the next morning after a pleasant breakfast during which they made plans to return soon. A note from them the following week referred to the nightmarish snowstorm as a blessing in disguise because of what they discovered in Bethany. "A haven of rest, peace, and comfort, a literal shelter in the midst of a storm. The whole experience was like a dream I shall never forget," wrote Jane, "especially that goodnight kiss from an angel in the form of a golden cat."

The following spring, for my sixtieth birthday I received from Jane this lovely framed picture of Hosanna, which had been used as a cover for *Four-Footed Friends* magazine that Christmas. Each time I look at it, it reminds me not just of him, but of Jane whose need he sensed and met years ago on her first night in Bethany.

Sister Brenda had trouble always catering to her appetite. One Advent she decided to ask someone else for help with her problem. She agreed to have another person serve her plate at each meal and choose her snacks for her with the understanding that that person would at times deliberately choose for her foods that she would not necessarily pick herself.

I was the person chosen—not an easy task for someone who knew all her likes and dislikes and had my own problems with palate pampering. So this task was a challenge to both of us. From time to time, usually when she was least expecting it, I would give her something that I knew she really enjoyed.

Around this time I made a cake that was very popular with guests and retreatants, and I often served it as a lunch dessert. It was a moist one-layer cake with a crunchy brown-sugar bottom, topped with finely chopped walnuts and generously flavored through and through with nutmeg. Anyone fond of nutmeg automatically fell in love with it. Mrs. Buckworth, our guest, was one of those people.

Sometimes parents are very supportive of their child's interest in a religious vocation. Sometimes they are not, and this is understandable. They often see such a vocation as a mere waste of a talented life, especially if they have preconceived ideas and plans for the child. This was true of Mrs. Buckworth, who was now visiting us. Her little Susie was a popular, attractive, gifted young woman, and Mrs. Buckworth's aspirations were that Susie would become a Miss America who would eventually marry and produce beautiful grandchildren for her enjoyment.

When parents are of this conviction, little will convince them otherwise, except their witnessing, with time, the satisfaction their offspring experiences in his or her chosen profession. A novicemistress is often viewed as the parents' rival, and all one can do is love the parents, answer their questions, and try to assure them that their offspring will be free to make his or her own decision (though they always suspect that this is not really the truth).

One slight thing I had in my favor was that Mrs. Buckworth was a good cook, loved food, and very much enjoyed all the meals served to her at Bethany. She shared with me many of her cooking tricks and secrets, and in no time I discovered that she had a real sweet tooth and cared little for heathful, wholesome foods.

Mrs. Buckworth was determined to take Susie shopping and then go for a drive around the Cape. I offered them a snack to take with them and she took me up on it, adding, "You know what I'd love, Sister Irene," casting a glance at the two pieces of nutmeg cake left on the table from lunch.

Later in the afternoon I returned to the Retreat Kitchen and found a note to me from Sister Brenda on the counter where I regularly left her snacks.

"My faith was mega-multiplied today," it read. "I can't tell you how I felt when I opened my snack this afternoon. If there was ever a day when I needed such a boost, it was today. Thank you so much!" Puzzled, I set the note aside, wondering how apple slices and celery sticks could have had such an effect on her, since she cared for neither. Perhaps her tastes were changing.

As I went about making dinner preparations, I turned the matter over in my mind, still perplexed about it. "Why are so many towels missing?"

I asked the other Sister helping me.

"Oh, Sister Brenda came by earlier than usual today to collect the kitchen laundry and took everything off the racks to make a clean sweep of things. I just haven't replaced them yet."

Sister Brenda came by early? She usually came at 3:00 PM to collect the towels and pick up her snack at the same time. "What time did she come?" I asked.

"Not long after lunch," was the answer.

"Oh, no!" I wailed. "Don't tell me she picked up the snack I'd packed for Mrs. Buckworth and Susie and they've gotten hers that I set out later?" A quick phone call confirmed my fear, and while Sister Brenda reveled in God's love for her in giving her her favorite cake, I inwardly groaned, imagining how Mrs. Buckworth was accepting God's love to her through apple slices and celery sticks, neither of which would ever have been her choice.

I hung up the phone and began turning over in my mind how best to fix this situation. Bake another cake quickly? Come up with another treat? Plead guilty and ask for pardon? I didn't even feel guilty. Before I could arrive at any solution, Sister Marie came into the kitchen with a snack bag in hand.

"Just returning this from Mrs. Buckworth and Sue," she said. "They came across a tea shop and couldn't resist stopping there so they never even opened this bag, but they said to thank you very much anyway."

Could I really trust my ears? "Why are you looking so dumbfounded?" asked Sister Marie.

"Me? Dumbfounded? I'm looking dumbfounded? I *am* dumbfounded! And my faith in God has just been mega-multiplied today."

For over twenty years, Sue has been a solid, productive Sister, never having regretted her life's choice. Mrs. Buckworth, who for years grieved over her daughter's choice, recently returned to Bethany. Though still a large woman, she was less forceful and robust than when we had sat together at this table so many years ago. I poured her tea and cut her a piece of warm nutmeg cake. Then I asked her about her family.

Painfully, she related some very disappointing experiences with each of her other children, and I felt compassion for her and for the heartache her family obviously had caused her. "You know, Sister Irene," she said, "I never was in favor of Susie becoming a Sister."

"Yes, Mrs. Buckworth," I replied, "I do remember that."

"Well," she went on, "her life has turned out to be the most satisfactory of any of my three children, and I want to thank you for your part in helping her make that decision. I think, now, that it was the right one for her."

"Yes," I agreed, "I do too."

Then with a slight grin, she added, "I really shouldn't do this, but give me another little sliver of that cake. I just love it."

NUTMEG CAKE

2 cups brown sugar
2 cups flour
½ cup butter, softened
1 egg

1 teaspoon ground nutmeg
1 cup sour cream
1 teaspoon baking soda
½ cup chopped nuts

Yield: Makes 9 servings

Preheat oven to 350°F. Grease a 9-inch pan. Blend together brown sugar, flour, and butter to make a crumb mixture. Spread half the mixture in the pan. Stir nutmeg, sour cream and baking soda into the remaining crumb mixture. Pour batter over the crumbs in pan. Sprinkle with nuts. Bake for 35 minutes.

DECEMBER 31

As the year draws to a close, I take time late in the day for
reflection on the year gone by, and anticipation of another
year coming, full of God's blessings.

People who come to Bethany often say, "There's something about this place that's different, something I can't quite put my finger on that makes it so special to me. It's the way I feel when I'm here and what I take away with me when I leave. It makes me want to come back."

I'm wondering whether what these people feel is the dedication or commitment of the people in the Community. We have a commitment not only to the running of this place, but to each other, so that when someone comes here, it is almost like coming into a home or family where you can sense the love people have for each other. They may have their struggles and differences, but you can tell there is a strong bond that holds them together and makes them care for each other.

Two years ago, I celebrated my sixty-fifth birthday. One of the Brothers sent me a greeting in which he thanked me for the many ways in which he felt I had been a real sister to him over the past twenty-five years. "We've seen each other at our best and our worst," he said. "We've shared some of the struggles of life, and you've been a true friend through thick and thin."

I had never thought about it quite that way, but that comment sums up our life together in the sisterhood, the brotherhood, and the Community as a whole. We work, we play, we laugh, we cry, we fight, and we make up. We know each other's strengths and weaknesses, but when all is said and done, we stick with each other, and I can't help thinking that the effect of this commitment must be felt by those who come here.

"There's so much peace in this place," we often hear people say. "It must be wonderful to live in such a peaceful atmosphere all the time." Such remarks always bring a smile, because the atmosphere is never peaceful *all* the time. Living in community is not a magical remedy for getting along with others. It requires a lot of give-and-take, a lot of deferring to one another and considering others over oneself. Life in community is a process, and in the midst of the process, disagreements and outbursts of strong feelings often occur, causing lots of tension and stress. The peace comes only after these problems are worked through and a resolution comes about.

While I was out walking this morning, I was overwhelmed with what a wonderful life I have, how glad I am to be where I am, to do what I'm doing, and to be with the people I'm with. It is not that we all have a natural liking for each other, and even where that may be the case, it sometimes wears thin when we live so closely, but we work things through. The process is not always easy, and it often involves both pain and joy.

But for myself, I would not trade the life God has given me for any other.

Whenever people come to Bethany, we thank God for having brought them, and we thank God for what he intends to do for them while they are here. Then we go about our business during their stay, affirming his love and care for them and his activity in their lives. Sometimes we get to see or hear about the results. Other times we don't. It doesn't really matter. It is a very satisfying experience to be able to pray for people in this way without telling God what to do for them.

I waved one last goodbye as Sandy's car disappeared down the driveway. Going back into the house, I picked up the lovely wrapped box of chocolates she had left for the Sisters and read the attached card. "How can I tell you all that is in my heart as I leave this place? I came here empty and despairing. I was received and cared for in a way I had never before experienced."

Sandy had come to Bethany for a personal retreat. It was her first time here. That she had experienced deep hurt was evident, though the details were unknown to us. At her request she received personal counseling from one of the clergy, but our association with her came simply through serving her meals, cleaning her room, and attending to whatever practical needs arose during her stay. By the time she left we shared a warm friendship that made us sad to see her go.

I read on. "This was a painful retreat for me. I cried off and on most of the time, but surprisingly, I was not self-conscious doing so in your presence. I felt no judgment, only love and acceptance and a strong sense of quiet, but loving, support. Leaving now, I'm still not without pain, but because of what I've received while here, my heart is full and I feel strengthened to go through the rest of the healing process that lies ahead of me. I was hungry and you fed me, a stranger and you took me in, and somehow my life will never be quite the same."

Now it was my turn to cry.

ABOUT THE COMMUNITY OF JESUS

Through the centuries, many Christians have gathered to form communities in which they support one another in prayer, work, and daily living. In that enduring tradition, members of The Community of Jesus are joined in a common commitment of love and service to God, to each other, and to the world.

The Community of Jesus is an ecumenical Christian community dedicated to the transformation of individual lives through a way of life centered on God. An order of daily worship—Holy Eucharist and the Liturgy of the Hours (short prayer services)—sustains both its internal life and its mission. Together with the praises of God, daily intercessions are offered for reconciliation and healing, for other Christian communities, and for world leaders.

The community is made up of Brothers, and Sisters, married couples, and single adults. The Brothers live in Zion Friary and the Sisters live in Bethany Convent. The Brothers and Sisters maintain the Community church, facilities, and grounds, care for the retreat house, provide meals for visitors, and sew liturgical vestments and monastic habits. Both the Brothers and Sisters pursue studies in Gregorian chant, contribute to the many outreach ministries of the community, and aid in the community's Christian education. In addition, they participate with the community adults and children in a variety of activities.

Members of the community come from many walks of life and different denominational backgrounds including Presbyterian, Episcopalian, Congregational,

Baptist, Roman Catholic, Lutheran, Pentecostal, and Methodist. They have discovered both enrichment and strength in their diversity, as well as a common bond of Christian faith as expressed in the Apostles' and Nicene creeds.

"Extended families" (couples, single adults, and children) live in privately owned homes near the community church. Household members share meals and tasks of the home. They work at a variety of occupations: authors, musicians, artists, salespersons, teachers, businesspersons, medical personnel, architects, carpenters, plumbers, electricians, painters, lawyers, and many others.

Members also volunteer their time and talents to community activities. Several fundraising events are held during the year to provide support for the community and for its mission, including Fourth of July and Christmas celebrations.

Located in Orleans, Massachusetts, overlooking Cape Cod Bay, The Community of Jesus was founded by Cay Andersen and Judy Sorensen, who were joined by several families and the first Sisters. Named and incorporated in 1970, the community now includes over 300 people, including children.

(Adapted from The Community of Jesus brochure, published by The Community of Jesus, 1997.)

INDEX

Sour Cream–Apple Crunch
   Kuchen   124
Southern Black
   Chocolate Cake   22
Sponge Cake   166

CHEESE

Bacon–Cheese Filling   154
Blueberry–Ricotta Pancakes
   with Blueberry Syrup   191
Cheese Blintzes   81
Creamed Spinach with
   Chèvre   138
Mascarpone Cream   139
Potato and Wild
   Mushroom Gratin   115
Romaine and Roquefort
   Salad with Herb
   Vinaigrette   106
Sausage and Cheese
   Strata with Tomatoes   61
Stilton Potato Gratin   107
Swiss Omelet Roll
   with Mustard Sauce   85

CHICKEN

Alpine Chicken   20
Barbecued Chicken   121
Cassava Pie   68
Chicken Heroes   63
Chicken–Mushroom
   Crêpes   77
Chicken Salad Filling   154
Coq au vin   170
Crispy Chicken   59
Cumberland Chicken   84
Orange–Rosemary
   Chicken   62
Poulet Jubilee   13
Spring Stuffed Chicken
   Breasts   83

CHOCOLATE

Black-Bottom Cappuccino
   Mousse Cake   116
Buckeyes   28
Chocolate Frosting   22
Chocolate–Brandy
   Frosting   122
Chocolate–Cassis Icing   78
Chocolate Kahlúa Layer
   Cake   122
Chocolate Rum Sauce   108

Chocolate Truffle Loaf with
   Raspberry Port Sauce   119
Crème de Cassis
   Chocolate Cake   78
Fudge Crostata   125
Southern Black
   Chocolate Cake   22
White Chocolate–Coffee
   Frosting   140

COCONUT

Coconut–Oat Crunchies   28
Lime Curd Coconut Cake   184
Pineapple–Coconut
   Napoleons   139
Toasted Coconut Soufflé with
   Chocolate Rum Sauce   108

COOKIES

Brandy Snaps   156
Cardamom Cookies   194
Coconut–Oat Crunchies   28
Cowboy Cookies   49
Crispy Sugar Cookies   81
Ginger–Molasses Cookies   177
Rosie's Biscotti   95

Vegetable Crown Sandwich
    with Basil Pesto   135
Wilted Cabbage with
    Carrots and Bacon   62
Zucchini Lasagna   60
Zucchini-Stuffed Tomatoes   98

VENISON
Venison Steaks   37

ZUCCHINI
(See Squash)

For more copies of this cookbook, ask for
Sister Irene's Culinary Journal
at your local bookstore.

You may also order additional copies by mailing or faxing the following order form

Sister Irene's Culinary Journal
$19.95 plus $5.00 for shipping/handling   Mass. Residents add 5% sales tax

Name _____

Address _____

City _____ State _____ Zip _____

Quantity _____

Method of Payment   VISA ☐   Mastercard ☐   Cash/Check ☐

Card Number_____

Exp. Date _____

Signature _____

 PARACLETE PRESS P.O. Box 1568 Orleans, MA 02653
Call 1-800-451-5006 or Fax 1-508-255-5705